Kirk Wilson is an investigative journalist, author, film producer and former police reporter who has won more than 100 awards for his work in various media.

"An accomplished amateur sleuth's handbook ... thought through with Holmesian passion."

Kirkus Review

"Wilson documents ten fabulous crimes in his well-researched account. A provocative, probing work."

Library Journal

"Well written and well researched ... combined with wry writing makes this a superior anthology. Highly recommended."

Booklist

"A fabulous book ... these masterfully recounted stories are alternately fascinating, surprising, suspenseful."

Times Record News

UNSOLVED CRIMES

THE TOP TEN UNSOLVED MURDERS OF THE 20TH CENTURY

Kirk Wilson

with a Preface by Colin Wilson

CARROLL & GRAF PUBLISHERS
New York

Carroll & Graf Publishers
An imprint of Avalon Publishing Group, Inc.
161 William Street, 16th Floor
NY 10038-2607
www.carrollandgraf.com

First Carroll & Graf cloth edition, 1990
First Carroll & Graf trade paper edition, 1991
Second Carroll & Graf edition, 2002

This revised and updated paperback edition first published in the UK,
by Robinson, an imprint of Constable & Robinson Ltd, 2002

ISBN 0–7867–1022–5

Printed and bound in the EU

Three monks – Seppo, Kinzan, and Ganto – were in the temple garden. Seppo noticed a pail of water and pointed to it. Kinzan said, "The water is clear, and the moon is reflected." "No, no," said Seppo, "it is not water, it is not moon." Ganto kicked over the pail.

Zen mondo

"Tell the truth and run."

Yugoslav proverb

This book is for Dylan and for Lisa.

Contents

Acknowledgments

The ground I have covered in these cases is by no means virgin soil. I am indebted to the authors of at least fifty books, and to the journalists responsible for more than a thousand newspaper and magazine articles. These works have been a priceless source of facts, leads, theories, and inspirations. They have also been a hell of a lot of fun to read.

I am grateful to all who have agreed to be interviewed, about matters that can involve a great deal of emotional pain. Murder does not leave its survivors unscarred.

My sincere thanks are due to all who have helped me with this book. There are many. I will mention only these: my long-time friend, fellow amateur sleuth and wily lawyer James R. Walker, Jr., who helped select the subject matter; researcher Ingrid Edison, who gathered background information on the Serge Rubinstein case; and, Cynthia Milne and Jim Shay, who spent countless hours running down leads.

Finally, I would like to thank Constable and Robinson for their unexpected and gratifying decision to offer this book in a new and revised edition. The opportunity to revisit these cases and to provide updates for them is much appreciated.

Preface

by Colin Wilson

I came across a secondhand copy of Kirk Wilson's *Investigating Murder* in the mid-1990s, and bought it simply because it contained three murder cases of which I had never heard – John Hill, Helen Brach and Cullen Davis. With the other cases in the book I was familiar, and felt no strong impulse to read yet more speculations about the Kennedy assassination, the death of Marilyn Monroe, or the disappearance of Lord Lucan.

But as soon as I began to read, I knew I was in the hands of a master of narrative, a man who knew exactly where he was going and what he was doing. This was the first paragraph I happened to read:

"In 1950, Frank Brach made some changes in his life. He divorced the woman he had been married to for seventeen years and started over with the red-headed hat-check girl he had picked up at a country club in Miami Beach. He did this knowing it could cost him a bundle, but that didn't seem to matter. Money was one thing he had plenty of."

But Wilson's skill is not simply a matter of a breezy style. He has another essential quality of a good crime writer: he has all the facts at his fingertips.

The Helen Brach case is followed by an account of the Lord Lucan mystery. I have always found this a rather boring case, because it involves the kind of people I find tedious: rich upper-class idiots with nothing between their stupid ears. Lucan used to sleep late every morning, then go to the Clermont Club in Berkeley Square and have his first martini, after which he always ate a lunch of smoked salmon and lamb chops. Then he sat at the gaming table until past midnight playing chemin de fer or baccarat, until he went home and slept until late the next morning . . .

Lucan's addiction to gambling had apparently taken hold after an early win of £20,000, which had convinced him that gambling was an easy and exciting way of making a living. He proved to be mistaken, and after inheriting his father's peerage, proceeded to throw away his fortune with both hands and sink into debt. It is not difficult to imagine what would have happened to him if he had not been forced to flee a murder charge in November 1974: he would have sold everything he possessed, been declared a bankrupt, and probably ending up blowing his brains out. It seems ironic that he should have been known as "Lucky" Lucan.

That luck had deserted Lucan becomes plain from the fact that he nerved himself to murder his wife, then made the extraordinary mistake of killing the wrong woman.

My only tenuous connection with the case lies in the fact that in the 1960s, when my own club, the Savage, was within a few minutes walk of the Clermont, I once met Lucan's friend Dominic Elwes, a charming painter whose name frequently appeared in the gossip columns. For me, one of the saddest parts of the story is that Elwes committed suicide after being blackballed by fellow members of the Clermont Club, because he was honest enough to admit that Lucan was probably guilty. But I find it hard to imagine why a witty and talented man should have killed himself merely because a few upper-class gamblers decided not to speak to him. It argues that his sense of values was as flawed as theirs.

It seems fairly clear that Kirk Wilson regards the long opening chapter on Kennedy as its most important in the book, and I agree with him. What this generation has forgotten is that at the time of the assassination, Kennedy was regarded as a kind of saint, and America went into shock that anyone should want to kill such a paragon. In 1960, I was at a dinner in Georgetown, Washington, given by a hostess who had been one of Kennedy's closest friends. I tactlessly raised the subject of Kennedy's womanising, and my out-raged fellow guests assured me that it was a vicious calumny; it was not until 1976, when one of Kennedy's mistresses, Judith Campbell

Exner, announced that she had been having a simultaneous affair with Kennedy and the Chicago mobster Sam Giancana, that it began to emerge that Kennedy was, in fact, a kind of sex maniac.

Over the years, I had myself written about the Kennedy assassination, and thought of myself as thoroughly familiar with it. Kirk Wilson's revelatory chapter made me aware that there was a great deal with which I was unfamiliar, and it ended by convincing me completely that both the Kennedy brothers were murdered by the Mob.

I should note that I read it in 1995, three years before the death of Frank Sinatra, and the candid appraisal of Sinatra's career that has since become possible. Now we know just how much Sinatra's Mafia friends – like Giancana – were responsible for Kennedy beating Nixon in the presidential race, which Kennedy won by a slim margin, and how Sinatra's support for Kennedy during the election led the singer to believe that he would in future become a favoured guest at the White House, and play host to the president at his own home at Palm Springs.

But Sinatra was failing to take into account Bobby Kennedy's detestation of the Mob, and his determination to break the power of the Mafia. Just before the weekend JFK was due to fly to Palm Springs to stay with Sinatra, the president was told that on no account could he accept Sinatra's hospitality, since Sinatra was a close associate of Giancana and other Mafia figures – all of whom were waiting for Kennedy to demonstrate his gratitude for past favours by telling Bobby to adopt a more friendly policy towards the mob. At the last minute, the president cancelled his visit to Palm Springs, and Sinatra exploded into a screaming rage (when angry he had as little self-control as Adolf Hitler) and went around the newly installed facilities, which had cost him around a million dollars, smashing them with an axe.

From that moment on, Sinatra ceased to be a Democrat. Giancana regarded him as a welsher for failing to deliver Kennedy's support (in exchange for Giancana's gift of a crucial vote in Chicago). And the Kennedy brothers were suddenly on the Mob's death list.

Kirk Wilson dots the i's and crosses the t's. "If the assassination had not happened and both Kennedys had served a second term, it is possible that organised crime could have been effectively crippled as a national threat."

As it is, the world's greatest democracy continues to be virtually a hostage to Cosa Nostra.

This theme of Mafia influence continues to dominate Wilson's article on the disappearance of Teamster union leader Jimmy Hoffa, who rose from being a teenage strike leader to being the most powerful union boss in America. But Hoffa then went on to make the same mistake that Kennedy would make: accepting a helping hand from the Mob. It was the Mob link that eventually made Hoffa the target of Robert Kennedy, and landed him in jail. He emerged from the Lewisburg penitentiary determined to regain his position as the Teamsters' boss. That was enough to make him a target of rivals like Tony Provenzano.

But according to Wilson, the reason behind his murder may have been more sinister than that. Hoffa had promised to clean up the Teamster's union and get rid of Mob influence. And, as Wilson comments, his disappearance may have "deprived . . . the rank and file members of the world's largest labour union of the best chance they have had to get the Mafia out of their business and off their backs".

The Mob rears its head again in the mystery of the murder of Sir Harry Oakes. His body was found at his home in the Bahamas in July 1943, bludgeoned to death and partly burned. Meyer Lansky, close friend of Lucky Luciano, was interested in establishing a gambling casino in the Bahamas, and needed support from influential residents. Sir Harry Oakes was apparently unwilling to give that support. This alone could provide a reason his murder, and probably did. What Wilson does not mention is that in 1972, an American law professor named Marshall Houtts, who had been a wartime undercover agent, wrote a book called *King's X* in which he claimed that Sir Harry Oakes and his friend Harold Christie had made a late night visit to the boat of Meyer Lansky, virtually the accountant of "Murder Incorporated", to discuss the casino idea, and that Oakes had lost his temper, and been struck on the head by one of Lansky's bodyguards. The intention, Houtts claims, was merely to subdue him, but the blow was too hard, and Oakes died on his way back to his own house. So the "murder scene" was arranged.

While this scenario could well explain the murder, it does not explain why the governor of the Bahamas, the Duke of Windsor, insisted on taking over the investigation, and appointed two incompetent policemen, who bungled it. In recent years, an interesting and convincing theory has emerged.

Edward, Duke of Windsor, as everyone knows, gave up his throne in 1936 to marry an American, Mrs Wallis Simpson. It was known at the time that he was sympathetic to Germany and the Nazis. What was not generally known is that he felt that democracy is inefficient, and was determined not to be a mere constitutional monarch, but a ruler and a leader, like Hitler or Mussolini. The British Government was anxious to get rid of him for this reason, and the constitutional crisis over Mrs Simpson was merely an excuse.

If Edward had remained on the throne the Second World War might never have taken place, because he would have appeased and supported Hitler. As it was, he was packed off to the Bahamas in 1940, to keep him out of trouble, and spent much time in contact with Nazi sympathisers like the Swedish billionaire Axel Wenner-Gren. And he proceeded to engage in illegal currency dealing on a massive scale. He also closed his eyes to drug smuggling – Bahamian residents used their yachts to transport morphine and opium to the American mainland – as well as gold.

So when Oakes was killed, the Duke had good reason not to call in Scotland Yard, and to try to impose a news blackout about the murder. A competent police investigation might uncover his own activities.

Whoever killed Sir Harry Oakes – and the Mafia is bound to figure among the chief suspects – the Duke of Windsor certainly played an active part in covering it up.

The death of Marilyn Monroe was another mystery in which I had never taken much interest, although I had very sincere regrets.

I had met her twice in London in the 1950s, together with her husband Arthur Miller. I liked her, and got the impression that she liked me. When I knew I was going to Los Angeles on a lecture tour in 1961, I thought idly about renewing the acquaintance. But it was a crowded trip, during which I saw something of Aldous Huxley, Christopher Isherwood, Henry Miller, and actor Charles Laughton and his wife Elsa Lanchester, and had no time to wonder where to find Marilyn Monroe. So when I heard that she had died – a possible suicide – in August 1962, I was saddened. If she was as lonely and miserable as most accounts suggested, she might have been glad to renew an old acquaintance.

However, if Kirk Wilson is correct, her death was not the result of emotional problems and deep-seated insecurities, but of her intention of calling a press conference. And although at first glance it looks as though Wilson is pointing the finger at Robert Kennedy as the man behind her "murder" – she was in love with Kennedy and deeply hurt by his abandonment of her – it quickly becomes clear that what Wilson really has in mind is – once again – Sam Giancana and the Mob. Giancana was involved in a CIA–Mafia plot to kill Fidel Castro, which Wilson also suggests may have had something to do with the disappearance of Jimmy Hoffa. If Giancana suspected his name might figure in Marilyn's revelations, then she was certainly playing an incredibly dangerous game. In *His Way*, her "unauthorised" biography of Frank Sinatra, Kitty Kelley records that "by 1960, Giancana had eliminated more than 200 men". Giancana himself was assassinated by gunmen in his Chicago home in 1975.

It is obviously because of his analysis of these Mob-related cases that Kirk Wilson received the Byliner's Award for the best non-fiction book of the year. But it would be a pity to discount his superb analysis of less known cases, such as the crooked financier Serge Rubinstein, the Danish "boulevardier" Claus von Bülow, the one-time hat-check girl Helen Brach and the born-again million-aire and murder suspect, Cullen Davis. All in all, this book is a classic of true-crime reportage.

Colin Wilson 2002

Introduction

Since Cain picked up the jawbone, people have been settling their problems by killing other people. The choice of such an extreme solution is generally regrettable, for most murderers enjoy no more success than Cain. They kill in anger, feel bad about it, and suffer the punishment.

The killers in these stories are different. They are, in the pure sense of the word, *assassins*. They do not kill in passion or in the throes of some derangement. They plan to kill. The end is the calculated achievement of an objective, and the means is murder.

There is another, more striking difference that separates these killers from the common murderer. Though their victims were among the most famous people of our era, though their crimes have been exhaustively researched and rehashed and written about, though every lead has been followed and every clue has been turned a thousand ways, they remain – if not unknown – unpunished.

They got away with murder.

They killed our President, and our favorite Hollywood sex symbol, and the richest man on earth, and all the other victims you will meet here, and walked away scot-free.

Aside from whatever judgments we may wish to pass on them, we do owe these exceptional evildoers one debt of service: they have created the most intriguing unsolved murder mysteries of our time. The very best of these sordid creations – the Top Ten – are presented here.

Who decided which ten are the Top Ten? I did. Working from a lengthy list of nominees supplied by fellow crime addicts, I was contest judge, jury, and, some may say, executioner. I can only beg for leniency in your judgment of my selections of the tales and my telling of them.

Some of the choices were obvious. Others were a matter of weighing, in an altogether subjective way, factors that seemed to tilt the scales of interest. These considered choices were not easy. I would have preferred, like Pooh Bear counting his honey pots, to have come to a stop at a higher number. But a rare outbreak of good sense and an all too common outbreak of necessity conspired to demand a manageable cutoff point.

To qualify for consideration, a case had to be (1) a genuine page one sensation, (2) a first-rate tale of mystery, and (3) still unsolved and therefore still mysterious.

A serendipitous result of applying these criteria was that the stories they turned up tended to be not only great mysteries, but great histories as well. The murder of Sir Harry Oakes is a particularly fine example.

As a whodunit the Oakes case is all but nonpareil: the world's richest man – a cantankerous old gold prospector – is found bludgeoned to death in the bedroom of one of his Bahamian mansions. The body has been partially burned and is covered with feathers!

The old man's son-in-law, a yacht-racing French playboy-count, is clumsily framed by the island authorities (for reasons that are, yes, shrouded in mystery) and declared not guilty in a sensational trial.

The governor of the islands, and the character who appears to be at the center of the cover-up, is none other than the Duke of Windsor, the former King of England who had made the century's grandest romantic gesture by giving up his throne for the woman he loved.

All of this occurs in an earthly paradise against the dramatic backdrop of the height of World War II, a stage setting replete with Nazi spies, arms dealers, forbidden romances, American Mafiosi out to expand their Cuban gambling empire into Nassau, and even, if you buy one theory of the crime, a witch doctor or two.

And this case, in my ranking anyhow, could do no better than third place!

Other than their shared status as members of the Top Ten, the cases were not required to be related. As it happens, several of them tie into one another in interesting ways. John Kennedy and his brother Robert seem to have had affairs with Marilyn Monroe, and may have known more than they ever told about her death and the cover-up that followed it. The Kennedys were tape-recorded in their diversions with Marilyn by arch-enemy Jimmy Hoffa, who may have known who was behind the assassination of John Kennedy. The Cosa Nostra figures who weave their shadowy ways through the stories of Kennedy, Hoffa, and Monroe are directly descended from the mobsters who figure prominently in the story of Sir Harry Oakes, and so on.

Though there is a good deal of previously unpublished information – more in some cases than in others – to be found here, the thrust has been to gather what is known, and the best of what is theorized, about the great murders and murderers of our age for scrutiny under one cover. Some years have been given to this effort, but it has not been unrewarding.

In some cases the sifting and probing have gradually revealed the features of a killer with a name and an address, features so clear that we can only feel outrage that the guilty party has never – and probably will never – come to justice. In other cases all that remains is a shadow, a disturbing sense that the killer or killers have turned the corner just ahead of us.

In any event, each of these tales is first-rate evidence for the old argument that truth may be stranger than fiction. It may also be more frightening. In a way, I suppose, the chronicles of our most celebrated crimes make up a kind of fun house image of the time and the place we live in.

Welcome in. And, please, do watch your step.

Postscript

Unsolved murder cases do not lie still like murder victims. They shift appearances as new information becomes available, and, because of the attention that is paid to them, celebrated cases like these tend to do so more than your average homicide. The passage of almost twelve years since the first edition of this book was published has brought developments worth mentioning in most of these cases, and it has been my pleasure to look into these developments and to provide updates where appropriate at the end of each chapter.

1

The Last Time We Saw Camelot

The Assassination of John Fitzgerald Kennedy

This is a story that haunts every American who knows it. To tell it is to invoke memories that challenge our most cherished assumptions, memories that will not leave us because, in all likelihood, we will never see the nagging questions answered and the guilty face punishment, and we know it. The crime involved was murder. A murder more terrible and more frightening than any before or since, because it touched us in a way we never wanted to be touched, almost as though it had happened in our own homes.

These feelings are compounded by the fact that our elected government, which could and should have helped us through our grief, instead engendered a self-propagating muddle that made the nightmare worse, and all but guaranteed that the crime would forever go unsolved.

Unquestionably, the assassination of John Fitzgerald Kennedy is the crime of the century. It changed our country and our world, at the same time changing forever, if in subtle ways, the way we think about that country and about ourselves as its citizens. To many it seemed the gate-opening event that set the decade of the 1960s on its shattering course – through the assassinations, the riots, the war, and the anti-war – and changed the lives and the lifestyles of more than one generation.

As an enduring tale of mystery, the assassination is as perfect as anything in history. Every theory has a hole, and every hole could spawn another theory. No scene is more than half lit. For every character visible in the drama, there are a dozen shadows moving just beyond our range of vision. And for every seemingly clear image there is a mirror image set and ready to contradict it in every particular.

The scene of the crime was in a large sense not limited to downtown Dallas. It was a national stage that surged with an unprecedented variety of plots and players. Never in peacetime had the country been so bitterly divided along ideological lines; the closest presidential election in history and the actions of the dynamic government that came to power in that election had split Americans into uncompromising camps of Kennedy lovers and Kennedy haters.

Black Americans, one hundred years after emancipation, were on the verge of coming into the full rights of citizenship, but not without the violent opposition of diehard racists throughout the country.

The Cold War was near the freezing point. In Europe, the Berlin Wall had gone up as an ugly symbol of the struggle. The American President had responded with his stirring "Ich bin ein Berliner" speech. No compromise seemed possible.

In the fall of 1962, the world had come as close as it ever has to the brink of nuclear war, in a Mexican standoff with intercontinental ballistic missiles where the six-guns should have been. It had been called the Cuban Missile Crisis, and it was only one of many Cuban crises of the era, brought about by the emergence of the first Communist government in the Western Hemisphere, with the victory of Fidel Castro's revolutionaries on January 1, 1959.

Within the United States, the elected government was locked in a bitter contest with a powerful rival the young Attorney General called the Private Government: organized crime. It was a battle the elected government would lose, in a war that has not ended. From outside the country, the bodies of American soldiers were beginning to come home from another losing cause, in an obscure Southeast Asian nation called Vietnam.

The man who led the country in these turbulent times was

seen in many quarters as the best example America could offer. He was young – the second youngest president ever – handsome, brilliantly intelligent, articulate, and rich. He was a war hero and a writer who had won a Pulitzer Prize. He had a beautiful wife and a beautiful family, and on its surface his administration was a perfect match for the storybook image his publicists created for it: he was the King of the brief and shining moment, and his court was held in Camelot. To this day John F. Kennedy wins straw votes as the most popular president in American history.

With cruel irony, the story of this glittering figure did not end when his head was blown apart by gunshots on November 22, 1963. The story went on, and in it we learned he was as given to human flaws – to lust and clouded judgment – as any of us. Worse, within that story he was in company with the seediest denizens who inhabit the underside of America. These violently desperate characters – crooks and killers, malcontents, fanatics, double agents, whores, and strippers – own and rule these pages as much or more than he does.

Whatever else he may have been, John Kennedy was an ardent politician. When he and his entourage arrived in Texas on Thursday, November 21, his purpose was purely political. The stakes were twenty-five electoral votes in the 1964 election. The gamble was that the presidential visit could smooth over a factional squabble between liberal Texas Democrats, represented by U.S. Senator Ralph Yarborough, and conservatives, led by Governor John Connally, in a state where the Kennedy–Johnson ticket had squeaked through by the barest of margins in 1960.

The trip itinerary was grueling. On the twenty-first, a motorcade and building dedication in San Antonio, followed by another motorcade and a dinner speech in Houston. Sleep in Fort Worth, followed by an early-morning speech, a breakfast meeting, a motorcade in Dallas, a luncheon speech, then to Austin for an evening fundraiser and finally to Vice-President Lyndon Johnson's ranch.

The reception in San Antonio was worshipful – 125,000

cheering people had lined the motorcade route; Houston went nearly as well. But no trouble had been expected in these cities. It was Dallas that most worried the people close to the President.

The Dallas of the early 1960s was a hotbed of extreme right-wing sentiment. It was the headquarters of H. L. Hunt, the rambunctious billionaire oilman who was perhaps the best known and certainly the most well-heeled spokesman of the far right, and of his sons Bunker, Lamar, and W. Herbert, who shared his fortune and his politics.

During the 1960 campaign, tastefully dressed and perfectly coiffed young Dallas matrons had showered Lyndon and Lady Bird Johnson with spit, and as recently as October 24, Adlai Stevenson, the former presidential candidate and the Ambassador to the United Nations, had been assaulted during a celebration of UN Day.

The city was dotted with billboards that said IMPEACH EARL WARREN. On the day of the motorcade, a leaflet designed like a wanted poster was passed out downtown, with the headline WANTED FOR TREASON and two pictures of Kennedy arranged like police mug shots. That morning, a full-page ad appeared on page fourteen of *The Dallas Morning News,* with the headline "Welcome Mr. Kennedy to Dallas," followed by a bill of a dozen particulars that charged the visiting President with selling out to Communists in Cuba, Latin America, Europe, and Asia.

Given this atmosphere, a number of influential people advised the President not to go to Dallas. The Democratic National Committeeman from Texas, Byron Skelton of Waco, felt so strongly about it that he followed up a letter with a trip to Washington to plead his case in person. Kennedy answered the warnings with his conviction that it was absurd for an American president to be afraid to travel anywhere in his own country.

Hindsight has shown that a certain measure of fear would have been prudent. It has also shown that Dallas is not entirely deserving of its rap as the city that killed the President. Dallas is the city where the assassination happened to happen. There is evidence that John Kennedy had barely escaped death by gunfire in both Miami and Chicago during the same month he died in Dallas. His death had been planned. The people who had planned it were only waiting for the right place and the right time.

Skies had been overcast and drizzling as the presidential party awoke that Friday morning in Fort Worth. But by the time the short hop had been made to Love Field in Dallas, the skies were clearing and it was decided not to bolt the clear bubble top over the President's Lincoln convertible. This seemed a good political omen, as the Dallas crowds would be afforded a good view of the dashing young couple they had come to see.

The Texas trip was Jackie Kennedy's first public appearance since the death of an infant son the previous August, and the first real campaign trip she had made since the 1960 election. Sitting in front of her and her husband in the Lincoln's jump seats were Texas Governor John Connally and his wife Nellie. In the front seat were two Secret Service men.

The motorcade moved without incident toward downtown Dallas, stopping twice on orders from the President so he could shake hands – first with a group of children, then with several nuns and their small charges. The crowds were thickest along the Main Street shopping district. A quarter of a million people had turned out to see the Kennedys. The motorcade route then veered from Main to avoid taking the President through a shabby neighborhood.

As it turned into Houston Street, the spectacle was coming to an end. All that remained was a zigzag through Dealey Plaza and a quick ride on Stemmons Freeway to the waiting luncheon at the Dallas Trade Mart. The procession slowed to eleven miles an hour to negotiate the hairpin turn from Houston onto Elm, passing beneath a nondescript, seven-story red brick building housing the Texas School Book Depository.

The crowd in the Plaza was thinner but still substantial. The President's car straightened after coming through the turn. It was 12.30 p.m., Central Standard Time.

There was a gunshot. The limousine slowed to a crawl as the surprised Secret Service driver looked around. Had he sped away in that instant, John Kennedy might have served his full term. Another shot, perhaps two close together. The President's hand had gone to the back of his neck. Less than two seconds later Governor Connally twisted abruptly sideways with the impact of a hit. The Lincoln drifted aimlessly in the street as the Secret Service men looked back at their passengers. Another shot, or another group of two. The top right side of the President's head exploded. He was thrown violently backward, then rocked up into a sitting position, then thrown forward and down.

Finally the big convertible rushed off behind a police car to Parkland Hospital.

It left pandemonium in its wake. The eyewitnesses are sharply divided over what had occurred. Of the 266 witnesses now identified, thirty-two believe the shots came from the Texas School Book Depository. Fifty-one heard shots from a grassy knoll in front of the approaching limousine. Some heard shots from both directions.

Some heard two shots, some three or four, up to as many as seven. Several of the people on the grassy knoll had thrown themselves flat on the ground, terrified by the shot or shots coming from the stockade-style fence and bushes close behind them. Some parts of the crowds surged toward the knoll, others toward the Book Depository.

The policemen present also went both ways. Officer Joe Marshall Smith, who had been standing in the Elm and Houston intersection, went to the bushes behind the grassy knoll. Officer Bobby Hargis, who had been riding a motorcycle to the left rear of the President's car, dismounted and ran up the railroad embankment above the knoll. Another motorcycle officer, Clyde Haygood, followed with his pistol drawn. M. L. Baker, an officer riding behind Haygood, ran to the Book Depository.

At Parkland Hospital a team of doctors spent a feverish half-hour in what each of them knew was a hopeless effort to save the President. They noted "slow spasmodic respiration" when he first arrived, but found no pulse or heartbeat. They used what they took to be a small entrance wound on the front right side of his throat as the starting place for a tracheostomy. Though they had more urgent matters to attend to in the crisis, they could not escape noticing the massive head wound that made their struggles futile. No photographs were made of the President's body at Parkland – the object then was to save his life, not document his wounds – and the historical record of his injuries at this point depends on the doctors' recollections.

The problem is that several of the doctors in Parkland's Trauma Room One that day remember the head wound as being in a different place than the place where it was described and photographed in the official autopsy at Bethesda Naval Hospital late that night.

In notes written three hours after the President was declared dead, the surgeon who headed the team at Parkland, Malcolm P. Perry, wrote that "a large wound of the right *posterior* [my emphasis] cranium was noted, exposing severely lacerated brain." The autopsy doctors noted the head wound to be larger and further to the front of the skull than the Parkland doctors. This discrepancy would give rise to a great deal of controversy and to speculation that the President's body was altered prior to the autopsy, the object being to eliminate forensic evidence of a hit from the front. The Parkland doctors did not have occasion to turn the President over, and never had a clear look at the wound the autopsy doctors said was an entrance wound at the back of the skull, or another and equally controversial wound on the back of the neck.

The President was pronounced dead at 1.00 p.m. In the meantime Governor Connally had been saved by another team of doctors in the adjacent Trauma Room Two. A bullet had entered the Governor's back near his right armpit, cut through his chest, shattered his fifth rib, then gone on to break the radius bone in his right wrist, finally coming to a stop in his left thigh.

About 1.45 p.m., a hospital engineer named Darrell

Tomlinson was moving a stretcher in a Parkland corridor when he noticed a bullet fall out from under the stretcher pad. He turned the bullet over to the head of hospital security, who turned it over to a Secret Service man, who stuck it in his pocket.

The projectile had no visible blood or tissue on it, and seemed barely damaged, with only a small deformity at its base. This bullet would become the centerpiece of the lone gunman theory of the crime, and one of the most controversial elements in the case.

Under Texas law, an autopsy should have been performed on John Kennedy, as on any other homicide victim, before a death certificate could be issued and before the body could be released for shipment out of state. On the day of the assassination, that law was broken. Kennedy aides and Secret Service men literally shoved aside protesting Dallas County Medical Examiner Earl Rose and took the body back to Washington. Given the deep emotions of the moment, their actions are understandable. But understanding does not change the fact that, had they waited the three or four hours necessary for the Texas autopsy, some of the great mysteries of the crime might never have become mysteries at all.

Back at the School Book Depository, local police had found an old Italian military rifle, a 6.5 mm Mannlicher-Carcano, partially hidden among some boxes near the stairwell on the building's sixth floor. They also found three empty 6.5 mm cartridge cases near a stack of boxes, described as a "sniper's nest," by a window in the southeast corner of the sixth floor.

A floor-laying crew had been at work in that area of the building, but had gone down to the street along with almost all the Depository employees to watch the noon-hour motorcade.

Police also claimed to have found a handmade paper package, presumably used to carry in the weapon, on the sixth floor, although the first three policemen on the scene did not report seeing the package. The Depository supervisor was asked if any employees were unaccounted for, and a headcount turned up one missing person. His name was Lee Harvey Oswald.

At 1.16 p.m., the Dallas police dispatcher heard a civilian talking over a police radio. The excited man was saying that a police officer had just been shot dead in the Oak Cliff section of Dallas. The dead officer was J. D. Tippit.

Several witnesses provided a description of the killer that roughly matched the description of a suspect in the assass- ination, which the police had apparently picked up from someone in Dealey Plaza and had been broadcasting to squad cars.

About twenty minutes later, the manager of a shoe store six blocks from the Tippit killing saw a man ducking out of view of a passing police car and watched the man run into the Texas Theatre without buying a ticket. At 1.51 p.m., police arrested Oswald in the theater. He pulled a .38 caliber Smith & Wesson revolver but was disarmed during a struggle.

Oswald was taken to the Dallas city jail and interrogated for a total of about twelve hours between 2.30 Friday afternoon and 11.00 Sunday morning. He never admitted guilt in either the Tippit or the Kennedy killings. As he was brought from the jail to the interrogation room, he twice shouted, "I'm just a patsy!" to the reporters who packed the corridor.

At 11.20 Sunday morning, the Dallas police set out to trans- fer Oswald from the city to the county jail, a standard procedure in homicide cases. As they reached the basement garage with their prisoner, they walked into chaos. Bright television lighting and exploding flash bulbs half blinded them as they felt their way through the 125 reporters and police packed into the small space between the jail office and the garage.

The cordon of detectives that was supposed to have formed to protect Oswald was nowhere to be seen. The car that was sup- posed to be there to pick him up couldn't make it through the crowd.

Standing behind Blackie Harrison, a big plainclothes officer from the Juvenile Bureau, was a stocky little man in a suit and a fedora. He looked like a cop, and he knew a lot of cops well, Blackie Harrison among them, but the .38 he held had been pulled from his hip pocket. When Oswald moved within reach, the stocky little man – whose name was Jack Ruby and whose business was the operation of a striptease joint and a bar – stepped out and fired one shot.

It was a deadly shot. The bullet ruptured the aorta and the vena cava in the heart and passed through the spleen, the pancreas, a kidney, and the liver. Oswald was worked over by three of the same doctors who had tried to save the President, and pronounced dead at Parkland Hospital at 1.07 p.m., almost exactly two days after Kennedy.

Ruby's timing had been perfect. He had not only entered a supposedly secure area without police or press credentials, he had come within two minutes of the time Oswald had entered the basement. During interrogation, Ruby denied that anyone on the police force had told him when Oswald would be brought down, or helped him enter the basement. A lawyer named Tom Howard – the first attorney to see Ruby after his arrest – allegedly told him to say he had shot Oswald to spare Mrs. Kennedy the grief of coming back to Texas for a trial, and that is exactly what he said thereafter.

Ruby's murder of Oswald was seen live on television by millions, and replayed and reprinted as a photograph many times thereafter, becoming the most witnessed homicide in history. There was no question that he killed Oswald. The only question was why, and the answer did not emerge during the three years Ruby had left to live.

Ruby went on trial for killing Oswald in March of 1964. His lawyer at the time of the trial was the colorful Melvin Belli – Belli was one among a parade of lawyers the Ruby family hired and fired – and Belli chose to base his client's defense on the argument that Ruby was a victim of "psychomotor variant epilepsy" and thus not legally responsible.

The ploy didn't work. Ruby was found guilty and sentenced to die in the electric chair. He died instead in Parkland Hospital, of cancer, just after the Texas Court of Criminal Appeals had ordered a new trial of his case.

The shooting of Oswald occurred at a high point of national emotion, just as the televised funeral Mass for John F. Kennedy was coming to an end. Rumors and wild speculation abounded, and the bits of information that found their way into the press only fed the flames. Oswald, for example, had defected to Russia in 1959 and spent two years there, returning with a Russian wife.

Was Oswald part of a conspiracy? If so, who was behind it? Did Ruby kill Oswald to keep him from talking? The questions were disquieting. Their implications could feasibly lead to the kind of national hysteria that could start a war, or – just as serious to the political mind – cost an election. It was clear that answers would have to be provided. There was talk of a Texas commission to investigate, headed by state Attorney General Waggoner Carr.

As a shrewd politician, the new President, Lyndon Johnson, felt an urgent need to take control of the situation. One week after the assassination, he named a blue-ribbon panel of prominent Americans, headed by Earl Warren, the Chief Justice of the Supreme Court. From its inception, the purpose of the Warren Commission was to smooth troubled waters by answering the assassination questions for all time, and the more palatable the answers the better.

The Commission staff found itself under considerable pressure to provide these answers with plenty of time to spare before the 1964 election. The original deadline was June 30. This proved to be impossible, but the Commission did file its 888-page report by September 24, providing a small but adequate cushion prior to the election in November.

Seen in retrospect, the Warren Commission established a pattern that has been followed by almost all the assassination investigators who followed: establish a thesis, gather all the evidence that supports your thesis, and ignore or debunk all the evidence that does not. The thesis the Commission settled on was, not too surprisingly, the most comforting one. There was no conspiracy. Lee Harvey Oswald was a lone, misguided nut.

So was Jack Ruby. The assassination could be written off as a sad episode for which no one was really responsible.

The members and staff of the Warren Commission cannot be wholly blamed for taking this view. They had no investigators of their own, and were forced to rely on information supplied by the FBI and the CIA. Asked to reveal the truth, these two agencies did what they could to hide it. The top brass in both cases seemed more concerned with self-preservation than with their roles as public servants.

This was blatantly true of the FBI. Director J. Edgar Hoover was too busy covering his own tracks and protecting the image of his agency to direct a competent investigation.

Within hours of the assassination, Hoover had good reason to defend the lone nut theory: he learned the Dallas FBI office had a file on Oswald, knew he was a returned defector who claimed to be a Marxist revolutionary, knew he was dangerous – he had in fact threatened to blow up the bureau office in Dallas – and knew he was working at the School Book Depository with a perfect gunsight view of the motorcade route.

Hoover even learned there was evidence of a connection between Oswald and Soviet intelligence. Yet with all this information (and perhaps more that has never been revealed), Oswald had not even been placed on the FBI's Security Index, a failing Hoover found unforgivable. Nothing had been passed along to the Secret Service, and no meaningful attempt had been made to check out Oswald or his connections.

When Jack Ruby's name hit the news, Hoover learned that Ruby had been an FBI informant, had long-standing connections to organized crime, and had traveled suspiciously back and forth to Cuba.

To the pugnacious little Director, airing facts like these in public would disgrace the police agency that was his lifework. He started an internal investigation of breakdowns in the Oswald case that led him to secretly censure seventeen FBI men, including two headquarters section chiefs and the Assistant Director.

He fumed in writing that the slipshod Oswald investigation "resulted in forever destroying the bureau as the top-level investigative organization." Accordingly, Hoover set out to make sure that the Warren Commission did not learn all that he knew about the assassination. In Dallas, Agent James Hosty, who held the file on Oswald, was ordered to destroy evidence of the threat Oswald had made at the bureau's local office.

Other evidence was withheld or destroyed, and much was simply changed to better match the FBI version of events. When interviewed later, sixty-six assassination witnesses complained that the FBI had in some way altered what they had said during questioning before presenting it as evidence to the Warren Commission.

Hoover decided on the day of the assassination that Oswald had acted alone, or at least that it would look better for the FBI if he had. Oswald's killing by Ruby was a threat to this theory. Almost immediately after news came that Oswald was dead, Hoover had a conversation with a top aide to President Johnson, in which he said, "The thing I am most concerned about . . . is having something issued so we can convince the public that Oswald is the real assassin."

The FBI rushed through a report, delivered to the President and to the Warren Commission on December 9, 1963. The report argued that there was conclusive proof both Oswald and Ruby had acted alone.

On the surface, the CIA was more cooperative with the Warren Commission. Though it did not volunteer information, it did supply answers to questions. The problem was believing that the answers were true. As Allen Dulles – who had headed the CIA until he was fired by President Kennedy after the failed Bay of Pigs invasion in Cuba – warned his fellow Commission members, the CIA was after all in the secrecy business. If asked about sensitive information, a CIA man could be expected to lie.

Given this disclaimer, little credence might be given to CIA-supplied information. The intelligence agency did, in fact, have a great deal to hide from the Warren Commission, but just how much was not learned until the Church Committee Senate hearings in the mid-1970s. The most striking revelations included CIA assassination plots against Fidel Castro and agency use of the Mafia to carry out some of these plots.

Perhaps the most amazing thing about the conduct of the federal police and intelligence agencies before and after the assassination is that there has not been more public outrage about it. A great deal of information about the assassination is still kept secret from the public. According to the CIA, roughly one-fourth of its assassination documents are still classified. There is no way of knowing how much – or what – information is held by government agencies.

The Freedom of Information Act, passed by Congress in 1966 and strengthened in 1974, has provided researchers with most of the previously classified assassination evidence that has come to light. Even these documents are more often than not delivered to those who request them in heavily edited versions.

At the time the Warren Commission released its report, its comforting lone nut theory was widely accepted. The case against Oswald seemed conclusive enough. He was a malcontent who made no secret of his opposition to government policies. He had had an unfortunate upbringing and craved attention. He had been trained as a marksman in the Marine Corps.

His violent nature was shown by the fact that he beat his wife, had allegedly taken a shot at General Edwin Walker, a right-wing extremist who lived in Dallas, the previous spring, and was accused of killing Officer Tippit.

Mail order sales receipts made out to one of his aliases, A. J. Hidell, were found for the Mannlicher-Carcano rifle and the pistol he had been carrying when arrested, his palm print had been found on the rifle and his fingerprints on the "sniper's nest" boxes, eyewitnesses had seen a man who looked like him in the Depository window with a gun, and he had fled the scene.

But for all its apparent cohesiveness, the one-man, one-gun story proved to be more remarkable for what it left out than for what it included. The more that is known of the evidence the Warren Commission either ignored or never saw, the less credible its version of events becomes.

A Growing Case for Conspiracy

Soon after Ruby killed Oswald, reports began to surface of associations between Oswald and Ruby, and Ruby and/or Oswald and officer Tippit, and so on. Most of these reports were discredited, but there were much more serious challenges to the lone gunman theory.

The first of these came to light just after the assassination. A dress manufacturer named Abraham Zapruder, whose offices were near Dealey Plaza, was a home movie buff and happened to have been set up in the Plaza with his camera, complete with a telephoto lens. Zapruder was positioned to the President's right, between the Book Depository building and the famous grassy knoll. His film clearly shows the effect of the shots on the people in the presidential limousine.

At the instant of the fatal shot to the head, the Zapruder film shows the President's head being slammed violently backward and to his left. In other words, it looks very much as though he has been hit by a shot fired from the front and to his right. Oswald's gun was found behind and above the President's position. If someone was shooting from the front, there was another gun and thus a conspiracy.

The Warren Commission did what it could to explain away this disturbing sight and then transposed the prints of the Zapruder film frames that it published, making it appear that the President's head was moving forward. FBI Director Hoover, whose agency was responsible for the transposition, explained it had been "a printing error." The twenty-two second film itself was not seen in public until 1967, and not shown on television until 1975.

In 1978, the House Select Committee on Assassinations

(HSCA) concluded that the President's backward motion was caused by an involuntary muscle spasm, and produced a film of a goat being shot to prove its point. The unfortunate goat experienced a spasm in all its muscles. The President did not. His head snapped sharply backward, and portions of his skull and brain traveled behind him, some landing on the car trunk and some reaching far enough to splatter the motorcycle cop riding behind him and to his left.

Various tests using melons and skulls stuffed with melon showed that an object can fall backward toward the gun that shot it. But in no case did the melon material fly backward toward the gun, as did the material from the President's head.

Analysis of the Zapruder film did show the President's head moving forward a fraction of a second before it snapped back, leading some to credit the shot from the rear and others to conclude that there was not one shot to the head, but two – the first from the rear and the second from the front. The latter view may help explain some of the confusion over the autopsy findings.

For the one-gun theorists, the Zapruder film was to pose an even peskier problem. Film moved through Zapruder's camera at eighteen frames per second. Each frame therefore represents the passage of one-eighteenth of a second of time, providing an absolute time clock of the reactions of the people in the limousine to the shooting in Dealey Plaza that day.

The FBI established that 2.25 seconds were required to work the bolt on the aged Mannlicher-Carcano, take aim, and fire a shot. Working the gun this fast did not allow shots to be fired with the accuracy seen in the assassination, but this difficulty was overlooked. The Zapruder film shows John Kennedy and John Connally reacting to hits less than two seconds apart.

This allows for only two possibilities. Either Kennedy and Connally were hit by two separate shots – Governor Connally swore they were – or they were hit by the same shot, with the bullet passing first through Kennedy and then through Connally. Since two shots could not have come from Oswald's gun that quickly, the Warren Commission took the latter view, accounting for the time discrepancy by theorizing that Governor Connally had a delayed reaction to his wounds. The HSCA also bought the two hits with one shot theory.

The bullet found on the stretcher in Parkland Hospital provided a convenient ribbon to tie up this theoretical package. The Warren Commission said the bullet was found on the stretcher that had been used to carry Governor Connally into the hospital, even though the man who found the bullet, Darrell Tomlinson, said he was not sure what stretcher it had come from. The bullet became known as Warren Commission Exhibit 399.

Since only bullet fragments, but no large slug, were found in the Governor's body, the Warren Report concluded that bullet 399 had passed through the President's neck and gone on through Connally's back, chest, wrist, and into his thigh, shattering a rib and a wrist bone on its way. Then it had fallen cooperatively out of his thigh and onto the stretcher.

Anyone familiar with shooting or with ballistics would expect a bullet that has done this much damage to be severely mangled. Indeed, government testing showed that firing 6.5 mm bullets into cadavers and striking bone produced an amorphous glob of lead. Only firing into cotton produced a relatively unscathed bullet. But bullet 399 was in near pristine condition, misshapen only a bit near its base and missing little if any of its lead. It was not even marred by blood or tissue.

There was a final, seemingly inescapable problem the Warren Commission and subsequently the HSCA managed to ignore: the Parkland doctors had seen more lead in John Connally's chest and wrist than could possibly have come from bullet 399. The Governor carried bits of this lead to his grave.

The issue was further complicated by the fact that the man Tomlinson handed the bullet to, Parkland Hospital Security Director O. P. Wright, insisted that the bullet he was given on November 22 was not bullet 399. He said the bullet found on the stretcher had been sharply pointed. The nose of bullet 399 is blunt. The Secret Service men who had handled the bullet could not positively identify bullet 399 as the one found on the stretcher.

For those interested in proving Lee Harvey Oswald was a lone assassin, bullet 399 had one overwhelming virtue that made it easy to overlook its many problems as a piece of evidence. FBI ballistics tests showed it had been fired from the Mannlicher-Carcano rifle found on the sixth floor of the Book Depository.

For advocates of a conspiracy, bullet 399 became equally important. Since it could not have performed the feats attributed to it, and since there was no other explanation for so perfect a bullet fired from Oswald's gun turning up at Parkland Hospital, it seemed reasonable to assume the bullet was planted to frame Oswald or to seal the case against him. The plant could have been made at the hospital, or the bullet could have been switched for another sometime between the discovery in Dallas and the delivery of bullet 399 to the FBI lab in Washington.

Hundreds of people had rushed to the hospital after learning the President was there, and one of these people was Jack Ruby. Ruby steadfastly denied going to the hospital, but he was seen there by two people, one of them a veteran newspaper reporter named Seth Kantor who knew Ruby well. Kantor later wrote a book called *Who Was Jack Ruby?* that thoroughly documents Ruby's connections with organized crime and with Dallas policemen.

Other bullet fragments were found in the presidential limousine, and testing showed that these had been made from the same material as bullet 399. The fragments were too small to ascertain what gun they had been fired from.

Here, too, the possibility of planted evidence exists. The open limousine was left unattended in the hospital parking lot for an hour or longer after the President had been taken inside. There is another possibility. Conspirators sophisticated enough to kill the President and successfully frame Oswald could have used hand-loaded fragmentation bullets molded from the same lead as the bullet fired through Oswald's rifle.

They would also have been sure to establish better escape

routes for themselves than for their patsy. In Dealey Plaza, there was no better place from which to fire on a motorcade and then escape than the grassy knoll. A shooter could fire from cover behind a stockade-style fence and foliage at the back of the knoll, walk a few feet to a parking lot behind him without being seen, and drive away. As a place to shoot and hope to escape, the knoll is an obvious choice over the sixth floor of an occupied building.

It is also a better stand to shoot from. At the time of the shot – or shots – to the head, the fence on the knoll was less than half as far from the President than the southeast corner of the Depository sixth floor.

All this would be pure conjecture but for the considerable evidence that sustains it. The HSCA went to great lengths to establish acoustical proof of where the shots had come from, using a tape recorded by a microphone that had been open on a police motorcycle and an aural reconstruction of events in Dealey Plaza.

The Select Committee's conclusion was that there had probably been a total of four shots – three from the School Book Depository and one from the grassy knoll. This was the first and only time a U.S. government investigative body stated that there was a good possibility of a conspiracy in the Kennedy assassination, and this hedging admission did not come until 1978 – fifteen years after the fact. The acoustical findings caused great controversy and were later disputed by the Justice Department.

The great acoustics debate amounted to little more than a red herring. With or without acoustics, there is a convincing body of evidence of shooting from the knoll. People standing on or near the knoll swore they heard shooting from behind them. Several instinctively threw themselves to the ground because the gunfire sounded so close.

One of these was a Korean War veteran named William Newman, who was standing on the curb between the knoll and the motorcade with his wife Gale and two small children, close enough to the limousine to hear some of what was said in the car during the shooting. Newman's testimony before the HSCA is especially interesting because it seems to establish the timing and effectiveness of the grassy knoll shot.

The first two shots sounded to the Newmans like firecrackers. They did not duck down in response to these shots. They saw the President and Governor Connally react as though they had been hit. Then they saw the President's head explode at the same instant in which a loud boom came from immediately behind them. It was then that Newman fell to the ground out of the line of fire, pulling his wife and kids down with him.

Amateur cameraman Abraham Zapruder, standing to the left of the Newmans further from the knoll, told the Warren Commission he heard at least one shot that "came from right behind." The other shots he heard were like car backfires, but this one was much louder, echoed, and shook him physically.

In the car, Mrs. Connally heard the first two shots that hit the President and her husband as "pops." The shot to the head, which came as she was bending over the Governor, was different. She "felt" the sound.

A railroad supervisor named S. M. Holland, who was on the railroad overpass above the knoll, heard a shot from the fence on the knoll (the third of four shots he heard) and along with several co-workers, saw a puff of smoke rise among the trees there.

The suspicious activity behind the knoll fence was not limited to gunfire. Jean Hill was standing on Elm Street directly across from the knoll when the President's head exploded in front of her. Her eye was immediately drawn to movement on the knoll. She saw a man in a brown overcoat running from the knoll toward the railroad tracks.

Witnesses Tom Tilson and J. C. Price also saw a man running from the knoll, Tilson remarking that the man threw something in a car, got in, and sped away. But it was Mrs. Hill who tried to catch the man. She ran across the street and up the knoll, but was stopped in the parking lot behind the fence by a man in a suit who showed her Secret Service identification.

A Dallas Police patrolman named J. M. Smith had a similar encounter. He was directing traffic at Elm and Houston when the shooting started and a woman ran up to him screaming, "They are shooting the President from the bushes!" Smith ran up the knoll and behind the bushes and the fence. He found a man in a suit there, and pulled his service revolver. The man showed him a Secret Service ID and Smith holstered his gun.

A few minutes later, D. V. Harkness, a sergeant in the Dallas Police Traffic Division, ran into several "well-armed" men in suits behind the Book Depository building. The men identified themselves as Secret Service.

A young man named Gordon Arnold, just back from Army basic training, wanted to take pictures of the President and went up the grassy knoll with his camera just before the motorcade arrived. As he stepped behind the fence on his way to the railroad overpass, he was stopped by a man in a suit who was armed with a pistol. Arnold told the man he was on his way to the overpass and the man produced a Secret Service badge and said no one was allowed in the area.

Subsequently, Arnold was watching the motorcade from the top of the knoll about a yard from the fence when he felt a bullet whiz past his left ear and heard the explosion of rifle fire immediately behind him. Arnold dropped to the ground as he had just been trained to do and then heard a second shot from behind the fence. It had been, he told author Henry Hurt, "just like I was standing there under the muzzle."

The only Secret Service men in Dealey Plaza on November 22, 1963, were the ones in the motorcade. None of them were, at any time, behind the fence on the knoll or behind the Book Depository.

The conclusion is inescapable. The bogus Secret Service men were in place to protect firing positions for assassins and to cover their escape routes. It was a brilliant tactic in an extremely well-planned operation. During a presidential visit, the presence of the Secret Service would be expected and its authority would not be challenged by either the ordinary citizen or the local police. The only threat of exposure would be from real Secret Service men, and their attention would be focused on the protection of the President and the Vice-President.

S. M. Holland, the railroad supervisor, located what may have been the second "sniper's nest" in Dealey Plaza when he arrived at the spot behind the fence where he thought shots had come from. With Holland were two other railroad men, and the three were soon joined by several other people who had run to the identical spot.

On the ground still damp from the drizzle that morning, the group found a short and narrow strip completely trampled by footprints. "It looked," Holland told author Josiah Thompson, "like a lion pacing a cage." There were no cartridge cases or rifles to be seen, and with good reason. The man who had fired from this position was nobody's patsy.

The bulk of the most credible grassy knoll testimony has been brought to light by independent researchers. The Warren Commission ignored what it heard about the knoll, and the HSCA chose to emphasize its controversial "scientific" proof of a knoll shot – throwing its already inconclusive report into question. As the century's greatest mystery story has unfolded, this strange pattern has been seen at every turn: in the vacuum left by official obfuscation, ineptitude, and outright lies, the burden of truth-seeking has fallen on individual citizens.

The scene at the officially established sniper's nest is another case in point. The Warren Commission seized on the testimony of one witness who had seen a lone gunman resembling Lee Harvey Oswald waiting for the President and later firing. But several witnesses, who had widely varying vantage points and spoke independently of one another, have reported seeing not one man waiting on the sixth floor, but two. One of these men had a rifle. The other – according to two people – wore a brown sports coat. One or both of the men was dark-complected.

At one point the two men were seen working together to adjust the scope of the rifle. In another view – a motion picture tracked down by researchers fifteen years after the FBI had rejected it as worthless – simultaneous movement is seen in two different sets of windows on the sixth floor. A photographic consultant reported to the HSCA that the moving figures were working together to build the sniper's nest of boxes.

Then there is the "getaway car." Three witnesses, one of them a Dallas deputy sheriff, saw a man come out from the back side of the School Book Depository about fifteen minutes after the shooting, hurry down the grassy incline, hop into a light green or gray Rambler station wagon with a luggage rack, and be driven away. The driver was a Latin or dark-complected man. The sheriff's deputy and one of the other witnesses swore the man who got into the car was Lee Harvey Oswald or "his identical twin."

Another witness saw a man wearing a brown sports coat come out from the rear of the building shortly after the shooting, walk south on Houston Street, kill time by circling the block, and then get into a gray or green Rambler station wagon. Still another person confirmed the view of the sports-coated man leaving the building, but watched him only to the point when he headed south on Houston.

It is interesting to note that all these reports indicate an escape route at the rear of the building – the same side where Dallas Police Sergeant D. V. Harkness ran into his bogus Secret Service men at about the same time.

The Warren Report concluded Oswald had left from the front of the building, though not a single witness saw him do so. A black and white press photograph of Dealey Plaza shows a light-colored Rambler station wagon with a luggage rack passing in front of the Book Depository. Like everything else about the assassination, it is a teasing picture, a half-fact, as much of the view of the supposed escape route is blocked by a city bus, and the license number on the Rambler cannot be seen. A clock shown in the picture establishes the time. It is 12.45 – exactly fifteen minutes after the shooting.

These reports were left out of the official reconstructions of the crime not only because they reeked of conspiracy but because, by the official reckoning, Lee Harvey Oswald was somewhere else at the time.

He is supposed to have caught a city bus blocks from the scene, transferred to a cab, and alighted near his rooming house, where he picked up the revolver that was later used to kill Officer Tippit. The witnesses who place him on this route are a former landlady – who saw him on the bus in shirtsleeves without a jacket – and the cab driver, who saw him wearing *two* jackets. Oswald himself reportedly confirmed his route home during his interrogation.

This is only one of many instances in which the alleged assassin showed an alarming tendency to be in more than one place at the same time. When the Warren Commission has him in Mexico, he is positively identified in company with two Cubans in Dallas. While he is quietly visiting his family for the weekend, he is seen taking target practice at a distant rifle range. He cannot drive a car and has no money, and he test-drives an expensive new model. And so on. The numerous reports of Oswald replicates have led to speculation that an impostor was used to call attention to the patsy and frame him for the crime. Another and perhaps more likely explanation is that there was a second man involved who strongly resembled Oswald.

Was Oswald framed? He was almost certainly used as a fall guy, though it seems impossible to determine how active his own role in the assassination may have been. It is possible he never fired a shot.

He claimed to have been eating in the second-floor lunch-room of the Depository when the shooting started. About ninety seconds after the last shot, he was seen in the lunchroom by his boss and Dallas policeman M. L. Baker. According to both men, he seemed perfectly undisturbed, despite the fact that the policeman had drawn his gun.

Less than a minute later, a clerical supervisor saw Oswald walking with a full bottle of Coca-Cola in his hand, presumably just purchased from the vending machines in the second-floor lunchroom. A secretary named Carolyn Arnold had seen him in the second-floor lunchroom, casually having his lunch, as late as 12.15. (Mrs. Arnold's account was one of the sixty-six that were significantly distorted by the FBI before presentation to the Warren Commission.)

To have shown so calm a demeanor immediately after killing the President, Oswald must have been an actor of consummate gifts.

To have killed the President alone, he must have been an even better rifleman. The evidence says that he was not. To those who knew him in the Marine Corps, his marksmanship was a joke. His performance on the Marine firing range was never better than mediocre. His bolt-action Mannlicher-Carcano rifle, first manufactured in 1891, was a notoriously inaccurate and undependable weapon that would not have been the choice of a skilled assassin.

Both the Warren Commission and the HSCA tried and failed to duplicate Oswald's alleged feat of marksmanship using teams of expert riflemen shooting at fixed targets, not at targets moving away and downhill. It may not be impossible to work the bolt on the Mannlicher-Carcano as quickly and still fire as accurately as Oswald supposedly did, but it is difficult enough that no expert has yet done it.

Oswald was a bad shot using a lousy gun. He is a poor candidate for the role of lone gunman, and not a good candidate for the role of one gunman in a two or three-gun team.

The one clear fact about Oswald is that he knew enough to make it imperative that he be stopped from talking. Though no tape recordings were made during his twelve hours of interrogation, we are told he had said nothing to implicate anyone before he was silenced by Jack Ruby's gun.

Ruby stalked Oswald for an entire weekend, waiting for his opportunity, before killing him on Sunday. He almost certainly had help in doing this from someone within the Dallas Police Department – his timing and his access to Oswald were too perfect to have been coincidence – though Ruby went to his grave without saying who had helped him or why. The suspicion that some Dallas lawmen may, for whatever reason, have tipped Jack Ruby off does not necessarily implicate police in a conspiracy, though the official handling of evidence did little to clear the air.

Lee Oswald was the one visible moving part in an intricately hidden mechanism. The ongoing debate over how many shooters there were and where they shot from has become no more than window dressing for the genuine issue, which is not what happened in Dealey Plaza, but who made it happen. Here the real mystery begins. And here the investigator of the crime enters a never-ending labyrinth of mirrors. Convincing cases can and have been made to support a number of theories. The problem is that one convincing theory tends to cancel out another.

There are only two sure things about the conspiracy. One is that the people behind it had substantial resources. It was well planned, well funded, and well executed. It involved the coordinated activities of a dozen or more people – at least eight in Dealey Plaza alone – in several cities. The other sure thing, at least up until this point, is that the conspiracy worked and the conspirators won. They killed the President of the United States and got away scot-free.

Considering the enormous body of claims and counterclaims that make up the assassination literature, the tragic fact is that the truth could not be clearly recognized today even if it were told.

Had the Warren Commission been an investigation and not a whitewash, had our police and intelligence agencies done their jobs instead of – no doubt unwittingly – serving the interests of the conspirators, the crime might have been solved soon after it was committed. At this point far too much water, from too many twisted streams, has flowed under the bridge.

Still, each of the more credible theories of the crime is, if nothing else, entertaining in its own way. Here are the best of the lot.

The Body Chopping Off the Head

Conspiracy in the Executive Branch

This one is not so much a theory as a jumble of suspicions based on mysterious activity in a number of government camps.

As previously noted, FBI Director J. Edgar Hoover did everything he could to limit the assassination investigation to the conclusion that Oswald acted alone. Presumably Hoover did this to cover up what he thought was an embarrassingly bad performance by his agency. Could he have had other motives, and could he have been covering the tracks of assassins whose actions he supported?

Hoover did not particularly like John Kennedy and intensely disliked his brother Robert, who, as Attorney General, was Hoover's boss. The Attorney General was much more aggressive than his predecessors, and was pursuing an all-out war on organized crime with his own Justice Department strike forces, preempting Hoover's territory and stealing his established glory. Though Hoover was a notoriously vain man, this hardly seems grounds for an assassination.

It is possible that Hoover – and others in government – thought John Kennedy's actions were dangerous for the country. The FBI director knew the President, a man possessed of a legendary libido, had carried on a torrid affair with a woman named Judy Campbell, who was literally in bed with at least two top Mafia figures, Sam Giancana and John Roselli. Hoover had learned that these same Mafia figures were being used by the CIA in plots to assassinate Fidel Castro.

It is remotely possible that an investigation of Oswald's connections to the KGB could have threatened Hoover's only source inside Russian intelligence: a mole code-named Fedora. There is evidence that Hoover may have disapproved of the President's aggressive support for civil rights. But all this proves nothing. Hoover's only established connection with the crime is the FBI's remarkable reluctance to solve it. The most sinister implication of the evidence is that the FBI's efforts may have extended to consciously framing Oswald.

Three of the investigators who first saw a rifle on the sixth floor of the Texas School Book Depository said it was a 7.65 mm Mauser, not a 6.5 mm Mannlicher-Carcano. The Mauser is a better weapon and would have been a more likely choice for the job at hand. The three men, one deputy constable and two deputy sheriffs, were all familiar with guns and would have been unlikely to make such a mistake. One of them noted the word "Mauser" imprinted on the gun's barrel. The Dallas District Attorney was still telling reporters the weapon was a Mauser as late as midnight that night. Thereafter references to the Mauser ceased. Assertions that the gun had been a Mauser could not be proved or disproved, because none of the evidence found in the Book Depository was photographed in place.

It was Lee Harvey Oswald's Mannlicher-Carcano that was examined for fingerprints at the Dallas police lab. Only partial prints were found during this first going-over, which was presumably a thorough one, and the press was duly notified that no definite prints of Oswald's had been found on the gun. The rifle was flown to Washington the night of November 22, where the FBI lab confirmed the Dallas finding. No Oswald prints. The rifle was returned to the Dallas police on November 24, the same day Ruby killed Oswald. That night, for the first time, the press was informed that Oswald's palm prints had been found on the gun barrel.

Earlier that evening, FBI agents with a fingerprint kit had visited Oswald's body at the funeral home. The funeral director told a reporter the "black gook" the agents put on Oswald had made "a complete mess of his entire hand." Oswald had already been palm and fingerprinted while alive. The explanation for the belated discovery of the palm print on the rifle was that the print was lifted from the gun with tape, rather than photographed *in situ,* and that the lift was not analyzed until November 24.

If it is true that guns were switched and prints were planted, the inference that the police agencies involved were part of a cover-up is hard to escape.

There were other suspicious developments in the case against Oswald for the killing of Officer Tippit. Tippit's killer made the thoroughly odd decision to empty the expended cartridge cases from his gun at the scene of the crime. Four bullets hit Tippit. Three of them were identified as Winchester rounds and one as Remington. The slugs could not be definitely shown to have come from Oswald's gun.

Of the four cartridge cases found at the scene – which *were* shown to have been fired in Oswald's gun – two were Winchesters and two were Remingtons. There is no evidence that Oswald owned or knew how to use ammo-reloading equipment.

The Dallas police officer who marked the shell casings with his initials at the scene, a standard procedure in the handling of evidence, could not identify his markings when later shown the shells from Oswald's gun.

Otherwise the evidence against Oswald in the Tippit killing is strong. Though Oswald insisted he had not killed anybody, two witnesses identified him as the killer, and six others said he was the man who fled the scene. (Two other witnesses said two men killed Tippit, and a third said the one man who killed him wasn't Oswald.) Oswald was certainly the man arrested in the theater nearby, and he was armed with a revolver.

There have long been attempts by assassination buffs to establish Tippit as a party to the conspiracy, without much success. The argument that Oswald and Tippit were working together is not, however, without its own mysterious nuggets of fact.

The best of these is the testimony of Oswald's landlady, who said that while Oswald was inside her rooming house just after the assassination – getting a jacket and a gun – a police car pulled up out front and honked as though signaling for someone to come outside. The only police car in the immediate vicinity was Tippit's. It is unclear what any of this might have to do with the possible planting of evidence against Oswald in the Tippit murder.

As previously noted, the FBI was interested enough in cementing the case against Oswald to revise the testimony of witnesses before releasing it to the Warren Commission. Most of the revisions were minor, and in almost all cases they tended to incriminate Oswald and to eliminate indications of a conspiracy. One particularly glaring case is that of a young woman named Julia Ann Mercer, who was tracked down by author Henry Hurt and interviewed for his book *Reasonable Doubt*.

Twenty-three at the time, Miss Mercer was driving through Dealey Plaza on assassination day, a little more than ninety minutes before the shooting started. Just past the grassy knoll, a green truck blocked her path, stopped in the road with its two inside tires up on the curb.

As she waited for the truck to move, she watched a young man get out of the truck and take what looked like a rifle in a case or package out of the tool compartment, then walk up toward the knoll. As she pulled around the truck, she saw a heavily built middle-aged man with a round face sitting behind the wheel.

She then drove on to a restaurant and had breakfast, remarking to several people she knew there that "the Secret Service is not very secret," and telling them what she had seen. As she drove away from the restaurant, she was stopped by two police officers who had overheard her comments and was told to get in their car. She then learned that the President had just been shot in Dealey Plaza.

Miss Mercer was taken to the Sheriff's office, where she was interviewed on and off over at least four hours by both uniformed police and men in civilian clothes. At 4.00 a.m. the next day, she was awakened at her apartment by two FBI men and taken back to the Sheriff's office, where she was shown about a dozen photographs of different men and asked to pick any who might have been the ones she had seen in Dealey Plaza. She picked two.

The next day, she was watching the assassination coverage on TV and, along with the rest of the country, saw Ruby kill Oswald. She immediately recognized Oswald as the young man and Ruby as the driver she had seen and later identified for the FBI.

The FBI report of the Mercer interrogation flatly states that Miss Mercer failed to identify Oswald when shown his picture, and omits mention of Ruby. The Sheriff's report adds the assertion that Miss Mercer said she did not get a good enough look at the driver to identify him.

On the strength of these reports, or lack of it, the Warren Commission declined to call Miss Mercer as a witness. Had she been called it is unlikely that her story would have been believed, since Ruby and Oswald were both supposed to be somewhere else at the time she says she saw them. The point is that the FBI, with the cooperation of the local police, apparently wanted to make sure the Warren Commission never had a chance to make this judgment.

If Miss Mercer's story is true, the most revealing point about it is not that she thinks she saw Ruby and Oswald together, it is that the FBI may have showed her a picture of Ruby as a suspected co-conspirator more than twenty-four hours before he killed Oswald.

It should be noted that Oswald's mother, Marguerite, also claimed an FBI man showed her a picture of Ruby before her son was killed. One possible explanation for both these Ruby picture stories is the fact that the CIA had given the FBI a picture of a man taken outside the Cuban embassy in Mexico City. The CIA originally thought this man was Oswald, and apparently took the picture during the time Oswald was supposed to be visiting the embassy. The man's true identity is one of the mysteries of the case. Though he is not by any means a dead ringer for either man, he looks more like Ruby than Oswald.

The FBI claimed the Mexico City picture was the one shown to Oswald's mother. It has never offered an explanation of the pictures shown to Julia Mercer, or of the fact that she and so many others swear their statements to the bureau were altered.

As for suspicions involving the CIA, there were rogue factions among both past and present employees of that agency who were bitterly displeased with John Kennedy over his handling of the Cuban situation in general and the Bay of Pigs invasion in particular.

There are enticing leads into the CIA, none of them indisputable, and there are sinister suggestions of intelligence activity woven throughout the assassination story. These are revealed in detail in the discussion of the spy conspiracy theory that follows.

One of the most thought-provoking tales of an executive branch conspiracy is told in David S. Lifton's book *Best Evidence*. Lifton's fastidiously documented argument is that President Kennedy's body was surgically altered between the time it left Dallas Friday afternoon and the time it arrived for the autopsy at Bethesda Naval Hospital that night. The point of the surgery would have been to eliminate forensic evidence of shots from the front, thus squelching further investigation of a possible conspiracy.

The cornerstone of Lifton's story is the fact that most of the doctors and nurses who worked to save Kennedy in Dallas saw substantially different wounds than were seen by the autopsy doctors at Bethesda.

The Dallas medical team members cited by Lifton saw a large wound in the back of the head, and interpreted the wound in the front of the throat as a wound of entry.

At the autopsy, the large head wound was seen in the upper right side of the skull, toward the front, and was much bigger than the one observed in Dallas. An entry wound was found in the back of the head, and the throat wound was thought to be the exit point for the shot that entered the President's upper back, though no path could be traced for the bullet.

Lifton bolsters his theory with testimony about the handling of the body. The deceased President left Dallas in an expensive bronze coffin. This coffin arrived at Bethesda accompanied by the President's wife and brother. But a number of people who handled the body at Bethesda reported it had arrived – earlier and at a different entrance than the bronze coffin – in a standard military coffin. One X-ray technician told Lifton he had already shot film of the President's body when he saw the bronze coffin come in. The personnel in Dallas had wrapped the body in sheets. The personnel at Bethesda found it in a body bag.

The theory is that the body was switched from the bronze coffin to a body bag while Mrs. Kennedy and others had gone forward in the presidential plane to attend the swearing-in of Lyndon Johnson.

There are some problems with Lifton's thesis. The first is the sheer size and complexity of the conspiracy required to carry it out. A medical argument against it is that, if the body had been altered just before the autopsy, the autopsy doctors should have recognized the difference between the surgical "wounds" created after rigor mortis had begun and the real wounds suffered while blood was still pumping through the body. And the Dallas doctors who subsequently recalled a wound in the right side of the head were not mentioned.

Some of the discrepancies in the medical testimony could be explained away by the perhaps unlikely possibility that the President's head was hit both from the front and the rear, with the front shot coming from a fragmentation bullet that exploded on impact.

Still, Lifton's story is too well argued to be easily dismissed. If it is true, the conspiracy to kill John Kennedy reached to a powerfully high level of the U.S. government.

The idea of an executive branch conspiracy is supported by a chilling fact. Certain pieces of key forensic evidence have unaccountably disappeared from the National Archives.

The HSCA investigated the disappearance, which was discovered in 1966, but came to no conclusion. The missing evidence includes the canister that apparently contained the President's brain, some autopsy photographs, laboratory slides of tissue sections from the areas around the wounds, and several bullet fragments taken either from Governor Connally or from the limousine.

During the autopsy, the President's brain was never coronally sectioned – a standard procedure in cases of death by gunshot wounds to the head – to establish the paths bullets took in passing through the brain. The evidence missing from the Archives is precisely the evidence that could prove the shots that killed the President came from more than one source.

Spy and Counter-Spy

The Intelligence Conspiracy

Lee Harvey Oswald was only twenty-four years old when Jack Ruby shot him down. Yet his short, apparently unhappy life was packed with activities more diverse and more intense than are experienced by most men twice his age.

As a youth, he had lived in New Orleans, New York, and Texas. He joined the Marines at seventeen, and saw Japan and the Pacific. At twenty, he defected to the Soviet Union and spent more than two years there. After his return to America, he was caught up in the outstanding political issue of his day, the struggle over Castro's Cuba. And by the last day of his life, he had been accused of killing the President.

In the meager, shifting light of the assassination story, Oswald is the prism. Turn him one way, and he is an indolent, incompetent boob. A ninth-grade dropout starved for affection and filled with the venoms of failure and despair. Turn him another, and he is a cunning operative, a skilled manipulator. A man sharp enough to teach himself the Russian language and to deceive everyone around him with his multiple identities.

To this writer, the most plausible view of Oswald is of a young man whose peculiar makeup and whose grandiose delusions made him the perfect front man in the crime of the century. Whether the people who used Oswald in the assassination were spies is uncertain. That he was involved to some degree with spies is not.

From a very early age – thirteen or fourteen – Lee Oswald took an avid interest in Marxism and in all things Russian. If this was adolescent posturing, it took a markedly different form than the teenage rebellions of Oswald's contemporaries in the early 1950s. By age sixteen, Oswald was spouting the virtues of Communism to his friends at every opportunity, sometimes within hearing of their outraged parents. He was kicked off the junior high football team for complaining that the coach had violated his constitutional rights.

By the end of ninth grade, when Oswald's mother moved him from New Orleans to Fort Worth, he abandoned formal schooling, settled into a pseudo-intellectual guise, and spent his time listening to classical music and reading Marx. His one career ambition was to join the Marines, as his brother had done before him.

This he did in 1956, less than a week after his seventeenth birthday. The notion of a Marxist Marine may seem a bit incongruous, but for Lee Harvey Oswald incongruity was par for the course. From basic training on, Oswald made no secret of his political preferences during bull sessions with fellow recruits. His unconventional attitudes earned him a number of Marine nicknames, not all flattering. For his clumsiness on the rifle range, he was "Shitbird"; for his timidity, he was "Mrs. Oswald"; for his Bugs Bunny imitations, he was "Ozzie Rabbit" or "Bugs"; for his Russophilia, he was "Oswaldokovich."

Oswald particularly liked and encouraged the Oswaldokovich tag, but this did not prevent him from being cleared to handle classified material upon graduation from radar controller training. His first orders were for Atsugi, Japan, a naval air station near Tokyo.

Oswald's career in the Marines and his later life as a defector have been thoroughly documented in Edward Jay Epstein's book *Legend*. According to Epstein and other sources, the base at Atsugi was more than a landing field for Navy and Marine aircraft. It was one of the largest centers of CIA activity in Asia, with twenty buildings housing agency operations. And it was a home base for the high altitude U-2 spy plane.

From his job in the air traffic control hut, Oswald could watch the U-2's come and go. The top-secret plane, codenamed Race Car, flew too high to show up on the radar screens except during takeoffs and landings, but it was possible to calculate its rate of climb and to approximate its altitude, speed, and other flight characteristics by listening in to communications between pilots and controllers. One former officer recalls Oswald showing particular interest when Race Car was in flight.

Oswald did not fraternize much with fellow Marines, and soon began spending his time off base with Japanese friends he had made on his own. The identities of these friends have never been learned, but their political leanings have. Years later, Oswald told a confidant that it was his affiliation with Japanese Communists that influenced him to defect to Russia.

Ozzie Rabbit had been teased about his inexperience with women, but now Marines began seeing him in the company of a pretty Japanese girl who worked as a hostess at the Queen Bee, a club a man of Oswald's rank could not afford. Dates with Queen Bee girls cost $60 to $100 a night. Oswald's take-home pay was $85 a month.

Naval intelligence suspected some of the Queen Bee hostesses were anti-American operatives. It was a well-established fact that certain girls who worked in clubs frequented by officers knew where units were headed long before the enlisted men.

Later, Oswald's frequent companion was a beautiful Eurasian woman who spoke fluent Russian. ("She was much too good-looking for Bugs," one Marine recalled.) Some speculated that Oswald was learning Russian from the woman, as his facility with the language improved. If this was true, Oswald wasn't saying. He did not discuss his off-base activities with anyone, even with his closest friends.

In September of 1958 Oswald's unit was briefly moved to

Formosa after Chinese Communists began shelling offshore islands there. The Marine radar controllers were surprised when Communist planes evaded their "friend or foe" identification system. The Chinese had apparently penetrated security and acquired the unit's secret code system. The source of the leak was never discovered.

After a month in the brig for spilling a drink on a sergeant, Oswald's pro-Marxist rhetoric increased noticeably. He referred to his fellow Marines as "you Americans," and complained of American imperialism. The decision to defect had apparently been made.

The opportunity was not long in coming. In late December of 1958 Oswald was assigned to a new Marine air control squadron based in Santa Ana, California. On New Year's Day, Fidel Castro took control of Havana and proclaimed victory for his revolution. Oswald followed the events in Cuba with great interest, and spoke of going there to join Castro's forces. He began to communicate with the Cuban consulate in Los Angeles – letters from the consulate were seen in his locker – and went into Los Angeles by bus to visit the consulate on several occasions.

During this period, a civilian visitor called for Oswald late one night from the Shore Patrol guard shack at the base gate. The visit was memorable for witnesses because the visitor was wearing a top coat in warm weather and because another Marine had to be called to relieve Oswald. Oswald's animated conversation with the man lasted about an hour. None of his family members were in California at the time.

In March of 1959 Oswald applied to Albert Schweitzer College in Switzerland, apparently to create an excuse to avoid Marine reserve duty, and was accepted for the following spring term. (He had passed a high school equivalency exam given by the Marines.) In August of that year, he filed for an early discharge from the service, claiming that he was needed at home to support his mother. The day after the discharge was granted, he filed for a passport.

He told his family he was going to New Orleans to enter the importing business, but instead boarded a freighter in that city bound for Europe. The freighter docked in France on October 8. One week later, Oswald was in Moscow. He had crossed eight borders with extraordinary ease, spending more money than he was known to have. The visa he obtained in Helsinki to enter the Soviet Union would have required at least a week's wait for an ordinary traveler of the period. Oswald got his in two days. The clear implication is that the wheels of Oswald's trip were greased by an unknown intelligence apparatus.

On October 31, Oswald appeared at the U.S. embassy and angrily renounced his citizenship. During this visit he told a CIA officer who worked under diplomatic cover that he was prepared to reveal classified information he had learned in the Marines to Soviet intelligence. The episode was typical of many in Oswald's strange career. He seemed to be consciously creating a scene guaranteed to make himself conspicuous.

At this point Oswald disappears from view for more than a year. The only known record of what may have happened during the period is his "Historic Diary," a handwritten document found in his effects after his death and employed by the Warren Commission to construct the official version of his time in Russia. Though it uses the present tense, handwriting experts have established that the diary was written in one or two continuous sessions, and the anachronisms it contains prove it could not have been written during the period it describes.

For whatever reasons, Oswald apparently wrote the diary after he decided to return to the United States. Given his well-established disdain for the truth, it can hardly be accepted as a factual account.

According to the diary, Oswald's offer to defect with his military secrets was at first rejected by the Soviets. This brought on an attempted suicide by wrist-slashing, which caused the soft-hearted Soviet government to change its mind. The odd thing about the alleged suicide attempt is that it came almost immediately after Oswald reached Moscow.

If the diary is to be believed, the would-be defector precipitately renounced his U.S. citizenship *before* he learned he would be allowed to stay in Russia.

Again according to the diary, Oswald was given work in a radio and television factory in Minsk, beginning in January of 1960. By Soviet standards, he lived lavishly. He was given a spacious and well-appointed apartment with lovely views from two private balconies. He enjoyed an abundant supply of cash, with his factory salary generously subsidized by the "Red Cross." His affluence made possible affairs with several attractive young women.

There are some things the diary does not mention. One is that "Red Cross" is a euphemism for the MVD, the Soviet internal security agency of the time. Another is that Oswald lived and worked within a short walk of both the KGB and the MVD training schools, and very near a polytechnic institute where about six hundred young Cubans studied. He was photographed socializing with Cubans and with younger members of some of the leading families in Minsk.

Perhaps the most curious omission from the diary was a historic event with which Oswald had some personal connection. On May 1, 1960, U-2 pilot Gary Powers was shot out of the sky over Sverdlovsk. It was a tremendous coup for the Soviets. The high-altitude spy plane had, by one knowledgeable estimate, been supplying the United States with more than ninety percent of its hard intelligence about the Soviet Union. The Soviets had long known about the overflights, but had been powerless to stop them. Their fighters could not come within thirty thousand feet of the U-2, and although their rockets could reach it, their guidance systems were not sophisticated enough to bring it down.

To improve their aim, the Soviets needed to know more about the U-2's flight characteristics and about its radar countermeasures. There were some indications the Soviets had gained access to bits of the needed data while Oswald was still in the Marines. There were only two U-2 flights over Russia after his defection, and the second was shot down.

Before he was swapped for a Soviet spy, the captured U-2 pilot was interrogated repeatedly by the KGB while watched by other Russian officials through a one-way window. Powers later said the Soviets seemed especially knowledgeable about U-2 flights from Atsugi, Japan, and dwelled on this base even though he insisted he had never been there.

Though the capture of the spy pilot was celebrated in Russia and became top news around the world, Oswald is known to have made only one reference to it. In a letter to his brother written two years later and referring to a mention of Powers in the news, Oswald said, "Powers seemed to be a nice bright American-type fellow when I saw him in Moscow."

How Oswald, the factory worker in Minsk, could have been allowed to see and presumably speak with or listen to the heavily guarded American spy in Moscow is not explained. Could the twenty-year-old American defector have been one of the people on the invisible side of the one-way window during Powers's interrogation? And could he have attained that status by supplying the information that brought the U-2 down?

Despite the fact that he was living far better than he ever had – or ever would – and was enjoying a real social life and the respect of his peers for the first time, Oswald's retrospective diary records an abrupt change in his attitude toward the Soviet Union in the spring of 1960.

The first negative entry occurs the same day the U-2 was shot down. Thereafter the diarist enters complaints against the regimentation of Soviet society, the privileges of Party members, the endless meetings, the drab work, and the lack of recreation. The possibility of redefecting begins to be mentioned. Considering that the diary may have been written long after the events it describes, the sudden change of heart has been seen by some as a convenient cover story for the reentry of an intelligence agent into the United States.

Nine months after the diary shows Oswald thinking of returning home, in February of 1961, he took the first step in that direction by declaring his intentions in writing to the same

CIA officer who had originally interviewed him at the embassy.

A month after writing this letter, Oswald met a pretty twenty-year-old named Marina Prusakova. After less than two months of courtship, in April of 1961, he and Marina were married.

With this another enigmatic character enters the drama. Marina testified at length before the Warren Commission, has been the subject of dozens of interviews and an authorized biography, and still lives in the United States. Still, indisputable facts about her background are as hard to come by as those about her former husband. Her story has changed with each retelling, and even her real name is in question.

One constant in the story is the fact that when she met Oswald she was living with her maternal uncle Ilya Prusakov, a lieutenant colonel in the MVD and a prominent citizen of Minsk. There are suggestions, though no proof, that Marina herself may have received some form of intelligence training while on "holiday," and that during one of these holidays before she met Oswald she was planted near another American defector – a man named Robert Webster – with the possible motive of striking up a relationship.

Shortly after the marriage Marina applied for permission to leave with her husband for the United States, while Oswald continued his correspondence with the American authorities.

The ease with which Oswald entered the Soviet Union had been exceptional. The ease with which he left with a Soviet-born wife was unique.

Through his position in the MVD, Marina's uncle almost certainly knew the young American was petitioning to go back to the United States, as correspondence with the American embassy was routinely read by Soviet intelligence. Yet he not only approved of the marriage, he threw a party for the newly-weds.

It was highly unusual for Soviet citizens in Marina's situation to be allowed to emigrate unless some intelligence motive was involved, yet she completed the complicated process with a minimum of trouble. American intelligence was wary of an established pattern of Soviets marrying U.S. citizens and subsequently becoming "sleeper" agents in this country. Yet the U.S. State Department overruled the official objections that were raised against Marina.

In Oswald's case, the United States was being asked to accept a man who had all but promised to offer military secrets to the Soviets, and the Soviets were being asked to let him go, taking a Soviet citizen along. Incredibly, all sides agreed that the young couple's new home would be in the United States.

The Oswalds spent the first year of their married life in Minsk. Only the barest facts of the period are known. The Soviet government, which routinely took years to issue exit visas for citizens in similar situations and often simply refused them, gave both Marina and Lee permission to leave by Christmas.

The American authorities engaged in a protracted debate over giving Marina an entrance visa, providing most of the delay. The couple's first child, a girl named June, was born in February. The family left Moscow on June 1, 1962, arriving in the United States twelve days later.

Marina set up housekeeping in Fort Worth, while Lee took a variety of low-paying jobs, never holding any job for long. He lived at times with his wife and child, and at times on his own in Dallas. Only he knew how he spent his time while living alone. The local Russian community took an interest in Marina which he seemed to resent. By several accounts, the Oswalds' domestic life in Texas was a battleground.

Sometime in the summer of 1962 Lee Oswald first made contact – ostensibly through the Russian exiles – with one of the more mysterious supporting actors in the assassination drama, an older man named George De Mohrenschildt. The two men struck up an unlikely relationship, which, according to some, had the look of a tutor and his protégé.

Before his suicide in 1977, De Mohrenschildt told at least three widely differing versions of the way he met Oswald, all of them demonstrably false. The deceit was typical of the man. If De Mohrenschildt was not an intelligence agent, he was the living image of the dashing spies of popular fiction.

According to one of his many and varied accounts of his own background, De Mohrenschildt was born in 1911 into the most purebred of the Russian noble families, the son of an official in the Czar's government. He was technically a baron, but never used the title. He escaped the chaos of the Revolution with his father, was schooled in Poland, and took advanced degrees in international business in Belgium before settling in the United States at the age of twenty-seven.

He was handsome, brilliant, and well built, the personification of the aristocratic playboy, reeking old-world charm. His chronic need for money and his sense of adventure led him, according to a number of sources, into the world of spies.

A seven-year-long FBI investigation begun in the 1940s indicated De Mohrenschildt was working for Polish intelligence as a propagandist when he first came to this country. During World War II he was employed by French counterintelligence to frustrate German efforts to buy oil in America. The British suspected, and he himself hinted, that he was doubling as an agent for the Nazis at the same time. Several of his associates were thought to be highly placed Nazi spies.

When he was briefly taken into custody in 1941 while sketching a Coast Guard station in Port Aransas, Texas, he had on his person two vastly different résumés. One said he was a Swede, the other a Greek Catholic. The various professions listed included insurance salesman, film producer, newspaper correspondent, and textile salesman.

Toward the end of the war, De Mohrenschildt stopped off at the University of Texas, breezing through a master's degree in petroleum engineering in less than a year. This opened the door to international travel on behalf of American oil companies. In Caracas, Venezuela, he met several times with the Soviet ambassador, for reasons that have never been adequately explained. After a trip to Yugoslavia on "oil business" in 1957, he was extensively debriefed by the CIA. In 1961, he was on a "walking trip" through Guatemala at the same time the CIA was training anti-Castro Cubans there for the Bay of Pigs invasion.

The CIA denied that he ever worked for the agency, though De Mohrenschildt claimed to have been in touch with CIA personnel at the time he knew Oswald, and even to have been asked to "keep tabs" on the returned defector.

With all this material in the files of at least three government agencies – FBI, CIA, and Navy intelligence – the Warren Commission stated flatly that its investigation "developed no signs of subversive or disloyal conduct on the part of . . . the De Mohrenschildts." The statement was an outright lie. The files on De Mohrenschildt were kept secret at the time.

De Mohrenschildt's worldliness and charm had placed him in some lofty social circles. While in New York, he had been a good friend of Jacqueline Bouvier Kennedy's parents, and knew Jackie and her sister Lee as children.

In Dallas, he was too unconventional to be accepted into high society, but cultivated anyone with wealth and was friends with a number of prominent oilmen. His close relationship with the sullen, impecunious Lee Oswald, who lived in a squalid little apartment with a quarrelsome wife and a young child, is difficult to imagine. Nonetheless De Mohrenschildt and his fourth wife Jeanne are said to have taken an intense interest in the Oswalds' welfare. Lee Oswald is said to have adopted George De Mohrenschildt as a father figure, and to have confided in him as in no one else.

Just as the Cuban Missile Crisis was unfolding, on October 7, 1962, De Mohrenschildt and his wife joined the young Oswald couple for dinner. The next day, Lee Oswald abruptly quit his job at Leslie Welding in Fort Worth. Less than a week later he found employment with a graphic arts company, Jaggars-Chiles-Stovall (JCS), in Dallas. JCS primarily did advertising work, but was also engaged at the time in classified work for the U.S. Army Map Service.

President Kennedy ordered the first U-2 overflight of Cuba on October 14, and the resulting photographs showed evidence of Soviet nuclear missile sites. As part of its Army contract, JCS was setting type of Cuban place names. The names could have shown the areas under spy-plane surveillance, though this has never been proved. If Oswald was a spy, he had been placed, again, in the right place at the right time.

In March of 1963, according to the official accounts, Oswald made preparations for his first attempt at assassination. There is evidence that he cased and photographed the Dallas home of General Edwin A. Walker, a prominent member of the John Birch Society who had been fired by President Kennedy for distributing right-wing literature to his troops in Europe. Receipts for Oswald's Mannlicher-Carcano rifle show it was ordered that same month, under the name A. Hidell.

On the night of April 10, someone fired into Walker's study from outside the house, barely missing the General. This botched assassination became a prominent exhibit in the Warren Commission's case against Oswald. The problem is that there is no conclusive proof he did the shooting and, even if he did, there is evidence it was done with the help of other people – with a conspiracy all its own.

The bullet could not be shown to have come from Oswald's gun. The evidence against him included the photographs of Walker's home and the testimony of Marina Oswald and George De Mohrenschildt.

But one witness saw two men peeking in the General's windows two days before the shooting, who drove off in a Ford sedan; and another witness saw two men leave the premises immediately after the shooting and drive off in separate cars, one of them a Ford sedan. Oswald, according to the official story, couldn't drive.

In one of the photographs of the General's home found with his possessions, the license number of a car parked on the street has been torn out. Various advocates of conspiracy theories have suggested that, if Oswald was involved in the potshot at Walker, the operation was a dry run to test Oswald's mettle as an assassination patsy.

In an "if I am caught" note left for Marina, presumably in connection with the Walker shooting, Oswald tells his wife the "Red Cross" will help her with money. He instructs her to forward any newspaper clippings on his role in the shooting to "the Embassy," presumably the Soviet embassy. To the Oswalds, of course, "Red Cross" meant the Soviet MVD.

In this connection, it may be significant that correspondence from both the Oswalds to the Soviet embassy in Washington was routed to a consular officer named Vitaly Gerasimov. At the time, Gerasimov was suspected by both the FBI and CIA of being the paymaster of a nationwide network of Soviet spies.

The instructions in Lee's note never had to be put to use, because the attempt on General Walker was not "solved" until after Oswald's death.

Just nine days after the Walker shooting, the De Mohrenschildts left Dallas bound for New York, Washington, and finally for Haiti, where George had a contract with the Duvalier government to "develop natural resources."

The HSCA established that De Mohrenschildt met with the CIA while in Washington, though the purpose of the meeting has never been revealed. Neither has the purpose of a CIA "expedite check" on De Mohrenschildt run by the agency's Office of Security at about the same time.

So far as is known, there was no contact between Oswald and De Mohrenschildt during the seven months that would pass before the Kennedy assassination. On March 29, 1977, just after the first of four scheduled interviews with author Edward Jay Epstein and on the day he was first contacted by an HSCA investigator, De Mohrenschildt committed suicide in Palm Beach, Florida. Not long before, he had reportedly told another journalist he had been a part of the conspiracy that killed the President.

Having been fired from his job at the graphics company, Lee Oswald left Dallas about a week after De Mohrenschildt. By

April 25, he was in New Orleans. Here, the inferences of an intelligence operation become stronger.

The New Orleans of 1963 was a hotbed of intrigue. Thousands of recently exiled Cubans lived there, involving themselves in scores of schemes to reclaim their homeland. The intense patriotic feelings of these people were manipulated by opportunists and fanatics of all stripes, by the American CIA, and even at times by Castro's own intelligence apparatus, the Cuban DGI.

Lee Oswald lost no time in making himself conspicuous in this environment. He formed a one-man chapter of the pro-Castro Fair Play for Cuba Committee, without the blessings of the national organization. He got himself arrested in a scuffle with anti-Castroites while passing out his FPCC literature, and took the pro-Castro side in a radio debate on Cuba.

The official explanation is that Oswald was laying the groundwork to defect to Cuba, and wanted a track record to show Cuban authorities. The problem with this explanation is that it fails to consider Oswald's curious associations with people he was supposedly struggling against.

Several witnesses have established that Oswald was involved with a former FBI man named Guy Banister, who worked as a private investigator in New Orleans and who was rabidly anti-Castro. Almost certainly in association with CIA handlers, Banister helped coordinate the activities of the various Cuban exile groups in New Orleans. Banister's secretary insists that Oswald and Banister were working together, and a number of other witnesses connect Oswald with Banister and with his associate David Ferrie. The address stamped on some of Oswald's FPCC literature is the same building that housed Banister's office, and had recently housed a prominent anti-Castro CIA front group.

Another Oswald sighting places him at the Habana Bar, a hangout for anti-Castro forces, in the company of a Latin man. This is one of many reports of Oswald's associations with Latin or Cuban men during the New Orleans period and afterward.

Oswald's one known job in New Orleans seems innocuous enough. He oiled equipment at a coffee company, less than a block from Banister's office. This job was not demanding, and Oswald spent a good deal of his working time hanging out in the Crescent City Garage next door, where he became friends with the garage owner. The garage had a contract to service government vehicles. One day the garage owner had just checked out a car to a man who showed him FBI credentials when he noticed the car stop where Oswald was standing. The driver handed Oswald a white envelope, and Oswald walked back toward the coffee company.

Oswald was estranged from Marina, who was living with a friend in Dallas. She joined him for a brief and unhappy attempt at reconciliation in New Orleans. During this period, Lee was apparently encouraging Marina to return to Russia. At his urging she wrote to the Soviet embassy that both she and her husband wanted to return, but, according to her, Oswald's real interest at the time was getting into Cuba. This explanation has been used to account for Oswald's trip to Mexico City and his visits to the Cuban and Soviet embassies there.

In June of 1963 Oswald applied for a passport that would allow travel to Cuba, the Soviet Union, and elsewhere. He received this passport in just one day.

Normally, an ex-defector could expect, at the very least, to have his passport application for travel to Communist countries flagged by the FBI and mulled over by the State Department. If this was simply an oversight, it could be easily dismissed. But the FBI, in a memorandum reviewed by a Senate committee, explained that its failure to flag Oswald's application was not an oversight, but a conscious decision. The reason given is revealing: "We did not know definitely whether or not he had any intelligence assignments at that time." The clear implication is that the FBI either knew Oswald was an agent for someone or thought his background showed he was.

Oswald applied for a tourist card to enter Mexico at the Mexican consulate in New Orleans on September 17. When the

Warren Commission tried to establish who else had applied for tourist cards that day, it was informed by the FBI that no record existed for the card issued immediately before Oswald's.

Many years later, a document released under the Freedom of Information Act revealed that the mystery traveler was William Gaudet, the publisher of *Latin American Report* and a man with a long-standing history of work for the CIA. Gaudet vehemently denied any connection with Oswald, but the curiousness of the coincidence and the FBI's effort to cover it up did little to stifle speculation.

The Mexico trip provides one of the better and more complex examples of Oswald's troublesome tendency to be in two places at once. The Warren Commission produced a number of witnesses who placed Oswald on a bus journey to Mexico City, and ignored equally convincing testimony that placed him in Dallas in the company of two Cubans at the same time. The Mexico Oswald made several visits to the Cuban embassy, where, the story goes, he was told he could not have a transit visa until he presented a Soviet entry visa to prove he was only stopping off in Cuba.

There are conflicting versions of what happened during these visits. According to one of them (Fidel Castro's), Oswald threw a tantrum and intimated that he might show his support for the Cuban revolution by trying to shoot President Kennedy.

For five days, Oswald shuttled back and forth between the two embassies in an attempt to resolve his dilemma. At one point, he was heard on the phone telling the Soviet embassy that his contact there was Comrade Kostikov. This would have been Valery Kostikov, a KGB officer whose specialty was handling Soviet agents working within the United States. Kostikov was thought to be a member of the KGB's Department 13, which dealt in sabotage and assassination. For whatever reasons, the Oswald who was in Mexico City was apparently frustrated in his attempts, and arrived in Dallas on October 3.

The entire Mexican episode is thrown into question by the CIA's failure to prove Oswald was there. Since the Soviet embassy in Mexico City was thought to be the primary control point for espionage operations throughout North America, the CIA was intensely interested in everything that happened there. CIA surveillance cameras were trained on both the Soviet and Cuban embassies. Why are there no photographs of Oswald's frequent comings and goings? The reasons given are hardly credible.

The Cuban embassy camera, it seems, was broken, and was allowed to stay that way during the entire (Friday through Tuesday) period of Oswald's visits. The Russian embassy camera was turned off on weekends because the building was then officially closed. The fact that Oswald visited the Russian embassy on Friday and Tuesday without being photographed was not explained. CIA wiretapping tapes said to be recordings of Oswald talking on the phone between the two embassies were destroyed before they could be compared with genuine recordings of Oswald's voice.

There are other disquieting aspects of the Mexican visit. The two people who primarily dealt with Oswald at the Cuban embassy say their Oswald was definitely not the Oswald whose image is known to the world, but a man who was shorter, blonder, and more gaunt.

Two independent reports show Oswald socializing with Cubans in Mexico City, though the official version has him alone and friendless there. One Cuban defector, whose stories check out otherwise, even claims that Oswald had "a relationship" with a woman who worked in the Cuban embassy. Set against the fact that Oswald lived near and socialized with Cuban students being trained in Minsk for two years, these reports may not be as far-fetched as they sound.

As with so many other aspects of the story, it is hard to avoid the conclusion that a full disclosure by U.S. government agencies would do much to clear up the mysteries of Mexico City. This disclosure will not be forthcoming. The HSCA produced a three-hundred-page report on Oswald's visit to Mexico City, and then ordered the report sealed in the national archives. Why? To protect the "sensitive sources and methods" of the CIA. The citizens of the United States were again judged incompetent to know the facts about the murder of their President.

Back in Dallas, Oswald continued to live separately from Marina, moving into a boarding house under the name O. H. Lee. Apparently through a tip from Marina's friend Ruth Paine, he secured the job at the Book Depository and worked diligently filling book orders until assassination day. The apparent randomness of the way Oswald got the job overlooking Dealey Plaza is a link missing from all the conspiracy theories.

Apart from weekends, when he customarily visited his wife and children (a second daughter was born on October 20), almost nothing is known of his activities during the last six weeks of his life.

Oswald's curious actions from his days in the Marine Corps onward add up to a rather powerful suggestion that he was an intelligence agent, or – at the least – that he thought of himself as a spy and was thus easily manipulated by real spies or by people he thought were spies. Given the information at hand, there is no answer for the most important question: who was he working for?

Predictably enough, the KGB, the CIA, and the FBI all have denied any association with Oswald. The KGB made the incredible claim that it had never even interviewed him, despite the fact that he was an American defector who knew genuine military secrets. The Soviets appear to have gone to the trouble of planting their own defector in early 1964, a KGB officer named Yuri Nosenko, who said he had managed Oswald's file, in an attempt to substantiate their claim. Nosenko's bona fides has been endlessly debated. The motives for his defection have never been clearly established.

For its part, the CIA said that it had never so much as debriefed Oswald on his return from Russia, despite the fact that it was routinely debriefing and copying the snapshots of ordinary tourists – 25,000 of them a year – returning from Communist countries. The idea that the agency had so little interest in a possibly traitorous man who had lived for over two years in Soviet society is preposterous.

The Oswald case is complicated by the fact that allegiances are seldom clear in the world of intelligence. A defector may be genuine, or he may be a plant for the other side. Information may be disinformation. And any given agent may be working against the cause he appears to be working for. Oswald's activities in New Orleans are a case in point. He appears to be pro-Castro, but he associates and works with anti-Castro elements. He may be building a cover for one side to penetrate the other. But which is which?

A surface view of Oswald seems to show a man with connections to Soviet intelligence. There is no doubt that assassination had long been a common tool of the Soviet government, common enough to rate its own euphemism within the KGB. Political killings were *mokrie dela* – "wet affairs" – because blood was spilled. But there are two good arguments against the notion that Oswald was working for the KGB: (1) the Russians would have been unlikely to risk destabilization and war to kill an American president, and (2) Oswald's pro-Communist posturing would have been poor cover for a Soviet agent.

As for the CIA, there are many suggestions that the agency knew a great deal more about Oswald than it has ever revealed. One enticing report, if accurate, connects Oswald directly to the CIA. Antonio Veciana, who worked closely with the CIA as the leader of the prominent anti-Castro group Alpha 66, told HSCA investigators he saw his CIA handler, a man known to him as Maurice Bishop, meeting with Oswald in Dallas in late August or early September of 1963, when Oswald was supposedly in New Orleans. Veciana said that Bishop asked his help after the assassination in providing a cover story to explain Oswald's associations with Cubans in Mexico City.

Veciana was the victim of an unsuccessful murder attempt soon after he testified in a closed session to the HSCA. He was struck in the head by one of four bullets that were fired at his car, but recovered.

If Veciana's story is true, it helps explain the CIA's less than forthcoming attitude about the evidence of Oswald's time in Mexico. It also establishes a possible connection between a CIA employee and the assassination conspiracy, and a definite connection between the CIA and the post-assassination cover-up.

Allegations that Oswald may have worked as an FBI informant are tantalizing, but remain unproved. His relationship with ex-FBI man Guy Banister has been relatively well established. There is the reported envelope exchange at the Crescent City Garage. There is the testimony of Orest Peña, the owner of the Habana Bar, who said an FBI man he knew well met several times with Oswald at the bar. The FBI man denied this. And a former security clerk in the New Orleans FBI office has claimed he saw an informant file on Oswald, but his claim has never been substantiated. Established connections between Oswald and the FBI would do a great deal to explain J. Edgar Hoover's urgent efforts to portray Oswald as a lone assassin.

Another possibility is that Oswald was working for U.S. military intelligence. Other young soldiers of his time were recruited by military intelligence for missions inside Communist countries. Oswald's interest in Marxism and the Russian language could have made him a potential recruit for a Soviet mission. While in Japan, he could have been feeding his Communist contacts bits of information designed to build his credibility for the eventual defection.

It would have been a great coup for an American intelligence agency to have had an agent accepted as a genuine defector and subsequently returned to the United States as part of a Soviet spy network. A role in military intelligence – presumably for the Navy – would explain the hands-off attitude toward Oswald that seems to have been taken at various times by the CIA and FBI.

The existence of an Army intelligence file on Oswald, under his alias A. J. Hidell, was revealed to the FBI the day of the assassination. Oddly, the FBI showed no interest in the file, it was not turned over in response to the Warren Commission request to all intelligence agencies for background on Oswald, and it was reported destroyed in 1973. If anyone living today knows what was in the file, they have not come forward to say so.

Any of these possibilities would mean Oswald had intelligence experience and was conditioned to intelligence assignments. The hottest intelligence assignments of his time had to do with Cuba.

The Left Hand and the Right Hand

The Cuban Conspiracy

When Fidel Castro took control of Cuba on New Year's Day of 1959, much more than a change in the Cuban government was set in motion. The major political events in the Western Hemisphere over at least the next four years were predetermined by the revolutionary victory.

The United States could not abide a Communist government in its own backyard. But the forces aligned against the new Cuban regime were not limited to recognized governments. The losers in the Cuban revolution included many thousands of bitter Cuban expatriates, most of them taking refuge in the United States and most of them aligned with one or more of the seven hundred militant factions dedicated to the overthrow of Castro.

In terms of hard coin, the biggest single loser in Cuba was the American Mafia, which had operated an empire of lucrative casinos, hotels, prostitution rings, and narcotics routes within the island nation.

American right-wing extremists, already incensed over desegregation, were outraged over the loss of Cuba and the sight of an outpost of the red peril so near America's shores.

In short, virtually all the forces suspect in the killing of John Kennedy had an interest in Cuba. Cuba is the hub around which the more plausible conspiracy theories turn, connecting in manifold ways.

President Kennedy did not create the Cuban problems; he inherited them. The United States formally broke relations with Cuba eighteen days before he was inaugurated. The CIA training of Cuban exiles that led to the Bay of Pigs invasion was begun under President Eisenhower. But Kennedy took up the campaign against Castro with characteristic enthusiasm. His contests with Khrushchev and Castro became personal trials of will and cunning, like those of his brother Robert, his Attorney General, against the Mafia and against Teamsters Union boss Jimmy Hoffa.

Of all those who had motives to kill John Kennedy, Fidel Castro had the best. His was simple self-defense. The American government was literally out to kill the head of the Cuban government. Between the day Kennedy took office and the day he was assassinated, no fewer than eight documented attempts on Castro's life were set in motion by employees of the United States government. These were only the attempts that have come to light in the course of subsequent investigations; Castro claims there were a total of twenty-four U.S.-inspired assassination plots against him.

On the very day of the Kennedy assassination, at about the same time, a CIA officer named Desmond Fitzgerald was meeting in Paris with a Cuban official code-named AM/LASH, subsequently identified as Rolando Cubela, to pass along a poison pen supplied by the CIA as the murder weapon to be used on Castro.

In its efforts to kill the Cuban Premier, the CIA took in some strange bedfellows. In the mid-1970s, the Senate Select Committee to Study Government Operations with Respect to Intelligence Activities, commonly known as the Church Committee for its chairman, Frank Church, revealed that the intelligence agency had enlisted the Mafia in several of its anti-Castro schemes. The mob was eager to take its Cuban territory back, and some of its more prominent members took part in the plotting. The CIA–Mafia alliance was formed just before Kennedy took office, in August of 1960, but continued well into his term.

The dirty tricks used against Castro were not limited to murder plots. The largest CIA field operation in the world was established on a 1,500-acre tract in south Florida. No fewer than fifty-four bogus corporations, all in the business of the violent overthrow of the Cuban government, were created to cover the covert activities of this field station, code-named JM/WAVE. The CIA trained, armed, and funded many of the Cuban exile groups, coordinated their activities, and directed their raids and invasions.

Some of the more colorful CIA brainstorms included plans to spray Castro's radio studio with an LSD-like drug, so that he would embarrass himself before the Cuban nation; to sprinkle chemicals in his shoes that would make his trademark beard fall out; to put deadly bacteria in his diving suit; and to poison his cigars.

Meanwhile, a U.S. trade embargo damaged the Cuban economy to the extent that Castro was forced to announce rationing of food, clothes, shoes, and soap.

The most blatant American move against the Castro regime came on April 17, 1961, on a beach facing Bahía de Cochinos – the Bay of Pigs – on the southwest coast of Cuba. A 1,400-man force of invading exiles, known as Brigade 2506 and trained by the CIA in Guatemala, walked into a disaster. The American air power that had been promised to support the landing never showed up. The Cuban defenders, well prepared for the invasion and rumored to have been under the command of Castro himself, took 1,200 prisoners. The last of these was not released from Cuban jails until October of 1986.

President Kennedy had given the go-ahead for the invasion and took full responsibility afterward. Several of the top men in the CIA – including Director Allen Dulles, who later served on the Warren Commission – lost their jobs in the aftermath.

The exiles blamed Kennedy for the debacle and for the lack of air support. So, it is said, did some factions of the CIA. The Bay of Pigs was the first blow against the love affair between the American President and the Cuban exiles. It would not be the last.

In October of 1962, American intelligence detected the presence of Soviet missiles in Cuba. Kennedy demanded their removal, and in the standoff that followed, the world braced for nuclear war. Finally the missiles were removed, in a deal that the exiles thought was treacherous. Kennedy had promised not to invade Cuba.

From this point on, the administration's attitude toward the exiles became ambivalent. The anti-Castro rhetoric was heated and the covert operations, including the assassination attempts and some CIA-backed guerrilla raids, continued. But the Coast Guard began to stop anti-Castro operations in the Florida straits, an anti-Castro training camp in the Bahamas was broken up by the British on a U.S. tip, and an anti-Castro arms cache was seized in Louisiana by the FBI. Support for Brigade 2506 and other U.S.-based exile groups was officially withdrawn in February 1963. The President's frequently repeated promise to return the exiles to a free Cuba had been broken. Among the most militant exiles, well armed and conditioned by years of fighting, John Kennedy became a man who needed killing almost as much as Fidel Castro.

This was the prevailing atmosphere into which Lee Harvey Oswald relocated in the spring and summer of 1963.

Only Miami had more Cuban exiles than New Orleans. The city was swarming with bitterly frustrated and suspicious expatriates, with CIA handlers and freelance contractors, with mercenaries, and even with double agents affiliated with Castro's DGI. In just five months the young and, by all appearances, unimpressive Oswald managed to make contact with an amazing number of the more prominent people on the Cuban scene. Curiously, considering Oswald's pro-Marxist and pro-Castro rhetoric, all these poeple were very much on the anti-Castro side.

In August Oswald presented himself to a Cuban exile leader named Carlos Bringuier, asking for membership in the militant Cuban Student Directorate. He said he had been trained in the Marines and that he wanted to fight against Castro. He even dropped off a copy of his Marine training manual, claiming it contained useful pointers on guerrilla warfare. Four days later Bringuier saw Oswald distributing pro-Castro literature on the street, and the resulting scuffle got Oswald arrested and led to his radio appearance and his local notoriety as a pro-Castro misfit.

Also in the late summer, a private detective who worked for Guy Banister met Oswald in a restaurant. Oswald's companion there was Sergio Arcacha Smith, the exile leader who headed the New Orleans chapter of the largest CIA-run exile group, the Cuban Revolutionary Council. Arcacha, a close associate of Banister's, says the meeting never happened.

On several occasions, Oswald was seen in the Habana Bar, the favorite meeting place of anti-Castro Cubans. During one visit he sat with an unidentified Cuban man and created a spectacle that stood out later in the minds of witnesses. Oswald is said to have ordered a lemonade. The bartender was accustomed to more daring beverages, and had to ask how a lemonade was made. He seems to have produced a very bad lemonade in his first effort, as Oswald vomited the drink across his table.

At the end of September, when the Warren Commission says he was en route to Mexico, Oswald was seen in Dallas touching base with yet another anti-Castro faction. A young woman named Silvia Odio, whose parents were jailed in Cuba as co-founders of the Junta Revolucionaria Cubana (JURE), said two Cubans came to her Dallas apartment in the company of a young American. The Cubans gave the correct JURE passwords, identified themselves by their "war names," and asked for help with a JURE fundraising letter. They introduced the American as "León" Oswald, and said they wanted Silvia Odio to help him make contacts in the anti-Castro movement. The men said they had come from New Orleans and were about to leave on a trip (if the trip was to Mexico, a new dimension is added to that part of the story). Mrs. Odio suspected the men of being pro-Castro agents.

The next day one of the Cubans called and explained why the

American had been taken into their confidence. "León" was an ex-Marine who knew how to shoot and was "kind of loco," the Cuban said, claiming that Oswald could be used to kill Castro and quoting him as saying, "President Kennedy should have been killed after the Bay of Pigs." When Silvia Odio saw Oswald on television after the assassination, she recognized him as "León" and fainted. Her sister Annie supported her entire account. The two sisters' description of one of the Cubans matched that of the unidentified man seen with Oswald in the Habana Bar.

Of all the glimpses of Oswald's Cuban intrigues, none is stranger or more sinister than his association with the ex-FBI man Guy Banister and his freelance investigator David Ferrie. Banister had put in twenty years with the bureau and had run the FBI office in Chicago. He was a hard-drinking tough guy with a violent temper and a well-established hatred of Communism, integration, and liberal politicians, Jack Kennedy in particular. Almost all his work in 1963 was dedicated to the overthrow of Castro: he ran background checks for anti-Castro groups, gave advice on guerrilla tactics, bought and shipped guns, and raised money. Banister died of a heart attack in 1964, without testifying before any investigatory body about the assassination.

Compared with Ferrie, Banister was the boy next door. The best Surrealist would be hard pressed to create a David Ferrie; in a story studded with castoffs and grotesquerie, he is by far the most bizarre creature. Forty-five years old in 1963, Ferrie was afflicted by a rare disease called alopecia, which had left him without body hair of any kind. To compensate, he glued shaggy patches of an orange-tinted substance that has been variously described as mohair and monkey fur to his scalp and where his eyebrows should have been. Sometimes the eyebrows were simply, but thickly, painted on. With his beaky nose and thin-slit lips, Ferrie looked like something that had just pecked out of an egg it should have stayed in. The eyes were piercing and the face was haunted. The brain behind it all was said to be brilliant, if in a demented sort of way.

Ferrie had made a lifelong study of medicine, and considered himself an expert on that subject. He claimed to be a psychologist and a master hypnotist, and listed the title Dr. beside his name in the New Orleans phone book. A seminary dropout, Ferrie also used the title Bishop, in his own obscure, ultraconservative religious order known variously as the Orthodox Old Catholic Church of North America and the Holy Apostolic Catholic Church of North America. Professionally, he had been an airplane pilot, some said a very good one. In 1961, he had lost his job with Eastern Airlines because of the exercise of his sexual preference, which was for teenage boys.

By 1963, Ferrie was said to be making a living by freelance flying – sometimes with a cargo of guns, for anti-Castro Cubans and probably the CIA, and sometimes with a cargo of gangsters, for New Orleans Mafia boss Carlos Marcello – and by investigative work for Banister and for Marcello's lawyer G. Wray Gill. Ferrie was rumored to have participated in the Bay of Pigs invasion, and was known to be involved in the training of Cuban exile military forces. There is some evidence that he was the go-between for Marcello with the Cuban exiles, supplying them with Mafia money at various times.

David Ferrie hated John Kennedy. After the Bay of Pigs, he was forced to stop in mid-speech before a New Orleans veterans' group because of the virulence of his attack upon the President.

Oswald's connection to Ferrie extended back into his boyhood. As a junior high school student in New Orleans, Lee had been a member of a Civil Air Patrol unit commanded by David Ferrie. As far as is known, there was no contact between the two from that time until the summer of 1963.

Three witnesses – and the street address on Oswald's pro-Castro leaflets – connect Oswald to Banister and his associates. There are numerous reports of Oswald and Ferrie together, one of them involving a "military training maneuver" with a number of Cubans near Bedico Creek, about fifty miles north of New Orleans.

Six witnesses, among them a state representative, a deputy sheriff, and a registrar of voters, saw Oswald and Ferrie together with another man in Clinton, Louisiana, about 130 miles from New Orleans. Oswald, who was out of work at the time, had apparently been driven by the other two to apply for a job at a nearby state hospital. When advised that he had to be a registered voter in the parish to get the job, he was taken back into Clinton, where he presented his Marine discharge papers as identification.

Was David Ferrie the evil genius behind the assassination? There is only circumstantial evidence to suggest that he may have been. He is the only visible connection between several of the primary suspect groups – the far-right fringe, the Mafia, and the Cuban exiles. There are tenuous connections between Ferrie and Jack Ruby. Ferrie was in Galveston, Texas just after the assassination, when Ruby placed a call there. And Ferrie seems to have made an unexplained and lengthy phone call in September 1963 to a woman who had dinner with Ruby the night before the assassination.

Ferrie was capable of devising a plan as intricate as the assassination conspiracy seems to have been. He seems to have known Oswald well, and was cunning enough to manipulate him. Of course another view of all this, equally supported by circumstantial evidence, is that Oswald was exploiting his connections with anti-Castro elements on orders from Communist or Castroite handlers.

Ferrie's connections with Oswald were brought to light by the bizarre assassination investigation conducted by New Orleans District Attorney Jim Garrison. Between 1967 and 1968, Garrison made a great but unsuccessful show of putting on trial a prominent New Orleans businessman named Clay Shaw for conspiracy to assassinate the President. Shaw apparently did have connections to the CIA, making numerous reports to the agency on international trade, but Garrison's strange and inconsistent witnesses could not establish that he had anything to do with killing Kennedy.

During the trial, Shaw was said to have been overheard plotting the assassination with Oswald and Ferrie. He was also said to be the third man seen with Oswald in Clinton, Louisiana, but this man could just as easily have been Guy Banister, who resembled Shaw. Shaw's life was effectively ruined by the investigation. David Ferrie's life was apparently ended by it.

Four days after news of the Garrison investigation first hit the press, and the day after Ferrie was released from protective custody, his nude body was found in his apartment. He had concluded a four-hour interview with a *Washington Post* reporter just before he died. Despite the two possible suicide notes found near the body, the cause of death was listed as a brain hemorrhage brought on by a berry aneurysm. Ferrie, the medical expert and ersatz doctor, had boasted to friends that he knew ways to kill that could never be detected.

The same day Ferrie died, his close associate in the anti-Castro cause, a prominent Cuban exile named Eladio del Valle, was found murdered in Miami. Del Valle had been tortured, hit in the head with an axe, and shot through the heart. His murder has never been solved.

Several of the more ominous incidents supporting the Cuban conspiracy theories have no apparent connection to Oswald. Of particular interest, because it involves a plot reported before the assassination, is the case of Rose Cheramie. Rose was a prostitute given to overindulgence in narcotics and alcohol. On the night of November 20, 1963 – two days before the shooting in Dallas – a highway patrolman found her lying by the road near Eunice, Louisiana. Because Rose was obviously under the influence, her story was ignored by the patrolman and by the doctors who treated her.

The story was that Rose had been traveling with two Latin men she couldn't identify, who were driving to Dallas to kill President Kennedy on November 22. After Rose got high, the men lost interest in her and threw her out of the car. The story was not passed along to Dallas police until after the assassination, and by that time the only official interest was in proving

Lee Oswald was the lone assassin. Rose Cheramie was found on another roadside two years later. She had been run over by a car and left dead near Big Sandy, Texas.

A more specific pre-assassination report came from a bugged conversation involving a police informant in Miami. On November 9, 1963, the informant was talking to a rich right-wing extremist named Joseph Milteer, who was under investigation in the infamous September 1963 bombing of a black church in Birmingham, Alabama, in which four young girls were killed.

Milteer was recorded telling the informant that Kennedy would be killed "from an office building with a high-powered rifle." The patsy, he said, was already in place: "They will pick up somebody . . . within hours afterwards . . . just to throw the public off." Apparently because of the threat, Kennedy's scheduled motorcade in Miami on November 18 was canceled, but no information on the threat was passed along to the authorities in Dallas.

On the morning of November 22, Milteer called the informant and claimed he was in Dallas. He said Kennedy would probably never be seen in Miami again. After the assassination, Milteer told the informant the arrest of Lee Oswald meant nothing, because "he doesn't know anything." Some conspiracy theorists claim a photograph shows Milteer standing in Dealey Plaza during the assassination.

The day before the assassination, a Cuban exile named Homer Echevarria, affiliated with the militant Cuban Student Directorate, was setting up an arms deal in Chicago. Echevarria told an associate he had come into "plenty of money," and that the deal could be closed "as soon as we take care of Kennedy." An HSCA investigation disclosed that the source of Echevarria's money was probably the Mafia. His comments were passed along to the Secret Service by a reliable informant immediately after the assassination. When the Secret Service began to investigate, its efforts were cut off by the FBI, which by then had been designated the primary investigative agency for the Warren Commission.

A compelling epilogue for the Cuban conspiracy evidence is provided by the confession of a man named Robert Easterling. Easterling first contacted author Henry Hurt in 1981, and his story became the centerpiece for Hurt's book *Reasonable Doubt*.

A number of assassination "confessions" have been published, tending markedly toward the fantastic: an assassin named "Saul" is said to have worked for Lyndon Johnson *and* the KGB; a CIA contractor recounts his James Bondesque antics on behalf of agency renegades. Unlike its predecessors, Easterling's confession has the gritty feel of truth.

This is not because Easterling is an admirable character. He is an alcoholic with severe mental problems and a history of heartless violence. He may have been guilty, at various times, of everything from burglary and car theft to blowing up an airliner – with forty-six aboard – to child prostitution.

In 1963, Easterling was a sometime diesel mechanic and sometime criminal. He lived in a trailer near New Orleans and frequented the Habana Bar. He there met an old acquaintance he knew as Manuel Rivera, a Cuban who worked the numbers and prostitution rackets for the New Orleans Mafia and who cashed in on both sides of the struggle for his homeland. According to the story, Rivera enlisted Easterling as a bit player in the assassination plot.

The other players included a number of unnamed Cubans, David Ferrie, and a man who may have been either Clay Shaw or Guy Banister. The real weapon was a Czech-made semi-automatic rifle with a specially constructed catch box to collect ejected shells. The planted weapon was a 6.5 mm Mannlicher-Carcano, and the patsy due to take the blame was Lee Oswald.

A field behind Easterling's trailer was used for target practice with the Czech gun and for a strange exercise Easterling didn't understand. The Mannlicher-Carcano was fired into a barrel of water, and the slugs were collected. Author Hurt duplicated this feat and ended up with a slug that looks almost exactly like Warren Commission Exhibit number 399 – the bullet found, and very likely planted, on the stretcher in Parkland Hospital, and used to tie up the loose ends in the lone gunman theory. The episode of these water-shooting Cubans was confirmed by Easterling's ex-wife, who had no reason to support his story.

The operation was funded by $100,000 in laundered cash, provided by "a wealthy Dallas oilman." The bagman for the cash was Jack Ruby, who actually was, according to official accounts, visiting New Orleans at the time. Ruby had at least one known connection with oilman H. L. Hunt.

One of Easterling's chores was to drive Oswald and Rivera to Houston, at the time of Oswald's trip to Mexico. (While official accounts have Oswald on the bus to Mexico beginning in Houston, they have never provided for his transportation from New Orleans to Houston.) The hitch was that Oswald, because of his political activities, had come under FBI surveillance. A fire was set to create a diversion while Oswald slipped into the car. Hurt was able to establish through New Orleans Fire Department records that a suspicious fire did occur when and where Easterling said it did.

In Houston, the travelers met an Oswald look-alike introduced as Carlo, and Easterling returned to Louisiana alone. He claims Oswald, Rivera, and "Carlo" spoke Russian together. This would have been just before the three men appeared at Silvia Odio's apartment in Dallas. Her description of one of the Latins is a good match for Easterling's description of Manuel Rivera.

In Easterling's version of the assassination, the Czech rifle was smuggled into the Book Depository building in the false bottom of a wooden book crate. Hurt established that such crates were in use in the building. Manuel did all the shooting with the Czech gun. The Mannlicher-Carcano was left conveniently exposed, while the Czech rifle was put back in its box and later removed.

Easterling's role in Dallas was to pick up Lee Oswald, who left the Book Depository before the shooting and was replaced there by the double "Carlo," at the Dallas bus station and get him to Mexico. According to the official account, Oswald caught a cab at the bus station. If the Easterling story is true, he was forced to do this because Easterling did not show up. Fearing for his life, he created an alibi by committing a burglary, did his time for the crime, and laid low for the next ten years.

During a trip to Honduras in 1973, Easterling met a young man who recognized him and introduced himself as Manuel Rivera's younger brother Francisco. Francisco told a frightening tale. He said he recognized Easterling because he had seen his picture, among the pictures of the other conspirators, in Raul Castro's den. Raul is Fidel's brother and his intelligence chief. Most of the pictures of the other people had been crossed out with X's. Above Easterling's picture was a question mark. The Czech rifle was mounted like a hunting trophy, above a plaque that said only "Kennedy 1963." Francisco offered Easterling a plane ride home, but Easterling wisely declined.

There are several important points the Easterling story cannot account for. It does not, for example, provide for the second shooter on the grassy knoll, or for the involved cover-ups designed to protect the one-gun theory. But it does tie up a number of previously loose ends.

It shows how various apparently incongruent conspiracy theories – each with much to recommend it, but none a complete story on its own – can be put together in a reasonable reconstruction. Using right-wing money, members of a crime syndicate cooperate both with anti-Castro Cubans and with Cuban covert agents to accomplish a common goal. In doing this, the reconstruction touches base with the established facts at critical points.

Judged on his own credibility, Easterling is not much of a source. But judged purely on the merits of his story, he is either a man who is telling the truth or a damned clever storyteller.

Further evidence of a Cuban conspiracy surfaced when researchers used the Freedom of Information Act to gain access to previously classified CIA documents in 1983. The documents, together with information gathered by the Church committee in the 1970s, establish an unusually heavy pattern of

Cuban diplomatic traffic at the Mexico City airport on the night of November 22, 1963.

In one strange instance, a Cubana Airlines flight from Mexico City to Havana was held on the ground for five hours awaiting the arrival of a passenger. That passenger finally landed at the airport in a private, twin-engine plane and boarded the Cubana flight without going through customs. The CIA documents tentatively identify the passenger as one Miguel Casas, a man of about the same age and bulk – short and stocky – as Easterling's Manuel Rivera. Casas's private flight is said to have originated in Laredo after a car trip from Dallas, where Casas had gone with two other men. A report quoting Casas's aunt identifies him as "one of Raul's men," and confirms the trip to and from Dallas on assassination day.

A separate report quotes a Cuban scientist who was a CIA source as having observed a plane with Mexican markings landing at Havana airport the afternoon on November 22. Two men, "recognized as Cuban gangsters," emerged from the plane and went through the back of the airport, avoiding customs. This sighting could explain the escape route of Casas's two companions.

As for the possibility that Fidel Castro or his brother ordered the assassination, there are good arguments that can serve for either side. Some take the view that Castro is too smart to have killed Kennedy. If he had been caught doing so, he would have risked an American invasion, and the troops on his beaches would have been U.S. Marines, not paramilitary amateurs.

On the other hand, Castro had both the motive and the means to carry out the assassination, and gained more from it than any other man alive. The American harassment of the Castro regime came to a virtual standstill after John Kennedy died. Without American support, serious resistance to Castro dwindled to nothing. If Castro did kill Kennedy, the killing accomplished everything he could have hoped for.

The Hit on America

The Mafia Conspiracy

Fidel Castro was not the only one who benefited from the President's death. Within the United States, there was another "government" – the one Robert Kennedy called the Private Government – that benefited in a surprisingly similar way. This "government" too was under attack by the Kennedy administration. The assassination turned what had been a blitzkrieg into a running skirmish.

The HSCA report came to the conclusion that the death of the President probably was the result of a conspiracy, and strongly hinted that organized crime could be involved. The Select Committee's Chief Counsel, Robert Blakey, and Committee Editorial Director Richard Billings followed up with a book, called *The Plot to Kill the President,* which made a case for a Mafia hit.

Other well-publicized Congressional investigations in the 1950s had established the existence of powerful criminal organizations that controlled vast empires of legal and illegal business. But it was not until the early years of the Kennedy administration that a coordinated, national crime organization was revealed and known by its real name. An imprisoned hit man named Joseph Valachi, convinced he had been wrongly condemned to death by his former employers, decided to turn informant.

In an interview with the FBI on September 8, 1962, Valachi revealed that the crime syndicate popularly called the Mafia was known to its members as La Cosa Nostra. He confirmed that the organization was controlled by a national commission of nine to twelve members who were heads of prominent crime "families." Valachi's story was brought to the public in a book called *The Valachi Papers,* by Peter Maas, and his revelations before a Congressional committee were much in the news at the time of the assassination.

The high profile that La Cosa Nostra experienced – but did not enjoy – in the 1960s was due in large part to the efforts of John and Robert Kennedy. Beginning in the mid-1950s, Robert Kennedy had served as Chief Counsel for the U.S. Senate committee – known as the McClellan Committee for its chairman, John McClellan – that exposed the Mafia's involvement in the Teamsters Union and in many other enterprises. Senator John Kennedy was a member of the McClellan Committee.

Both brothers were aware of the political benefits that could accrue from the committee's sensational hearings. Presidential candidate Thomas E. Dewey, the Republican nominee of 1948, sprang to national prominence on the strength of his gangbuster reputation as a prosecutor in New York. In 1956, John Kennedy lost the Democratic vice-presidential nomination to Senator Estes Kefauver, who had established his own national image during the organized crime investigations of the Senate committee that bore his name, and had himself barely missed the presidential nomination in 1952. The lesson was clear. Attacks on the mob were good politics.

As they did everything in life, the brothers pursued their quarry with vigor. Never before or since has a federal assault on organized crime been as intense or as effective as it was during the Kennedy years. In one characteristic instance, Robert Kennedy became locked in an all-out eight-year war, beginning with the McClellan Committee and extending through his term as Attorney General, with Teamsters boss Jimmy Hoffa. Kennedy won, but not without a struggle. It took five federal trials and the full-time efforts of a 150 person "Get Hoffa" squad in the Justice Department to nail Jimmy. As he went down, one hundred other Teamster officials and hangers-on went down with him.

Another special target was close Hoffa ally Carlos Marcello, the Mafia boss in New Orleans. Marcello, who lived in the United States illegally, had been under a deportation order since the early 1950s, but had fought off the best efforts of the government with bribes and with the substantial power of his "office." It was a paddycake game Bob Kennedy wouldn't play.

Under heavy pressure from the Attorney General, the Immigration and Naturalization Service (INS) grabbed Marcello without warning on April 4, 1961, and dumped him in Guatemala City (he held a Guatemalan passport he had bought with a bribe) with only the clothes he had on his back. The Guatemalans in turn dumped him, along with a lawyer who had flown to his aid, in the jungle of El Salvador. There he was interrogated for five days by Salvadoran troops and then redumped further in the jungle. The chubby Marcello and his lawyer, both used to easy living and dressed in silk suits and alligator shoes, were forced to hike their way through the mountainous country to the nearest airport.

The journey cost Marcello two broken ribs, but it did bring him, illegally, back into his fiefdom in New Orleans. Attorney General Kennedy insisted the one-way ticket to Guatemala was legal. Marcello and his lawyers insisted, with some reason, that it was kidnapping. Carlos Marcello was not a good man to humiliate. In Hoffa, Marcello, and many others like them, the Kennedys were making deadly enemies.

In all, 116 indictments were handed out between 1960 and 1964 against Cosa Nostra members throughout the United States. At Robert Kennedy's urging, the FBI vigorously pursued the illegal wiretapping and bugging of mob figures. Up to a hundred different bugs produced hundreds of volumes of transcripts from these overheard conversations, which yielded a wealth of information during the Kennedy era and were mined for years to come.

The Kennedy forces were not only putting people in jail, they were threatening to dry up the mob's flood-level cash flow at its sources. The under-the-table take from Las Vegas alone was measured in tens of millions of dollars every year. Under Kennedy, the IRS opened a forty-agent office in Las Vegas, and FBI strength in Nevada was tripled. The implications were clear: if the mob lost Vegas, it would suffer its biggest financial setback since Castro took Havana.

If the assassination had not happened and both Kennedys had served a second term, it is possible that organized crime could have been effectively crippled as a national threat. No one realized this more clearly than the men in control of La Cosa Nostra.

The Kennedy war on crime had about it some odd and highly personal twists. Historically, the mob had not often struck back against outsiders. Even the most aggressive cops were left alone. It was betrayal by a cop "on the take" that brought swift and violent retribution. As Bugsy Siegel put it, in the memorable line that would become the title of his biography, "We only kill each other." As it happened, La Cosa Nostra did not consider John Kennedy an outsider, for several reasons.

Joseph Kennedy, the patriarch of the Kennedy clan and John and Robert's father, is said to have made a portion of his fortune doing business with the Mafia. The head of one of the New York families, Frank Costello, claimed to have been in the bootlegging business with Joe Kennedy during Prohibition. Sometime during this association, there was a falling-out that caused bad blood between the mob and the elder Kennedy. Some of the older Mafia chieftains even reasoned that the Kennedy administration's warlike attitude was based on "a personal grudge" that dated back to the 1930s. Sam Giancana, the mob boss in Chicago during the 1960s, told a girlfriend that Joe Kennedy was "one of the biggest crooks who ever lived." Giancana bitterly remarked that, despite what he saw as a birds-of-a-feather relationship, "If I ever get a speeding ticket, none of these fuckers, [the Kennedys] would know me."

Giancana had good reason to direct this particular epithet at John Kennedy. He was literally sharing with the President the girlfriend to whom he made the remark about Kennedy's father, a pretty young starlet named Judy Campbell.

John Kennedy's sexual appetite was legendary. Both before and after he won the Presidency, he was supplied a steady stream of girls, Judy Campbell among them, by his friend Frank Sinatra, whose friendships with Giancana and other Mafia figures were – according to a number of sources – close and long-standing.

It was through the Sinatra milieu that Kennedy may have begun his fabled affair with Marilyn Monroe, an affair that seems to have been taken up by the Attorney General where the President left off. There is evidence that Giancana's West Coast representative, John Roselli, did the President a favor by covering up his involvement with another starlet named Judy Meredith, though it is not clear who asked Roselli to do this.

It is possible that the Kennedy liaisons in Hollywood were part of a Mafia blackmail scheme. This type of shakedown was a favorite of West Coast gangster Mickey Cohen, who made a regular business of arranging the seductions of show business personalities and recording them in the act. Jimmy Hoffa reportedly held tapes of both John and Robert Kennedy in the act of lovemaking.

Just as likely, the pimping done for the President was quite literally a sexual favor, for which other favors were expected in return.

Following an FBI investigation and under pressure from Robert Kennedy and from J. Edgar Hoover, the President broke off his relationship with Sinatra in the summer of 1962. From the Mafia's point of view, the damage had already been done. By accepting its sexual favors, the President had been "on the take" as much as any crooked street cop. The continued attacks by his Justice Department were dirty pool, and could not be tolerated.

There was still another debt the Mafia felt owed by the President, and this was perhaps the greatest debt of all. Some members of La Cosa Nostra were convinced they had given John Kennedy the presidency. In Sam Giancana's Chicago, the mob-controlled political machine known as the West Side Block came up, apparently out of thin air, with the votes necessary for Kennedy to carry Illinois in the 1960 election. This, together with the equally suspicious disqualification of 100,000 urban votes in Texas, made the difference that made Kennedy the winner. Giancana bragged to Judy Campbell that her lover in the White House wouldn't be there "if it wasn't for me."

Why would Kennedy, with his gangbuster brother, merit such support? According to Mickey Cohen, Kennedy was simply seen as the lesser of two evils, as Republicans had – up to that time – been tougher on the mob than Democrats. The possibility of Bobby Kennedy turning up as Attorney General was never considered.

By the fall of 1962, the mob's simmering hatred of the Kennedys had come to the boiling point. Carlos Marcello, continually hounded by the IRS, the INS, and the Justice Department since his return from the unscheduled trip to Guatemala, let his anger spill over during a September meeting at Churchill Farms, his estate outside New Orleans. Marcello's tirade was quoted by one of those present to author Ed Reid, and repeated to the HSCA.

When Robert Kennedy's name was mentioned, Marcello is said to have exploded: "Don't worry about that little Bobby son of a bitch! He's going to be taken care of." He would be taken care of not by killing him, but by killing his brother the President. Marcello explained with a bit of folksy allegory. When attacked by a dog [the government], it does no good to cut off the tail [the Attorney General]. Cut off the head [the President], and the dog is out of business. It is significant that Marcello saw the government efforts against him as a personal attack directed by the Kennedys. He reasoned that killing John Kennedy would stop the attack, and as it turned out he was right.

According to the source, Marcello was quite specific about his planned dog-beheading. He could not afford to have his own people involved, so he would use "a nut" who could be easily manipulated to do the job. When presented with the story of the Churchill Farms meeting in 1967, the FBI did little or nothing to verify it. The HSCA staff accepted the story and interviewed Marcello, who denied that the meeting ever happened.

The Marcello threat seems to have been confirmed by another

source. Santo Trafficante, Jr. was reportedly in the drug trade with Marcello, and was closer to him than any other Cosa Nostra leader. Trafficante had ruled the mob empire in Havana and fallen back into his power base in Florida after the Cuban revolution. He may have been among the guests invited to the Churchill Farms meeting.

Shortly after the meeting, Trafficante reportedly told a prominent Cuban expatriate named José Alemán that the President "is going to be hit" because of his brother's harassment of Jimmy Hoffa, "a friend of the working man."

If Marcello did have plans to kill the President, he also had the means to carry them out. An estimate by the New Orleans Crime Commission put the annual gross income from the operations under his command at just over $1 billion. About $600 million of this came from gambling, prostitution, burglary, and other illegal endeavors, the rest from "legitimate" business interests. Marcello's influence extended across the southern half of the country, from California to Florida. The Mafia outfit in Dallas, for example, was run by men who were strongly allied with Marcello if not under his direct control.

Marcello also enjoyed a special status among his peers in La Cosa Nostra. In 1968, New York boss Joseph Colombo was heard explaining that New Orleans was the first Cosa Nostra family set up in the United States by the organization's Sicilian forefathers. With such historical distinction, the New Orleans family did not require the approval of the national commission on its actions.

This probably explains the fact that Marcello, while one of the most powerful Mafia leaders in the country, did not sit on the commission. As far as the assassination is concerned, the implication is that Marcello could have planned it and carried it out without the commission approval that would probably have been required of any other local chieftain. Significantly, the FBI's electronic surveillance program in the early 1960s concentrated on commission members and missed Marcello entirely.

One of the multitude of people who were, directly or indirectly, on Marcello's payroll was David Ferrie. Ferrie worked as an investigator for one of Marcello's lawyers. On the day of the assassination, he was in the courtroom when Marcello was found not guilty of defrauding the United States by carrying a bogus Guatemalan birth certificate. According to one source, Ferrie was the conduit for cash that helped support at least one Cuban exile leader, and the likely source of that cash was Carlos Marcello. Ferrie may have flown for Marcello. There is one report that he is the pilot who flew Marcello back from his trauma in the jungle. And whatever his relationship to the top Mafia man in New Orleans, Ferrie seems to have been the recipient of a sizable gift from Marcello after the assassination: he was set up in a gas station franchise.

Some have theorized that Marcello was the invisible power behind the Jim Garrison assassination investigation in New Orleans, the point being to divert attention from Marcello's involvement. The evidence to support this assertion is that District Attorney Garrison apparently used the investigation, at Marcello's bidding, to intimidate an enemy of Jimmy Hoffa's, accepted an expenses-paid vacation to Las Vegas and a $5,000 gambling credit from Marcello in 1967, and was accused, but acquitted, of taking mob payoffs in 1971. Ferrie was a star suspect in the investigation, but despite Ferrie's connection to Marcello, the Garrison probe ignored Marcello entirely. Garrison's allegiances can perhaps best be judged by his oft-repeated opinion that there was no organized crime in New Orleans.

In Chicago, and throughout his dominions in California, Las Vegas, and Florida, Sam Giancana was suffering under the same federal pressure as Marcello. In the summer of 1961, Giancana was harassed by FBI agents as he and his girlfriend Phyllis McGuire — of the singing McGuire sisters — stopped over at O'Hare airport. As agents interviewed his girl outside his hearing, their colleagues giggled at the sight of the mighty crime boss holding her purse, and the hot-tempered Giancana lost his cool. "Fuck you, fuck your boss, fuck your boss's boss," he screamed. "You know who I mean, I mean the Kennedys. I know all about the Kennedys . . . You lit a fire tonight that will never go out!"

The fire was still burning in the summer of 1963, when the FBI put Giancana under "lock-step," twenty-four-hour surveillance, effectively crippling his direct control of his empire. By the fall of the year, Sam Giancana was a very angry man, and there could be no mistake about who he was mad at.

Marcello and Giancana were big fish. But it was a very small fish, who swam in murky waters both of them dominated, that made the history books because of his role in the assassination story. His name at birth was Jacob Rubenstein. Since the day he became famous by killing Lee Harvey Oswald, he has been known to all the world as Jack Ruby.

The Warren Commission investigated Jack Ruby at some length and came to the remarkable conclusion that he had no "significant" connections with organized crime. To anyone with a passing knowledge of Ruby's life story, this statement is equal to the proposition that Goofy showed no significant signs of being a dog.

Ruby was born in 1911 in Chicago, and grew up in a tough Jewish ghetto that abutted a tough Italian ghetto. His father was an alcoholic and his mother emotionally unbalanced. Young Jack was a street hustler who made very early connections with the mob. His first known job was delivering envelopes for Al Capone. His formal education ended with the fifth grade. This is understandable, as Ruby, at age sixteen, must have made an uncomfortably large fifth grader.

Ruby survived the Depression through ticket scalping and gambling operations and, apparently, through work for a hoodlum outfit known as the Dave Miller gang. In the late 1930s, he was a gun-toting thug in the goon squad of a mob-dominated Scrap Iron and Junk Handlers Union local. During World War II, he served in the Air Force.

There is good evidence that Ruby was in Dallas because the

Chicago mob put him there. In 1946, a Chicago gangster named Paul Rowland Jones, who worked for Giancana's predecessor Anthony "Big Tuna" Accardo, began visiting Dallas to lay the groundwork for an invasion by the Chicago outfit. When Jones attempted a bribe on Sheriff-elect Steve Guthrie, a bust was set up and conversations were recorded. According to Guthrie, Jones said the Chicago mob would bring in a man named Jack Ruby in the spring of 1947 to run a restaurant that would be a front for gambling action and other syndicate business. The recordings on which Ruby may have been mentioned have unaccountably disappeared.

Ruby made his first visit to Dallas in the spring of 1947, moving there later that year. Years later he told two friends the mob had "exiled" him from Chicago. He had wanted to go to California in 1947, he said, but he "was directed" to Dallas.

Ruby's sister Eva Grant had opened a dance hall called the Singapore Supper Club, which was frequented by Paul Rowland Jones – while his bribery sentence was on appeal – and his associates. Jones was moving opium from Mexico to Chicago through Dallas, and there is reason to believe Ruby and his sister were involved. They were interviewed by narcotics agents, but not charged along with Jones. Ruby soon took over the Singapore and began his undistinguished nightclub career.

From 1947 to 1963, Jack Ruby operated six different clubs in Dallas, all failures in varying degrees. His best pals in the early years were safecrackers and white slavers. In 1956 he was mentioned in an FBI report as the mob contact who gave the okay for an out-of-town narcotics ring to operate in Dallas. This is a role that is normally played by a designated "enforcer" in a Cosa Nostra territory. He was said to be in control of the mob's "policy" gambling wheel in Dallas, and had well-established connections with gamblers from California to Louisiana. Ruby routinely carried a gun and had a Dallas record of nine arrests, mostly for brawls, but no serious convictions (there had been other arrests in Chicago). He served as his own bouncer in the clubs, and seemed to especially enjoy beating up drunks and women.

By the fall of 1963 there were two Ruby clubs in Dallas, the Vegas and the Carousel. The Carousel was the main focus of Ruby's interest. It was a sleazy striptease dive where the girls hustled customers for overpriced drinks in between perform-ances, and turned tricks on the side. The most favored patrons at the Carousel were Dallas police officers. Any cop friendly enough to call Jack Ruby by name could depend on free soft drinks, cut-rate liquor, and – as a special favor – off-duty visits with the working girls. When a Carousel stripper complained to her union rep about Ruby slapping her around, she was told to forget about it "because Ruby had too much on the Dallas police."

Ruby helped the cops in other ways. He was a regular informer and was looked upon as a dependable source of up-to-date street news. When the time came to kill Oswald, Ruby had plenty of chips to cash with the police, and they seem to have come in handy.

In the pageant of grotesque humanity that files through the assassination story, Ruby seems right at home. He was a nervous little bully who was forever conscious of his status as an outsider, super sensitive about his Jewish heritage, craving respectability but trapped on the slimy underside of society. His role models were flashy big-name thugs like Mickey Cohen.

Ruby dealt in women and booze, but never drank – he was given instead to eating binges when upset – and rarely had female companionship. What affection he had to give was lavished on his dogs, so thoroughly that some have suggested he indulged in bestiality. His dachshund Sheba was referred to as his wife, his other dogs as their children. Ruby was meticulous about his appearance, taking up to three baths a day and pampering himself with baby oils, but his living habits were slovenly, his apartment a wreck, and his business done in cash out of the trunk of his untidy car.

There were two outstanding features of Ruby's life at the time of the assassination: he desperately needed money, and he was a much busier man than usual. His clubs were not prospering. He owed the federal government about $60,000 in excise and income taxes and, these debts going back some six years, the government was making efforts to collect.

Just before the assassination, on November 19, 1963, Ruby's financial problem appears to have been miraculously resolved. According to author Seth Kantor, he told his lawyer "a friend" would take care of his debts, and took the uncharacteristic step of giving the lawyer power of attorney to deal with the government. Ruby had an equally unusual visit with his doctor on November 11. The patient, who was no stranger to drugs but normally took amphetamines, asked for and received a prescription to calm his nerves. The prescription was refilled four days later.

During the same period, Ruby dashed through an intense series of meetings – by phone and in person – with his old mob acquaintances. The Warren Commission explained this activity in terms of a labor dispute Ruby had with the union that represented his strippers. The dispute was real, but given what was to come, it could hardly explain all of Ruby's actions. From May through September 1963, Ruby placed twenty-five to thirty-five long-distance phone calls each month. In October, he placed seventy-five of these calls. During the first three weeks of November, the number of calls shot up to ninety-six.

The recipients of these calls included Nofio Pecora, a highly placed member of the Marcello organization in New Orleans, Irwin Weiner, a bondsman and insurance man in Chicago with ties to Jimmy Hoffa and to mob figures throughout the country, "Barney" Baker, a 370-pound monster who enforced business agreements for Hoffa and the Chicago mob, and Lenny Patrick, a Chicago-based bank robber and suspected mob triggerman.

On November 12, Ruby was visited by his old pal Paul Rowland Jones and by Alex Gruber, another old Chicago friend who lived in Los Angeles and had contacts with Teamster hoods and with Mickey Cohen's gang. Jones and Gruber, neither of whom had seen Ruby for years and who both claimed to have traveled hundreds of miles – coincidentally – just to drop in on him, spent two days meeting with Ruby.

On November 17, Ruby seems to have made an unexplained trip to Las Vegas. His known contacts there denied seeing him, but witnesses confirmed his presence. The most suspicious meetings of all came the night before the assassination.

Ruby dined that night with his longtime friend and "financial backer" Ralph Paul. The chosen restaurant was the Egyptian Lounge, owned by Joseph and Sam Campisi. Joseph Campisi, according to an FBI report, was said to be the heir apparent to the top man in the Dallas Cosa Nostra family, Joseph Civello. Campisi and Civello both acknowledged knowing Ruby, and Ruby was said to be a frequent visitor to Campisi's restaurant and to a store owned by Civello.

Campisi also acknowledged his close friendship with Carlos Marcello. His phone records, examined by the HSCA, showed up to twenty calls a day to New Orleans. Campisi admitted seeing Ruby in his restaurant on the night in question when first interviewed in 1963, but denied it before the HSCA. After dinner, Ruby left the Egyptian Lounge for another rendezvous.

Overlooking Stemmons Freeway, and less than two minutes from Dealey Plaza, stood the Cabana Motel. For mobsters in town to kill the President, the Cabana would have been a likely roost. It was convenient to the site of the hit, offered an easy getaway route, and seems to have been friendly turf.

The Cabana had been built in 1959 with a $3.6 million dollar loan from the Teamster Central States Pension Fund, approved by Jimmy Hoffa. The loan recipient and the nominal owner of the Cabana was Jay Sarno, a front man for Mafia ownership of several Las Vegas casinos.

Just before midnight on November 21, Ruby arrived at the Cabana to meet a Chicago businessman named Lawrence Meyers, who was sales manager for a sporting goods company. Meyers's traveling companion was a woman he claimed was a "party girl" he had picked up at a hotel and lounge in Chicago. This was Jean West, aka Jean Aase, a shadowy figure who has not been heard from since, despite the attempts of numerous investigators to locate her. What makes Ms. West intriguing is the fact that, according to telephone records, David Ferrie – of New Orleans fame – placed an unexplained fifteen-minute phone call on September 24, 1963, to the Chicago hotel where Meyers says he met her.

Meyers and Ms. West had arrived in Dallas on November 20 and checked into a Ramada Inn. On November 21, they checked out and moved to the Cabana Motel. Why? Perhaps to be nearer other people who were staying there.

Two of these people were Eugene Hale Brading, aka Jim Braden, a high-flying West Coast con man with longstanding ties to the Chicago Mafia, and Morgan Brown, another con artist who had been involved in at least one shootout with Los Angeles police. According to author Peter Noyes, Brading had worked at one point as a courier for mob kingpin Meyer Lansky.

Brading, traveling as "Braden," had checked into the Cabana with Brown on November 21, telling the clerk they would stay until November 24. Moments after the assassination, "Braden" was one of about a dozen people picked up by Dallas cops and briefly questioned. When arrested, he was in the Dal-Tex building across the street from the Book Depository. He claimed to have ducked into the building to use the phone. There an elevator operator thought he was suspicious and reported him to police. While Brading was being questioned, his companion Brown checked out of the Cabana – without explaining why he was leaving two days ahead of schedule – and left his friend behind.

Brading and Ruby crossed paths on at least two occasions during Brading's brief stay in Dallas. The first was on the afternoon of November 21, when both men visited the Mercantile Bank Building, which housed the offices of the arch-conservative Hunt brothers. Ruby claimed to be only dropping off a friend for a job interview with the Hunts; Brading was supposedly meeting with Lamar or Nelson Bunker Hunt on oil business. The second path-crossing was in the wee hours of November 22.

According to the Warren Commission account, Ruby's midnight get-together with Lawrence Meyers at the Cabana Motel lasted only a few minutes. But Ruby telephoned an employee at 2.30 a.m. and mentioned that he was still at the Cabana. Was he with Meyers, or with Brading, or with someone else who may have been at the Cabana on deadly business? The question has never been answered.

During the HSCA investigation, Brading – now legally known as Braden – denied any association with Ruby, organized crime, or the assassination. But a curious footnote to the Ruby–Brading story did come to light. It was established that on the night of June 4, 1968 – the night Robert Kennedy was shot to death at the Hotel Ambassador in Los Angeles – Brading aka Braden was a guest at the Century Plaza Hotel, less than fifteen minutes away.

One man who could have cleared up many of the mysteries of Dallas never chose to do so. Jack Ruby died of cancer January 3, 1967, without revealing any of his secrets. On one occasion, he hinted that he was ready to talk, but he was ignored. The Warren Commission, or part of it – Chief Justice Earl Warren and then Congressman Gerald Ford – traveled to Dallas to take his testimony shortly after his trial ended on March of 1964. The interview took place in a tiny room in the Dallas courthouse, in the presence of Sheriff Bill Decker, three lawyers, three Commission staff members, a Secret Service man, and an assistant DA.

The transcript of Ruby's testimony before the Chief Justice and the future President is painful to read. This is not because he rambles to the point of incoherence, as he certainly does, and not because he seems at times to be in less than full possession of his faculties. It is because he so clearly and repeatedly signals his questioners that he has something to tell them if they will just take him somewhere else to hear it.

The signals were in vain. In the midst of a disjointed monologue about his activities after the assassination, Ruby breaks off abruptly: "Gentlemen, unless you get me to Washington, you can't get a fair shake out of me." Later, Ruby asks the officers and his attorney to leave the room. Only the officers leave. He then addresses Chief Justice Warren directly: "I want to tell the truth, and I can't tell it here." Again, a few minutes later: "The only thing I want to get out to the public, and I can't say it here . . . is . . . why my act was committed, but it can't be said here." Later: "I am used as a scapegoat . . . I have been used for a purpose."

The rest of the testimony, with some paranoid fantasy thrown in, is basically a retelling of the same unlikely tale Ruby had repeated so often and would repeat again. He clearly had something to add to this tale that he never felt safe enough to say.

Why did he want to go to Washington? Maybe just to be on center stage. Or maybe for a better reason. Ruby almost certainly had police help in getting to Oswald. He was now in police custody. As he well knew, the Dallas police were not incorruptible. Not long after he was jailed, Joseph Campisi had visited him in his cell, at the invitation of Sheriff Decker. Campisi acknowledged to the HSCA that he was close to Decker, who had "no problems with the Italian families" in Dallas. In these surroundings, it is easy to imagine why Ruby might not want to sit in the Dallas County jail and discuss the "purpose" he had been "used for."

In Ruby's cluttered car after his arrest, investigators found a September 8, 1963 edition of a New York newspaper. In the paper was a column that sang the praises of the famous Cosa Nostra informer Joe Valachi. Valachi was under federal protection. He had been a small-timer who made a big name for himself by telling what he knew. Given the same federal protection, it is possible that Jack Ruby, another small-timer, was ready to make his own splash with revelations much bigger than Valachi's. He would never get the chance.

Like so many of the players in the assassination, Ruby had his own connections to Cuba. Although he told police and the Warren Commission he had only traveled once to Cuba, on a "vacation" visit to his pal Lewis McWillie, who managed the

Tropicana casino in Havana, the evidence shows he made at least three trips there in August and September of 1959.

These quick back-and-forth trips do not have the look of a casual vacation; they may have involved gun-running, and are likely to have involved the liberation of mob boss Santo Trafficante, Jr. from a Castro jail.

When Castro took power in Cuba, he briefly closed the casinos and locked up some Cosa Nostra figures who had been running them in Trescornia prison camp. The bigger names included Trafficante and Meyer Lanksy's brother Jake.

Shortly after the Castro victory, a Houston-based gunrunner named Thomas McKeown got a call from a man named "Rubenstein," who wanted to get three Cuban prisoners released and was willing to pay $5,000 a head. The money, the caller said, would come from someone in Las Vegas. McKeown demanded a $5,000 advance and never heard from the caller again. A few weeks later Jack Ruby showed up on McKeown's doorstep and talked to him about the possibility of selling jeeps to Castro. Ruby admitted the jeep scheme but denied the rest.

In April of 1959, for the first and only time in his life, Jack Ruby rented a safe-deposit box at a Dallas bank. This box was presumably related to his Cuban activities, as it was used six times over the next five months, and only sporadically thereafter. It was empty when opened after the assassination.

In May, Ruby sent a coded message to Lewis McWillie in Cuba via a mutual friend. In July or August, he had dinner in Dallas with Pedro and Martin Fox, two brothers who were the nominal owners of the Tropicana in Havana. Trafficante told the HSCA the Fox brothers were doing "their best to get me out" of Cuba at this point. On August 8, Ruby made the first of his three trips to Havana. He was back in Dallas using the safe-deposit box on August 21. Trafficante was released from Trescornia on August 18.

Shortly after the assassination, a British "journalist" named John Wilson, aka John Wilson-Hudson, who may have been an intelligence agent, reported that he had been in Trescornia, had known an American gangster-gambler named "Santos" (a variant of Trafficante's first name) there, and that "Santos" had been frequently visited by another "American gangster-type" named Ruby.

During roughly the same period, Ruby was volunteering as an informant for the FBI, though the bureau claims he was of no use in this capacity, and that the information he provided had nothing to do with Cuba.

During the Warren Commission investigation, a comedian named Wally Weston, who had worked for Ruby, was visiting him in his cell at the Dallas county jail. According to Weston, Ruby became agitated and whined, "Wally, they're going to find out about Cuba. They're going to find out about the guns, find out about New Orleans, find out about everything!"

Weston has been a questionable source on other matters, but there is no reason to believe he knew Ruby had anything to do with guns, Cuba, or New Orleans.

If Ruby had something to do with Trafficante's release, he becomes a minor link in a chain of circumstances that tied La Cosa Nostra into a joint venture with another secret organization, the CIA. Trafficante was to become a key player in the venture. The goal was to kill Fidel Castro.

In April of 1961, the FBI stumbled onto this strange alliance when it discovered that Sam Giancana had used CIA surveillance equipment in October 1960 to test the fidelity of his girlfriend Phyllis McGuire. Through CIA contacts, Giancana arranged the bugging of an apartment in Las Vegas that belonged to comedian Dan Rowan. The American citizenry would not learn the full implications of this discovery until the Church Committee hearings in the mid-1970s.

The CIA apparently first had the idea of an underworld hit on Castro in August of 1960, when it was busy with its many other schemes to eliminate the Cuban leader. According to Church Committee testimony, the agency's Operational Support Division approached Robert Maheu, a former FBI agent who worked for Howard Hughes and had good Mafia connections.

Maheu in turn took the proposition to Giancana's man John Roselli, and a meeting was set up between the CIA, Giancana, and Trafficante. The deal was struck.

Another version of the story maintains that Jimmy Hoffa was the original go-between for the CIA and the Mafia. Hoffa had reportedly used his Teamsters financial machinery to shuffle mob money to both sides in the Cuban revolution.

However the alliance first came about, a number of unsuccessful assassination plots followed. The first known one came in February 1961, when John Roselli passed some CIA-concocted poison pills to a Cuban official with access to Castro. This scheme fell apart when the official lost his job, and the pills came home. More pills were dispatched in April of the next year, with similar results, and a three-man assassination team sent by Roselli tried and failed to penetrate Castro's bodyguard protection the following September.

Church Committee testimony indicated the Kennedy brothers did not learn about the CIA–Mafia plots until well into 1962. Robert Kennedy, who was doing all he could to hang the same people the CIA was cooperating with, was said to be greatly displeased. Still, the alliance continued, indicating the depth of the split between the President – who was now seen as waffling on his attitude toward Cuba – and the militant factions at the CIA.

There is a strong possibility that the Mafia was playing a double agent role with the spy agency all along. Jimmy "the Weasel" Fratianno, a hit man turned government informer, claimed Roselli told him, "These fucking wild schemes the CIA dreamed up never got further than Santo [Trafficante]. He just . . . conned everybody into thinking that guys were risking their lives sneaking into Cuba, having boats shot out from under them, all bullshit."

Some have suggested the mob had a secret agreement with Castro to use Cuba in its drug smuggling plans, or to reestablish its casino operations. This theory proposes that Roselli and his bosses were only playing the CIA game to gain leverage against the assault of Robert Kennedy's Justice Department.

Roselli told a different story, beginning in 1971, to columnist Jack Anderson. Over a two-year period, Roselli – who had fallen from grace with La Cosa Nostra and was suspected of having turned informer – gave Anderson the details of the CIA–Mafia plots and, finally, told him the story of the mob hit on the President.

In Roselli's version of the assassination, Santo Trafficante, Jr. cut a deal with Fidel Castro to kill John Kennedy.

Trafficante put together a team of Cubans – possibly anti-Castro exiles – to do the job. Oswald was brought into the plot to be used, just as he claimed, as a patsy. He may have fired from the School Book Depository, but the fatal shooting was done from closer range, probably from the grassy knoll. Ruby had nothing to do with killing the President, but was brought in afterward to silence Oswald.

According to Fratianno, Roselli told him that this story, too, was "bullshit." Given present evidence, there is no way to know who to believe. Roselli may have made his remarks to Fratianno in an attempt to cover himself with La Cosa Nostra, or Fratianno may have been lying for his own purposes. Whatever the truth of the matter, the assassination story seems to have been the death of John Roselli.

Roselli went over his story before the Church Committee in April of 1976, adding this time that it was only a theory and he had no evidence to support it. Three and a half months later, his body was found floating in an oil drum in Dumfoundling Bay, near Miami Beach. His legs had been sawed off to fit in the drum, which had been weighted with chains. His decomposing body had apparently created enough gases to float the drum, which was found by fishermen about ten days after the killing. A newspaper story quoting a Mafia source reported that Roselli had been killed because of his appearances before the Church Committee.

The Church Committee investigation may have also been the end of Sam Giancana. On July 19, 1975 – five days before he was due to testify about the CIA–Mafia deal – Giancana was shot dead in the basement of his Chicago home. The fatal shot was to the back of the head, but the body showed a total of seven bullet wounds to the head, throat, and mouth. In Mafia tradition, a shot to the mouth is said to be a signal that a talker has been silenced. The murder was never officially solved. One of Giancana's daughters said the family was convinced her father had been killed "by the same people responsible for killing the Kennedys."

This opinion was reinforced by a former Giancana gunman named Charles Crimaldi, who told his biographer he knew positively that Giancana was hit by the CIA, using a Mafia triggerman. The name most frequently mentioned in the triggerman role is that of David Yaras.

Yaras was widely feared because of his reputation as a brutal, or – in Mafia terminology – "stone" killer. In one FBI tape, he was heard relishing the memory of a two-day torture session that preceded the killing of one of his victims. His associations give him the appearance of a significant, though seldom mentioned, link in the chain of events that may have led to the assassination.

He was an acquaintance of Jack Ruby's and a co-suspect in a gangland killing with Ruby's old Chicago pal Lenny Patrick. He had helped set up a Teamster local in Miami with one of Jimmy Hoffa's henchmen, and a second Hoffa henchman – Barney Baker, who spoke three times by phone with Ruby in November of 1963 – called him long-distance the night before the assassination. To add the cherry to the top of this suspicious concoction, Yaras was known as the courier of information between Santo Trafficante and Carlos Marcello.

Eleven days after Giancana died, another alleged participant in the CIA–Mafia plots, Jimmy Hoffa, disappeared and was presumed murdered.

Did La Cosa Nostra kill John Kennedy? According to authors Blakey and Billings, "The mob proved to be the principal beneficiary of Dallas." This is something of an overstatement, as successful prosecutions of Cosa Nostra members continued, albeit at a reduced rate, after the assassination, and have continued

to the present day. If nominations are in order for a principal beneficiary, Fidel Castro would make a better candidate. Still, there is
no doubt that several of La Cosa Nostra's most powerful members
had the motive and the means to kill the President.

If the mob did take part in the assassination, it almost certainly
did not do so alone. There is too much evidence of the involvement
of other parties. Interestingly, both Robert Easterling's confession
and John Roselli's "theory" show plausible ways in which La
Cosa Nostra could have cooperated with others – Cuban exiles
and/or Castro and/or CIA renegades and/or extreme right-wingers
– to eliminate a common enemy.

In the Cuban exile groups alone, the mob had a ready-made cast
of killers willing to do its bidding. Its connections to the exiles
were well developed. In one case, the Mafia was reported to have
put up as much as $30 million to back an invasion scheme, in
return for the Cuban gambling business if the invasion succeeded.
And the mob was not above playing both sides of the fence in
Cuba. It still had lines of communication open to Castro. During
the Cuban revolution, the Mafia had hedged its bets by giving
support to both sides in the struggle (as had, according to author
Tad Szulc, the CIA).

The HSCA reviewed the transcripts of FBI surveillance tapes of
Cosa Nostra conversations that took place for eleven months
before and eight months after the assassination, and found no
direct proof of an assassination plot. One significant disclaimer
attached to this fact is that the FBI logs contained nothing from
Carlos Marcello's domain, and very little that had any bearing on
Santo Trafficante, Jr.

The logs did reveal a few interesting tidbits from conversations
just after the assassination. One of these was on a tape recorded on
November 26, 1963, at a funeral home owned by mob boss
Stefano Magaddino in Niagara Falls, New York.

When one of those present suggested that congratulations were
in order, the group broke into laughter. The laughter was stopped
by the old Don. People would be "watching for their reaction," he
said, and they should not "speak in this fashion." Magaddino went

on to say that the assassination had been brought on by Robert
Kennedy, who had "pressed too many issues." Three days later the
old man was recorded saying that the killing of Oswald had been
"arranged in order to cover up things" which "might have led to
civil war."

A Case of Loose Ends

There are other theories of the crime, and other variations of the
theories discussed here. Each has its own collection of tantalizing
loose ends which will, in all probability, forever remain untied.

Here are two of the better ones, just for the record:

In 1975, a copy of a handwritten note arrived in the mail for
prominent assassination critic Penn Jones, Jr., editor of *The
Midlothian Mirror* in Midlothian, Texas. The envelope containing
the note was postmarked Mexico City. Only the note was in the
envelope. The sender remained anonymous. This is the text of the
note, in full:

> November 8, 1963
>
> Dear Mr. Hunt,
>
> I would like information concercding [sic] my position.
>
> I am asking only for information. I am suggesting that we
> discuss the matter fully before any steps are taken by me or
> anyone else.
>
> Thank you.
> Lee Harvey Oswald

The handwriting looked like Oswald's. The misspelling and the
phrasing were typical of his writing style. In 1977 *The Dallas
Morning News* had a copy of the note studied by three handwriting
experts, who unanimously agreed that it had been written by
Oswald. The HSCA had its handwriting experts study the note but
no "firm conclusion" was reached on its authenticity.

Speculation on the identity of "Mr. Hunt" has, as might be
expected, centered on the eccentric stalwart of ultraconservatism

H. L. Hunt and on the three most famous of his children, Nelson Bunker, Lamar, and Herbert. The Hunts made no bones about their dislike of the Kennedys and, as billionaires, had the means to do something about it.

Nelson Bunker Hunt was one of those who shelled out money to pay for the anti-Kennedy ad that appeared in *The Dallas Morning News* on assassination day, and H. L. Hunt had once lost a football gambling bet to Jack Ruby and one of his con man pals. Still, other than the implications of the note and the fact that Jack Ruby and Eugene Hale Brading happened to have been in or near the Hunt offices the day before the assassination, there is no known evidence that ties the Hunt family to the crime.

An FBI document indicates that the bureau investigated the possibility that the note was intended for Nelson Bunker Hunt, but the results of the investigation have not been made public. Aware that his name might come up in the course of speculation on the crime, H. L. Hunt even commissioned his own investigation of the assassination, using his security men. As far as is known, this investigation added nothing of value to the already substantial body of evidence.

A second possibility for the identity of "Mr. Hunt" has received less attention. E. Howard Hunt was a CIA man who had been a key political coordinator for the Bay of Pigs invasion. He would later become famous as the head of the "plumbers unit" in the break-in that became the Watergate scandal. This Hunt was once rumored to have been one of those picked up in Dealey Plaza by Dallas police and briefly detained after the assassination, although the allegation has long since been disproved. Other than his prominent place in the anti-Castro milieu, he has no known connections to Oswald.

Another untied loose end concerns the presence in Fort Worth, on November 22, 1963, of a known French assassin. This lead first surfaced in 1977, when Dallas assassination archivist Mary Ferrell was perusing a batch of documents newly released by the CIA in response to a Freedom of Information Act request. A 1964 document reported a request from French intelligence for help in locating a suspected OAS terrorist and assassin named Jean Souetre aka Michel Roux aka Michel Mertz. The French, according to the document, had been told Souetre was in Fort Worth on the morning of the assassination (so was John Kennedy), and had been picked up by American authorities after the assassination and expelled from the United States. The CIA document quoted the FBI as saying it knew nothing about Souetre.

According to author Henry Hurt, further investigation by assassination researchers revealed that, shortly after the assassination, the FBI interviewed and then tailed for several weeks an old acquaintance of Souetre's who had become a respected Houston dentist. The dentist had known Souetre while stationed by the U.S. Army in France, and thought of him as an interesting man of neo-Nazi political persuasions. He said the FBI agents told him they felt Souetre had either killed Kennedy or knew who had.

To further complicate the story, it turned out that each of Souetre's "aliases" – Michel Roux and Michel Mertz – were real people. Roux, a French Army deserter like Souetre, was in Fort Worth visiting friends on November 22, but left Texas for Mexico of his own volition, and so could not be the "Souetre" who was expelled from the country.

Souetre himself turned up in 1983 as the public relations director of a French casino said to be owned by the Mafia. He denied any involvement in the assassination. He even denied having known the Texas dentist. He claimed "Mertz" was an old enemy who had been known to use his – Souetre's – name. Mertz turned out to be a French intelligence agent said to be opposed to the OAS cause and to be involved in international espionage and narcotics smuggling.

To add a final enigma, as if one were needed, an old photograph of Souetre obtained from the dentist shows that he clearly resembles a man who had been photographed with Lee Harvey Oswald, apparently during his time in Russia. Oswald and the man are standing with their arms about each other's shoulders. Marina Oswald has told investigators her husband identified the man to her only as "Alfred from Cuba."

Despite what appears to have been an intense investigation by the FBI and, if nothing else, an inquiry by the CIA, the French assassin story did not make it into the records of any of the official assassination investigations.

The Hunt note and the tale of the three French musketeers are but two examples from the overwhelming tangle of trails to be followed in the assassination story. With each passing year these trails, which have never been distinct, fade further and grow colder. To follow any of them is to take a step through the looking-glass. To tie them together into a coherent whole now seems impossible, especially given the fact that any citizen who attempts it – and many continue to – must work against the deceptions of the police and intelligence agencies who are, in theory, the servants of the public. It is a safe bet that the crime of the century will forever be unsolved.

Postscript

My safe bet still seems safe. The Kennedy assassination continues to drive a cottage industry of rumour and speculation, but little that has shed useful light has emerged. There have been minor revelations: the notes of the Dallas homicide detective who interrogated Lee Harvey Oswald said Oswald denied killing Kennedy and denied owning a rifle; a former associate of Robert Kennedy's intimated that the Senator believed his brother had been killed by the mob; Dr. Charles Crenshaw, one of the doctors who treated the President's wounds at Parkland Hospital, published two books detailing his belief that Kennedy was shot twice from the front; and Marina Oswald has changed her tune and begun saying publicly that her husband was innocent. Despite moves to do so under both the (first) Bush and Clinton administrations, full government records on the assassination have yet to be released for public review.

2

With Friends Like These

The Disappearance of Jimmy Hoffa

Jimmy Hoffa was a tough guy and a smart guy. He didn't get his smarts from books. He'd only read one book by the time he went to prison at the age of fifty-five, and that one was about him.

It was a book by Robert F. Kennedy called *The Enemy Within*.

It said that the world's biggest labor union, the union that was Jimmy's lifework, his Teamsters, was "a conspiracy of evil" run for the benefit of the mob. It portrayed Jimmy as evil incarnate, and said he had made himself and his mob friends rich off the sweat of his union members. It said the Teamster leadership was mixed up in fraud, and extortion, and killings, and that the gangsters behind the Teamsters were infiltrating and taking over the national economy. Jimmy hadn't cared much for the one book he had read.

And he didn't take time to regret not reading any others. He had quit school alter the eighth grade to take a stockboy job in a department store, ten hours a day, six days a week. Sixty hours for twelve dollars. He liked hard work. He recalled his first job as "a happy time."

At the height of his power, Jimmy was working even harder – twelve to sixteen-hour days, six-and-a-half-day weeks – and liking it even better. The rewards were better, too. By one informed estimate, he was worth about $12 million in 1960s dollars.

Jimmy carried every detail of every complex financial

arrangement he was involved in and every forty-page contract he was negotiating around in his head for instant reference, never taking a note or referring to a document. When one of his 1.6 million union members called him, he took the call or made sure to return it, and if he had talked to the man before he remembered the name, and the number of the union local, and the nature of the problem.

He could argue economics with professors from Harvard and M.I.T. And when Bobby Kennedy started coming at him with a barrage of legal charges, he learned the law. At one trial he showed up with fourteen high-powered lawyers and told them all what to do, with instructions sometimes written and sometimes highly audible, throughout the proceedings.

And though one wonders where he found the time, he was said to be a dedicated family man and loving father. Wife Josephine was the object of forty years of devotion. Son James grew up as a high school football star who won a scholarship to Michigan State, where his father would not let him play for fear of injury, and went on to become a successful lawyer. Daughter Barbara Jo was doted over and given a storybook wedding, even if the storybook bore more resemblance to *The Godfather* than to a more conventional tale.

This *Good Housekeeping* version of the Hoffa household leaves out, as most such versions do, the juiciest details. Jimmy had been known to do his share of womanizing in his younger days, and it was one of these early liaisons that, as much as any single episode, shaped his destiny and sealed his fate. In the early 1930s, as a young union organizer in Detroit, Jimmy was taken by a striking femme fatale named Sylvia Pagano. Sylvia numbered among her friends and lovers some of the toughest hoodlums on the local scene, and Sylvia's connections would soon be Jimmy's connections.

At roughly the time of her affair with Jimmy, a son was born to Sylvia. The boy, called Chuckie, was supported by Hoffa through much of his life and treated as a foster son. Many who knew Hoffa assumed Chuckie was a biological son as well, though this was roundly denied by all the principals. Chuckie and his mother were frequent guests and sometimes residents in the Hoffa home, enough so that some have suggested a *ménage à trois* involving Jimmy, Sylvia, and Jo Hoffa, who became Sylvia's good friend.

Chuckie took his last name – O'Brien – from a long-dead gangster in Kansas City, Frank O'Brien, to whom his mother had been married. To further complicate the confusion over names and bloodlines, Frank O'Brien's real name had been Sam Scaradino.

Whether a foster son or a real one, Chuckie was by outward appearances the spitting image of Jimmy Hoffa, the man he knew as Dad. He was short, square-set, and quick with his temper and his fists. Jimmy helped rear him, gave him a union job at the age of nineteen, supported him through his peccadilloes, and took him along on union travels.

With his own drive and cunning, Jimmy Hoffa made himself the most powerful union man in America. But it was another man who made him famous. A man named Kennedy. Bob Kennedy wanted badly to put Jimmy Hoffa out of business, and the battle between the two was fought out before the nation.

For over ten years in the prime of his life the complex dynamo of a human being that was Jimmy Hoffa not only survived, he prospered through a prosecution/persecution that was probably the most prolonged and most intensive assault ever launched by the federal government against a single individual. By the time he finally lost a round and entered Lewisburg Federal Prison in March of 1967, he had spent a decade outmaneuvering the combined efforts of several U.S. government departments and a federal task force of forty investigators and forty-two accountants working day and night to find anything that would put him in jail; slipped through the nooses of several grand juries; seen four federal trials decided in his favor; and thumbed his nose at his pursuers all along the way.

There is absolutely no doubt that Jimmy Hoffa was as tough

and as smart as they come. But there was one thing he didn't do well enough to survive. He was lousy at picking his friends.

On the morning of Wednesday, July 30, 1975, Jimmy got into his Pontiac at his Michigan summer house on Big Square Lake and drove off to meet a couple of those friends. He never came back. There is just enough evidence of what may have happened to him that day to tantalize and to point a few fingers in a few highly suspicious directions.

In death – he was declared legally dead in December of 1982 – as in life, Jimmy kept them guessing. Hundreds of local police and FBI agents, several strike forces and grand juries, and countless reporters chased after mirages and up and down blind alleys for years after the disappearance. Foul swamps were dug up, garbage dumps were sifted through, incinerators and trash compactors were sniffed over by man and beast. A lot of dirt was uncovered – literally and figuratively – and a lot of unrelated charges were brought against suspects in the case, but no one has been charged with killing Jimmy, and Jimmy has never been found.

There are a couple of reasons why Jimmy Hoffa's disappearance is one of the most significant unsolved crimes of our time.

First, there are his friends. He knew and dealt intimately with the top gangsters of his era – knew not only who they were but the specific things they did to make a living, and the people who had died to keep their living profitable. He ran the lending institution – the Teamsters' biggest pension fund – that became known as "the Mafia bank." Through this connection he knew, as one example, who the people were behind the front men in Las Vegas and how the take from Vegas was divided, because he made the loans that bought and built the properties.

Then there are his enemies. The man he hated most in all the world was Bobby Kennedy. When politeness was required, he referred to Bobby as "the spoiled brat." When only friends were listening, he used a different set of appellations. Jimmy's hatred of Bobby was well earned.

Beginning with the McClellan Committee Senate hearings in

the mid-1950s, Kennedy had pursued Hoffa relentlessly. He had done everything within his considerable power to destroy what Jimmy had spent a lifetime creating, and had hung Jimmy's dirty laundry across the headlines of the nation. He was the reason Jimmy went to prison. Much worse, he was the reason Jimmy lost his union.

Jimmy Hoffa was convinced his worst enemy had done all this to make a national name for himself and for his brother John Fitzgerald Kennedy. He saw the Get Hoffa campaign as part of a master plan to create a presidential dynasty of Kennedys that would last "a whole generation": two terms for John, two for Bobby, then two for Ted. Hoffa may have been right about Bob Kennedy's political motives; he was certainly right about the Kennedy name growing in value at his expense.

Senator John Kennedy was a member of the McClellan Committee. Young Bob Kennedy, the driving force behind the Committee's investigation into labor racketeering, was its Chief Counsel. The Committee's sensational revelations helped make the names of both Kennedys household words across the country. The same wind of fortune that turned Jimmy Hoffa's course toward Lewisburg Prison turned John Kennedy's course toward the White House.

It may have also set both men on the course that led to their violent deaths. There is a school of thought that makes Jimmy an accessory to the President's murder, though there is only a smattering of circumstantial evidence to support this view. Jimmy's own death may feasibly have come because of what he knew about the Kennedy assassination or about the shady deals between the CIA and the Mafia that may have been a factor in the assassination.

There are a multitude of unanswered questions about Hoffa, and among these not even the entangling of his fate with the Kennedys' is more compelling than the mystery of the man himself.

There is a picture of Jimmy at about the age of eight, standing beside his brother and some other children in a Midwestern countryside. The other kids are looking stoop-shouldered and intimidated by the camera. Jimmy is standing ramrod straight, defiant and block solid and with an enigmatic righteousness. Even at that age, it looks like it could be difficult to knock him down.

But Hoffa in the flesh was more than physical tenacity, and more than brainpower. He was a man who could seem to embody simultaneously the good and the evil of the country and the times that spawned him.

His full name was James Riddle Hoffa. He was born on Saint Valentine's Day of 1913 in the community of Brazil, Indiana, where his father worked for a mine drilling company. His forebears were six generations of Pennsylvania Dutch. His father died when he was seven, leaving his mother to manage the lives of four small children.

She did this by holding one full-time job cooking in a restaurant, a second job cleaning houses of the well-to-do, and a third taking in laundry at home. When he was eleven, she moved the family to Detroit looking for higher wages on the production lines.

The stock market crash came when Jimmy was sixteen. He quit the department store and found a job on the 5.00 p.m. to 5.00 a.m. shift at the loading docks of a Kroger warehouse, reasoning that no matter how bad things got people would always need to eat. This was Jimmy's introduction to the working conditions that inspired the labor movement.

He and his fellow dockworkers were paid thirty-two cents an hour, but only for the time they were unloading boxcars. They sometimes sat idle for six hours at a time, without pay. An overbearing foreman, remembered affectionately as the Little Bastard, tilted the scales toward the unbearable.

With two others, the teenage Hoffa organized a sit-down strike of the 175-man night shift, refusing to unload a shipment of strawberries until the company agreed to talk. Hoffa was chosen to negotiate for the workers, and won the first of a lifetime of contract agreements. When the fledgling union affiliated with the Teamsters, young Hoffa was hired as an organizer for Joint Council 43 in Detroit. At seventeen, he had found his calling.

In the Detroit of the 1930s, union organizing was not a job for the fainthearted. Employers did not take kindly to the notion of unionized employees, and were known to retaliate with hired goons and well-armed, well-muscled strikebreakers.

The local Mafia soon discovered there was a lucrative market for the hiring out of its toughs to serve these purposes. The police also tended to line up on the employer side, and a favored police pastime was cracking heads along a picket line. In his first year on the job, Jimmy Hoffa's head was laid open wide enough to require stitches on six separate occasions. In one twenty-four-hour period, he was hauled off a picket line and down to the local precinct eighteen times.

These early experiences had two effects on Hoffa; both, given his nature, were predictable enough. First, he became a dedicated cop-hater, and for "cop" could be substituted anyone who represented the established order. Second, he learned to fight muscle with muscle, and the hired Mafia goons working for employers soon found themselves faced with hired goons from the Detroit Purple Gang, a Jewish outfit, working for Jimmy Hoffa.

According to one account, the Mafia grew tired of suffering casualties among its soldiers in this war and put the young Hoffa on "trial" for his life. The story goes that Jimmy was able to convince his judges that he was worth more to them as a contact in the growing union movement than as a corpse. For the next forty-odd years at least, this was true.

There are several versions of the tale in which young Jimmy Hoffa sells the first piece of his soul to the mob. In one of them, perhaps the best from a Grade-B movie point of view, he makes his first contact through Sylvia Pagano. When Jimmy was locked in an organizing struggle against the rival CIO and needed to neutralize the Mafia to save Teamster skulls, Sylvia and another of her boyfriends – a gangster named Frank

Coppola, who was little Chuckie's godfather – put him in touch with Santo Perrone.

Perrone was the Detroit Mafia's number-one strikebreaker and union-buster. He had the look of a man who could bust a union, or a mirror for that matter, just by staring at it. His right eyelid drooped half open and through it he looked out in a thoroughly deranged scar-faced glare.

Through his contacts with Perrone and his superior Angelo Meli, Jimmy made deals that got the Teamsters special favors and made them more successful than their competition.

By age twenty-one Hoffa had become, for all practical purposes, the top Teamster in Detroit. When he ran for president of the city's Joint Council of Teamsters locals, he got only four of twenty votes but took office anyway, the explanation being that nobody wanted to fool with the hard-case hoodlums he had already assembled around him.

His official job was business agent at Detroit Local 299, the largest local in the city and the one that would be his own until he died. In Teamster parlance, "business agent" often serves as a euphemism for hired goon. In May of 1936 he met a girl named Josephine Poszywak on – where else? – a picket line, during a strike at the laundry where she worked for seventeen cents an hour. Jimmy was smitten, and the two were married in September. He then left for Minneapolis, to work in the bailiwick of an unusual Teamster named Farrell Dobbs.

Dobbs was a Trotskyite Communist who, along with cohorts of the same political leanings, had interlinked Teamster locals throughout the Midwest with great success. Though he thought all Communists were "screwballs," Jimmy was as apolitical as he was amoral, and took his education along the road to power anywhere he could find it. There was an important lesson to be learned from Farrell Dobbs.

This was the "leapfrog strategy" Jimmy was soon to put to good use. Having unionized warehousemen in Town A, Dobbs would refuse to unload the trucks of an employer based in Town B until that employer agreed to unionize. Then he would cut off deliveries to employers in Town C until they unionized, and so on.

Jimmy perfected the tactic until it paid off in every possible way. Because Teamsters controlled deliveries, he could control other unions through the power to make or break another union's strike (if deliveries stop, the strike succeeds; if they continue, it fails). He could then "sell" this power to employers, preventing "labor trouble" for a fee, or to mobsters who paid for the privilege of working as "labor consultants."

The mob also paid well for Teamster power to expand and control the market for its jukeboxes and vending machines. A tavern owner who didn't want a Mafia jukebox or cigarette machine would suddenly learn that his beer deliveries had dried up. The great beauty of the whole scheme was that, the more Jimmy's power grew within the Teamsters, the greater was his ability to market these related services.

And his power in the Teamsters had become substantial. At age twenty-seven, Hoffa headed the Central States Drivers Council Dobbs had founded, and negotiated with employers in as many as twenty-three states. When Dobbs's faction was booted out of the Teamsters in 1941, Jimmy found himself the unchallenged union power broker for the entire Midwest. At about this time, he came up with a new invention that would add the final touch to his authority and make him all but invincible: the regional contract.

By making himself the sole negotiator for all Midwestern Teamsters, Jimmy brought not only his union members but the employers they worked for and, by extension, the other unions in their industries under his direct control. Jimmy would later extend the concept into his masterpiece, the national contract known as the Master Freight Agreement. Farrell Dobbs went on to run for president of the United States under the banner of the Socialist Workers Party in 1960. Jimmy Hoffa went on to become the most powerful union leader in the world.

Throughout his rise in the Teamsters, Jimmy cultivated four kinds of relationships, all designed to pay him dividends. The first was with his rank and file union members. While there is no question that Jimmy stole from and deceived these men, it is just as certain that he improved their lives, and they were grateful for it. An overwhelming majority were loyal to Jimmy and remained loyal even after his fall from grace. The second group was made up of local and regional Teamster leaders, whom Jimmy controlled with the carrot of fat, multiple salaries and the stick of the enormous power he wielded to control their destinies. The third group was the employers in Teamster industries who had no choice but to keep themselves in Jimmy's good graces. And the fourth group was the mob.

"Violence and union organizing," one old-time Teamster has said, "go hand in hand." In the early days, Jimmy used the gangsters to help fight the more physical of his battles. In the world he inhabited, torch jobs, beatings, and killings were little more than tools employed to convince a recalcitrant employer or scare off a competing union or a dissident within the ranks. Later, Hoffa used elements of the mob to expand his influence within the Teamsters and to gain the union presidency, and the relationship became complicated by the fact that the Mafia controlled a number of Teamster locals on its own.

The hitch in the relationship was that it was not one of partners, but of host and parasite. As time went by, the parasite took over. The balance had shifted so that the mob was getting more from Jimmy than he could ever get from it. The fact is Jimmy Hoffa did more to enrich the Mafia's coffers and to expand its influence across the country than any single member of the Mafia has ever done.

The venerable Teamster president Dan Tobin, who had held office since 1907, finally stepped down in 1952. He was replaced by Dave Beck, his longtime second-in-command, whose power was based in the Western Conference of Teamsters.

With the Midwest secure and with Beck holding the West, Hoffa began to covet control of the East. His first attempt to take over New York was rebuffed by honest Teamsters. Hoffa decided to improve the odds by stacking the deck. He persuaded Beck to create seven "paper locals" in New York which listed a union man as nominal charter holder but which were actually run by two members of the Thomas Luchese Mafia family, John "Johnny Dio" Dioguardi and Tony "Ducks" (for his agility in "ducking" convictions) Corallo, and staffed by gangsters who worked for them. Five of the seven new locals did not have a single member, but this did not prevent their voting in the Joint Council election of 1957, in which the Hoffa ticket triumphed.

Dioguardi and Corallo were already established in the labor business, running a number of laborers locals whose members were mostly poor blacks and Puerto Ricans. These unionists paid initiation fees and monthly dues and received absolutely nothing in return. Their "contracts" were for the minimum wage and there were no benefits.

Like Jimmy, Johnny Dio did not take kindly to criticism. He was charged in the acid blinding of New York labor columnist Victor Riesel, after Riesel had interviewed reform-minded Teamsters on his radio show. Dioguardi escaped conviction when the man who threw the acid was found dead and the witnesses concluded it would be unhealthy to testify.

Hoffa's sympathies were with his friend Dioguardi. He reportedly told friends "that son of a bitch Victor Riesel just had some acid thrown on him. It's too bad he didn't have it thrown on the goddamn hands he types with."

Corallo's union work helped him ascend to the top spot in the Luchese family, a position he enjoyed until he failed to duck a conviction on racketeering charges in November of 1986. Through Dioguardi and Corallo, the union movement added to its ranks forty men with an aggregate record of 178 arrests and seventy-seven convictions. In the two years from 1955 to 1957, twenty-five of these novice labor activists managed to add new convictions for bribery, extortion, perjury, and forgery to their records.

Meanwhile Hoffa's East Coast expansion got a boost in New Jersey, where a young captain in the ranks of the Vito Genovese family was getting his start in the labor business. Anthony Provenzano had just become a business agent for Teamster Local 560 in Union City.

In 1958, "Tony Pro" took over as president of the eight thousand member local and promptly turned it into a thriving family business. His brother Nuncio was vice-president; brother Salvatore was secretary-treasurer; sister-in-law Theresa was office manager; and several nieces were clerks.

The new president found it necessary to increase his salary from $20,000 to $95,000. He also put the local to work to serve the interests of a larger family. The union stewards doubled as numbers runners. The business agents ran a lucrative loan shark business from the union hall.

While these machinations were in progress, a new and most unexpected player entered the game. Investigating government procurement practices in 1956 as Counsel to a U.S. Senate committee, an energetic and ambitious young man named Bob Kennedy had fortuitously discovered a notorious gangster known as Johnny Dio running some union locals in New York.

Kennedy smelled big game. He put investigators on the hunt, and one of the promising trails led straight to the president of the International Brotherhood of Teamsters, Dave Beck. Kennedy and a committee accountant named Carmine Bellino gathered evidence that Beck had embezzled over $350,000 from the union. By the summer of 1956, other trails had led to Teamsters Local 299 in Detroit. Kennedy, his chief investigator Pierre Salinger, and Carmine Bellino showed up at the local to see its president, a man named Jimmy Hoffa.

It was the first of many confrontations between two prodigiously determined and aggressive men. As Hoffa told the story, Kennedy and his lieutenants forced their way past his secretary and disrupted a meeting he was holding with his stewards. Hoffa shoved them out in the hallway and slammed his office door in their faces. When the meeting was over, Kennedy reentered the room and went straight for Hoffa's files. Hoffa again blocked his way and had him escorted from the building.

The next day Kennedy returned with a subpoena. Teamster lawyers made him pay with several trips to court and Jimmy Hoffa made him personally sign for every single piece of paper, but he eventually got the files he wanted. The country at large had heard little of Kennedy and, largely because the Teamsters had aborted two previous congressional investigations, less of Hoffa. Within a year this situation would be drastically changed.

Armed with details of a plethora of Teamster misdeeds, Kennedy got his full-scale Senate hearings. As the committee began to show the cards it held against Beck, Hoffa was quick to see an opportunity. He began to covertly feed information that would help hang Beck to the committee staff. Beck was publicly disgraced and broken. His first conviction on criminal charges came later the same year. The next international convention was scheduled for October, and the heir apparent to the union presidency was Jimmy Hoffa.

One of Jimmy's weaknesses was a tendency to overkill the opposition. He seems to have made one of several mistakes of this kind by attempting, through an $18,000 bribe, to place a spy on the McClellan committee staff, a New York lawyer named John Cye Cheasty. Cheasty turned double agent and Jimmy was arrested with committee documents on his person.

He had been indicted in May for allegedly tapping the phones of his own lieutenants in the Detroit office. But the trial for the attempted bribe on Cheasty came first, in June of 1957, and established a bizarre pattern that would be played out with fascinating variations in subsequent Hoffa trials. Jimmy was fond of saying that he had "a way with juries." Until he finally lost a trial (his fifth) seven years later, he seemed to actually enjoy and thrive upon the public spectacle of courtroom competition.

The bribery trial was held in Washington, D.C. The American civil rights movement was still in its early days, the days of freedom rides and marches and church bombings and white politicians blocking the schoolhouse door. The jury consisted of eight blacks and four whites.

During the trial, copies of a black newspaper with a front-page ad praising Hoffa as a friend of working people and illustrated with a photograph of a black attorney on his defense team were delivered to the homes of black jurors. Just before the trial went to the jury, Joe Louis, the great heavyweight boxing champion, suddenly appeared in the courtroom and put his arm around Jimmy Hoffa, wishing Jimmy well in full view of the jurors.

The verdict was not guilty. Investigators later learned that Louis's travel expenses had been paid by a Hoffa man, and that Louis, who was down on his luck, had gone on salary as a public relations consultant for a Chicago record company whose owner had received a sizable loan from the Teamster pension fund.

Before the trial, Bob Kennedy had been sure enough of his case to offer to "jump off the Capitol" if Hoffa wasn't convicted. After the verdict, Jimmy's lawyer Edward Bennett Williams sent Kennedy a parachute.

The wiretap trial, held in New York, ended in a mistrial.

Meanwhile the Kennedy–Hoffa war continued to escalate. It was more than big boys playing cops and robbers. It was Brazil, Indiana, against Hyannis Port, the eighth grade versus Harvard Law, blue collar and white socks against French-cut suits. Sometimes the war could take an amusingly juvenile turn. When the combatants met at a Washington dinner party, they engaged in an arm-wrestling contest. Hoffa claimed to have won two falls out of two.

The next day Jimmy and Bobby compared the number of pushups they could do. And when Hoffa flaunted his disregard during the McClellan hearings by going to lunch with Johnny Dio at a Washington restaurant frequented by Kennedy, there was a shoving contest and Kennedy ended up against a wall.

For the next two years, the McClellan Committee concentrated its attentions on Hoffa, calling Jimmy back before the microphones, the television cameras, and the hungrily assembled press time and again. Hoffa held up under the ordeal remarkably well. A man in his position had more to fear than social disgrace.

If he testified truthfully, he would be breaking the Mafia code of silence, an offense punishable by death. If he lied, he risked perjury charges and more questions in court. And if he took the Fifth Amendment, as Dave Beck and many other committee witnesses had before him, he sent a message to the Teamster rank and file that he was guilty.

Hoffa solved the dilemma by losing his memory. The man who never took a note, the man who negotiated massive contracts and closed multimillion dollar deals working purely out of his head, had forgotten every detail of every questionable activity.

This selective amnesia turned out to be a two-part strategy. If Hoffa was being questioned about a conversation, he would regret that he could not remember and would suggest that the committee ask the other party involved. When the committee did this, the other party took the Fifth Amendment. End of trail. Throughout two years of testimony, Hoffa never took the Fifth. Many of his associates did.

Wily as he was, Hoffa was damaged by the McClellan Committee hearings in ways that would prove fatal. The evidence that had been gathered would eventually put him in prison. And he would never overcome the stigma of the brazen corruption the committee had uncovered. Testimony established Hoffa's involved links with the underworld; showed how Hoffa and his gangster friends had grown rich off the misuse of union funds; how employers could get favorable treatment that cheated their union employees by paying off Hoffa, other Teamster officials, or a Mafia "consultant"; how those who interfered in Teamster business tended to die prematurely or to simply disappear.

In one scheme, Hoffa had poured at least half a million Teamster dollars into a disastrous Florida land development called Sun Valley, in which he secretly owned an interest, then allowed the lots, which were without roads and some of which were underwater, to be marketed to Teamster members with fraudulent advertising.

In another, an employer paid off Hoffa for fixing his labor trouble by setting up a trucking company called Test Fleet in the maiden name of Hoffa's wife. Jo Hoffa had no duties in the company aside from opening the envelopes that brought her dividend checks. The total take was said to be several hundred thousand dollars.

There were many other allegations, so many that the emerging picture of Teamster corruption reached ludicrous proportions. Before it was through, the committee had interviewed 1,525 witnesses and compiled fifty-nine thick volumes of testimony. Among those volumes it drew this conclusion: "Hoffa runs a hoodlum empire, the members of which are steeped in iniquity and dedicated to the proposition that a thug need not starve if there is a Teamster payroll handy."

In the thick of this barrage, Jimmy got on with the business of becoming international president of the Teamsters. He did this by taking control of the credentials committee at the international convention, then seating 561 delegates – more than half the total number – who had no business being there. The core of these delegates had dual allegiance to the Teamsters and to the Mafia. This led to a lawsuit which eventually brought about a Board of Monitors to oversee the union, with Jimmy chafing in the role of "provisional president" until the next convention in 1961.

Meanwhile Jimmy's greatest opportunity for wealth and power was growing ready for the harvest. In the late 1940s unions had begun negotiating fringe benefits such as welfare and pension funds for their members.

The Teamster Central States Health and Welfare Fund had been created in 1949, and Jimmy had used it to solidify his mob connections in Chicago. The business of underwriting the insurance for the welfare fund made a rich man of Allen Dorfman, stepson of a Chicago labor racketeer named Paul "Red" Dorfman, whose mob contacts were useful to Jimmy in a number of subsequent deals. The fact that Allen Dorfman had no previous experience in the insurance business was overlooked as a trivial consideration.

The real bonanza, the Central States Pension Fund, came into being in 1955 and had taken on gargantuan proportions by the time Jimmy got his presidency.

Contributions were made to the pension fund during each pay period of 400,000 Teamsters in twenty-three states. The resulting money tree seemed to bear more fruit with every harvest, and plenty of harvesting was done.

Most funds of this kind put their money in the care of financial institutions or professional money managers. Jimmy ran his fund through a board made up of three union and three employer representatives. But two of the union trustees had criminal records – one had to get furloughs from prison to attend board meetings – and two of the employers were borrowing from the fund themselves, and were beholden to Jimmy for labor peace into the bargain.

Hoffa ran the fund like his personal bank. When Jimmy was elected president in 1961, the cash in his bank was growing at the rate of about $100 million a year. When he went to jail in 1967, $325 million in cash was on hand; ten years later, $1.4 billion; and by 1980, $3.5 billion.

What does a man like Jimmy Hoffa do with so much investable cash? Two things: he lends money to his friends at ridiculously low rates, often without expecting it to be paid back, and he lends money to anybody else who needs it bad enough to pay 10 percent to 50 percent of the loan amount in kickbacks and finder's fees.

For the Mafia, Jimmy became the proverbial goose and his fund the golden egg. Here was money that was free for the asking; no scam had to be run, no job had to be pulled, no dope had to be moved. During Jimmy's tenure and afterward, the Teamster pension fund backed Mafia projects to the tune of hundreds of millions of dollars.

The mob used this free money to buy into highly profitable ventures like Las Vegas casinos and California real estate developments. When the borrower was non-Mafia, the required kickbacks fattened the already bulging pockets of those close enough to Jimmy to sell a Teamster loan. In Detroit, the loan arranger to see was Hoffa buddy and Mafia enforcer Anthony "Tony Jack" Giacalone; in Chicago, it was Allen Dorfman; in Ohio, "Big Bill" Presser, the father of a future Teamster president.

Given this style of lending, the Teamster pension fund did not establish much of a track record on its investments. By 1972, one-third of the fund's loans were in default. By 1976, $179 million worth of bad loans had been written off; on many of these, not a single payment had ever been made.

The supposed purpose of the fund was forgotten in the rush to spread the loot around. Faced with pension claims, Hoffa enforced restrictions that made it more than a little difficult to cash in at retirement time, One handy rule held that the pensioner had to put in twenty years of *continuous* service with a contributing employer; and even after twenty years, any break in service would send the pension out the window.

When the resulting scandals finally forced reform, Hoffa gained the distinction of having had two pieces of federal legislation written just for him. The Employee Retirement Income Security Act, or ERISA, was passed in 1974. The Landrum-Griffin labor reform act, known in its time as the Jimmy Hoffa Law, had been passed in the wake of the McClellan hearings in 1959.

Probably the most conspicuous monument to the Teamster pension fund is the glittering city of Las Vegas. Air travel to that city tripled after Jimmy Hoffa started pouring in money that belonged to his Teamsters. Teamster pensions bought or built the Stardust, the Fremont, the Desert Inn, the Dunes, Caesar's Palace, Circus Circus, and the Las Vegas Marina.

In some cases, Hoffa helped set up the holding companies that hid the real owners. He was widely suspected of holding hidden ownerships in some or all of the Vegas deals he financed. Some say his detailed knowledge of the underworld webbing beneath Las Vegas was the reason he was not allowed to live.

Another theory about Jimmy's undoing concerns his

flirtation with the world of spies. During the Cuban revolution, Hoffa had joined his mob friends in profiting on arms sales to both sides. Castro's victory in January of 1959 put the Mafia's extensive gambling, narcotics, and prostitution rackets in Cuba in jeopardy. The most powerful family bosses in the United States each had a piece of the Cuban pie, and stood to lose millions.

Jimmy tried to help out by financing – with Teamster money – the sale of a fleet of C-74 airplanes to Castro, to score a few points for his mob friends with the new Cuban government. But at the same time it was wooing Castro, the Mafia was covering its bets by plotting to kill him.

Its co-conspirator in this plot was the United States government. In August of 1960, according to revelations before the Church Committee of the U.S. Senate in the mid-1970s, the CIA decided to enlist the Mafia as a part of its many-faceted scheme to overthrow or assassinate the Cuban Premier.

According to one version of events, the original go-between the spy agency used to put the proposition to the mob was Jimmy Hoffa. A later and better-documented approach was made by Howard Hughes's aide Robert Maheu, an ex-FBI man who used his Las Vegas contacts to close the deal.

The story that Hoffa was the original contact came from a government informant and retired killer named Charles Crimaldi. According to the story, Jimmy made his first approach to Russell Bufalino. Bufalino commanded a Mafia family with interests in Pennsylvania, New York, and New Jersey. He had done profitable business with the Teamsters, and was a distant cousin of Jimmy's lawyer William Bufalino, and the godfather of William Bufalino's daughter. When Castro took over, Russell Bufalino lost a casino, a racetrack, and left behind at least three-quarters of a million dollars in cash.

Little that was useful came of the business between Bufalino and the CIA, and the actual assassination attempts were arranged by mobster John Roselli, with the cooperation of Chicago boss Sam "Momo" Giancana and Florida and Cuba boss Santo Trafficante, Jr. If Jimmy was a party to the plots, he was playing in a dangerous game.

Bufalino's business partners in Cuba, Salvatore Granello and James Plumeri, met sudden and violent ends just before and just after the first newspaper stories broke on the Castro plots. Five days before he was due to testify before the Church Committee, Sam Giancana was shot dead in the basement of his Chicago home. Jimmy Hoffa disappeared eleven days later. The next year, John Roselli was found sawed in half in an oil drum floating off Florida.

Informant Crimaldi told his biographer John Kidner it was the CIA that hit Giancana, using a Mafia killer. Crimaldi's information on other matters has proved reliable, and – as a Giancana gunman – he may have been in a position to know. The pattern of suspicious deaths that appears to be associated with the CIA–Mafia plots could well include the death of Jimmy Hoffa. According to one theory, discussed elsewhere in this book, it could also include the assassination of John Kennedy.

Be that as it may, Jimmy Hoffa might be living still if he had not lost the power that his union gave him. He owed that loss to an election. In 1960, John Kennedy faced Richard Nixon in a closely contested race for the White House. Nixon owed Jimmy: the Teamsters were the only big union supporting him, and Jimmy is said to have engineered a $1 million mob contribution to the Nixon campaign, half from Carlos Marcello in New Orleans and half from New Jersey and Florida gangsters. But Nixon didn't win.

When John Kennedy became President, his brother Bob became Attorney General. As Counsel to a Senate committee, Hoffa's worst enemy could only investigate and make headlines. As Attorney General, he became the biggest cop of all; he could chase Jimmy with the full force of federal law.

Jimmy did not take the attack lying down. In one especially dirty trick, he apparently contracted with electronic surveillance expert Bernard Spindel to tape Bob Kennedy and the President during their sexual adventures with Marilyn Monroe. The point was presumably blackmail, though Jimmy never used the tapes publicly. According to author Anthony Summers, Spindel may have even placed a bug in the Attorney General's office on Hoffa's behalf.

When 20th Century-Fox began work on the movie version of Robert Kennedy's book *The Enemy Within,* the studio was besieged with anonymous threats and told that the Teamsters would refuse to deliver prints of the film to theaters. The movie never got made.

Some believe Jimmy took his side of the battle to a deadly extreme.

It is a fact that phone records show calls between one of Jimmy's top henchmen – a 370-pound thug named Barney Baker – and others of his associates, and Jack Ruby – the man who killed the man who allegedly killed the President – during the days leading up to the assassination of John Kennedy.

Two of Jimmy's most fearsome Mafia allies, Carlos Marcello and Santo Trafficante, Jr., are said to have spoken openly of plans to kill the President. Trafficante was quoted as saying the Kennedys' harassment of Jimmy Hoffa, "a friend of the working man," was a reason for the "hit."

Jimmy himself was quoted by an unfriendly informant as scheming aloud about the murder of Robert Kennedy a year before John Kennedy's assassination. One alleged plan involved the firebombing of Kennedy's home. Another has taken on, in hindsight, an eerie aspect: the younger Kennedy would be killed *with a high-powered rifle while riding in an open car.* The possibility that the murder plan for one Kennedy became the death of another has not been lost on those who hold Jimmy and his bloody pals responsible for the President's assassination.

Jimmy clearly had something to gain from the President's death. Immediately after the assassination, he told an interviewer, "Bobby Kennedy is just another lawyer now," the clear implication being that Jimmy expected the Get Hoffa squad to lose its punch. In the autobiography published just after his disappearance, Hoffa professes to have "felt bad along with the rest of the nation" when JFK was shot. What he did the day of the assassination was chew out underlings who had lowered the flag at Teamster headquarters to half mast, screaming that Jimmy Hoffa was not going to be a hypocrite.

Neither was he hypocritical about the killing of Robert Kennedy five years later, summing up his feelings by repeating the story of Lyndon Johnson's favorite term for his inherited Attorney General: "the little shit."

If anyone in the underworld was behind the killing of the President – whether the Teamster President was personally involved or not – it is easily conceivable that Jimmy Hoffa went to his unmarked grave knowing who, how, and why. This knowledge could have been lethal.

Bob Kennedy's moves in the war with Hoffa were more a matter of record. The Get Hoffa squad he formed as Attorney General fielded a team of up to 150 federal employees, backed by the FBI and the Justice and Labor departments. The first indictment came in November of 1962. Given the vast assortment of Hoffa's alleged wrongdoings, it was a nit-picking charge: a misdemeanor violation of the Taft-Hartley Act involving the Test Fleet trucking company owned by Jimmy's wife.

The trial was held in Nashville, enlivened through an assassination attempt on Hoffa by a mentally unbalanced drifter who said he had "a message from a higher power" to kill Jimmy. Instead of ducking along with the rest of the courtroom when the shooting started, Jimmy turned around and knocked the man down. The would-be assassin's weapon turned out to be an air gun.

The jury reached a stalemate at seven to five for acquittal, and a mistrial was declared. The feds said Jimmy had tried to fix the jury, and Jimmy said the feds had eavesdropped on him illegally and had planted the main witness against him in the jury-tampering charge, a tough Louisiana Teamster named Edward Grady Partin.

The jury-tampering trial began two months after John Kennedy was shot dead in Dallas. This time Jimmy lost. He was sentenced to eight years in federal prison and fined $10,000. The Get Hoffa squad still was not satisfied.

Hoffa was put on trial in Chicago on charges of defrauding the Teamster pension fund in the Sun Valley land swindle. He was found guilty, sentenced to another five years and fined another $10,000. Hoffa's case in the Chicago trial was not helped by the local gangsters who took front-row seats and cast menacing looks at the jurors, taking advantage of recesses to physically threaten members of the federal team out in the hall.

Jimmy managed to forestall the inevitable for three years with legal appeals and political maneuvering. He finally entered prison in March of 1967, fifteen months before Robert Kennedy was killed in Los Angeles.

The Get Hoffa blitz got more than Hoffa. More than a hundred Teamster officials and hangers-on were convicted on a variety of charges. One of these awaited Jimmy's arrival in Lewisburg. "Tony Pro" Provenzano was doing time for extortion, having been convicted of selling protection from labor trouble in his northern New Jersey domain. By this time Tony Pro's union business had made him one of the most powerful Mafia figures on the East Coast.

Even with the best connections, Lewisburg was not a pleasant place to be. It held nearly twice as many men as it had been designed to hold, and the men thus packed together had not been gentle to begin with. Jimmy enjoyed the best available accommodations, in G Block – the maximum security section known as Mafia Row. A record of life on Mafia Row is provided in Tom Renner's biography of New England mobster-turned-informer Vincent Teresa. According to Teresa, Jimmy took his place as another luminary among a "Who's Who of the mob." The privileges of a Mafia Row address included decent haircuts, custom-tailored prison clothes, first place in line for lunch and laundry, and protection from homosexual attack and other violence.

Tony Pro helped Jimmy secure these privileges, and later Jimmy saved his old friend's life by badgering the warden until Provenzano, who was wasting away with a stomach ailment, was removed for outside medical care. But something happened during the prison stay that soured the relationship.

One story says Hoffa refused to let Provenzano have his union pension. But another story may be more revealing. There were at least two fistfights between Jimmy and Tony Pro, and the remarks passed during one of them, in the prison chow hall, seem to have a direct bearing on later events.

A bank robber redundantly named Edward Edwards, who claims to have been close to Hoffa, says Tony Pro was making luncheon conversation about his plans to get back in the swing of things at Local 560. Jimmy then "exploded": "I dealt with you guys . . . and it's got me so I'm in here now. And I don't like it in here. When you get out, you guys are going to have to be on your own."

Tony Pro's response, according to Edwards, was that if Jimmy did not "back off" he would "end up like Castellito [a union man Tony Pro was later convicted of killing] . . . they won't find so much as a fingernail of yours."

Another version of the split between Jimmy and Tony Pro has been offered by a convicted hit man who says he was given a contract on Hoffa. In an interview with *Playboy* magazine, "Tony the Greek" Frankos says the way he heard it Hoffa told Tony Pro, "When I come out, I want to go back as a leader of the union." Tony Pro said the mob would not allow this because Jimmy was "too hot." Jimmy then threatened to tell all he knew about mob shake-downs and use of union money if he was not allowed to take his job back. He then lost his temper and "smacked Tony Pro in the eye" in front of witnesses, a serious loss of face for a tough guy like Tony Pro. According to Frankos, this was Jimmy's fatal mistake. Tony Pro passed word to his brother Nuncio that Hoffa had to be hit, and the word found its way upstairs in the Mafia hierarchy.

Whether or not it was his death warrant, the break with Tony Pro would be permanent. The day Hoffa disappeared, he thought he was on the way to meet Tony Provenzano for a reconciliation sit-down.

These hard feelings were aggravated by a subsequent alliance between Jimmy and another Lewisburg inmate.

At this point – the fall of 1967 – the Mafia was distracted from its usual business by one of its periodic internecine blood-baths. The headman of one of the New York families, Joseph Bonanno, was feuding with Vito Genovese, Carlo Gambino, and others to settle an old score that involved a relative by marriage. The feud had become known as the Banana Wars, after Bonanno's nickname "Joe Bananas."

Bonanno had removed himself to Arizona and established an alliance with the reigning warlords of the South, Carlos Marcello of New Orleans and Santo Trafficante, Jr. of Miami. His heir apparent, Carmine "Lillo" Galante, was sitting out the war in Lewisburg Prison on a narcotics rap.

Without Tony Pro to protect him, Hoffa needed a powerful new friend in Lewisburg, and the most powerful man available was Carmine Galante, the cock of the walk on Mafia Row. Lillo Galante was a little man in his late fifties, but as tough and as mean as they come. He would later ascend to the top ranks of power in the Mafia, before being murdered in 1979.

By becoming friendly with Galante, Jimmy took a side in the Banana Wars. He was already close to Marcello and Trafficante, but by siding with Galante he became not just an enemy of Tony Pro's, but of the entire Genovese family from which he sprang. Perhaps significantly, the Detroit mob, run by Joseph Zerilli, stayed neutral in the Banana Wars.

Jimmy Hoffa did not intend to spend much time in Lewisburg. Even before he walked in a massive campaign was under way to get him out, and he expected these efforts to pay off anyday. Two million dollars was said to have been spread around in Marcello's Louisiana domain, in an attempt to buy off and/or intimidate witness Edward Grady Partin and a variety of others. A bribe was said to have been attempted on J. Edgar Hoover; and the brother of a Supreme Court justice, among others, was threatened. In the courts, Hoffa's lawyers pushed the argument that he had been illegally convicted.

Once again, Jimmy's fate got mixed up with the Kennedys', as his payoffs to officials in Louisiana were concurrent with New Orleans District Attorney Jim Garrison's bizarre investigation into the Kennedy assassination. At one point a story was leaked to the press that Edward Grady Partin had been seen driving Jack Ruby and Lee Harvey Oswald around New Orleans.

It was eventually a well-placed political contribution that succeeded where all other efforts failed. Las Vegas interests reportedly put $1 million into Richard Nixon's 1968 presidential campaign with the understanding that Jimmy would be pardoned when Nixon reached the White House.

The pardon did come, but much slower than expected and with deadly strings attached. Jimmy had only himself to blame. He had left the wrong guy running his union.

Jimmy had not given up his presidency when he had gone to prison. He had left a figurehead in charge and was using his lawyers to shuttle his orders on Teamster business back to the office. The figurehead was Frank Fitzsimmons, a phlegmatic man Jimmy had brought up through the ranks with him from Detroit to Washington. Fitzsimmons preferred golf to hard work and had none of his boss's charisma. He owed everything he had to Jimmy, so Jimmy figured him to be trustworthy and, for that matter, to be lacking in ambition and brains. Jimmy figured wrong.

The longer Hoffa was absent, the more Fitzsimmons grew to like life at the top of the world's biggest union. He liked the money and the power, and palling around the golf course with bigwigs like the President of the United States, who courted Fitzsimmons's favor because the Teamsters were still the only labor supporters he had.

Jimmy's old friends in the mob found Fitzsimmons a perfectly amiable union man. He proved to be easier to deal with, and less likely to demand a piece of the action, than Jimmy. And he was not nearly as hung up as Jimmy on the idea of enforcing a national Teamsters contract. Under Fitzsimmons's reign, local sweetheart contracts negotiated by mob middlemen put millions into the Mafia coffers. Other deals between the Teamsters and the mobsters proceeded at full steam without help from, or obligation to, Jimmy Hoffa. As Jimmy was siding with the Southern axis in the Banana Wars, Allen Dorfman – the man Jimmy had left in charge of his pension fund – was buying up allegiance to Fitzsimmons with huge loans to mob associates on both sides of the Mason–Dixon line.

Meanwhile Jimmy's people were paying President Nixon's old political mentor Murray Chotiner to lobby for a quick pardon. On several occasions Chotiner thought he had succeeded, only to find his way blocked at the last moment by someone else with access to the President. This someone else turned out to be the President's labor advisor, Charles Colson, who turned out to be working in the interest of Frank Fitzsimmons.

To no one's surprise, Colson was given the lucrative job of General Counsel to the Teamsters when he left the Nixon White House.

In this political tug of war over the pardon, timing was critical. If Jimmy was released in time to organize his forces for the 1971 international convention, it was a foregone conclusion that he would be elected to another five-year term as Teamster president. The Fitzsimmons forces won the tug of war.

Hoffa's parole board then made clear that his chances of parole were nil until he resigned his union office. He did so still believing that Fitzsimmons would hand the office back to him, and within minutes of the resignation's delivery to Fitzsimmons in Florida, Richard Nixon showed up from his Key Biscayne retreat to congratulate the new president of the International Brotherhood of Teamsters.

The presidential pardon came two days before Christmas in 1971. Before leaving prison, Hoffa signed the standard Conditions of Parole form and asked if there were any strings attached to his release. He was told there were none. He took the extra precaution of having a call made to the Justice Department pardons attorney in Washington, and was again assured there were no special conditions. He had reached his daughter's home in St. Louis before he learned the Nixon pardon stipulated that he was barred from all union activity until 1980, on pain of reimprisonment. Had he refused the pardon and remained in prison, he would have been released without restrictions in 1974.

One report published in *Time* suggested that yet another $1 million cash contribution to the Nixon camp – needed at this point as hush money for the Watergate conspirators – flowed from the Teamsters union and its Mafia friends as a payoff for the Hoffa restrictions. Half of the money was said to have come from Tony Pro, and the other half from Allen Dorfman.

For the rest of his life Jimmy Hoffa worked to get the conditions of his pardon lifted. He became a student of constitutional law, and the lawsuits that he filed were still before the courts when he disappeared. As long as he lived apart from the power of his union, Jimmy was living on borrowed time, and the conditional pardon was a death sentence.

At the time of his disappearance, Jimmy had information that the court of appeals was looking on his case with favor, and President Gerald Ford had just pardoned Dave Beck. Jimmy expected to return at any moment. His enemies expected the same.

If and when the restrictions were lifted, Hoffa's strategy was clear. His old friend Dave Johnson, who had been left holding the presidency of Hoffa's Detroit Local 299, would give Jimmy a business agent job with the local. He would then be elected to the local's presidency, and would challenge Fitzsimmons for the international presidency at the next convention. A poll taken in 1974 showed that eighty-three percent of the Teamster rank and file supported Jimmy over Fitzsimmons.

Even so, the international election would not have been a shoo-in. Jimmy himself had changed the rules so that only the fat cat local officers had a meaningful voice at the convention. The rank and file could only watch and wonder.

Because Local 299 was crucial to Jimmy's comeback, a violent struggle for control of the local began while Hoffa was in prison and continued after his death. Fitzsimmons's forces were commanded by Rolland McMaster. Like Fitzsimmons and Johnson, McMaster had come up through the ranks with Jimmy. He was an imposing man, six feet four and about 250 pounds, with a glass left eye that made his intense glare disquieting.

McMaster was not known for gentility. He had run fearsome goon squads for Hoffa, for Fitzsimmons, and, on occasion, to advance his own interests. Under Hoffa, he was known as Jimmy's primary ambassador to the mob. The struggle for 299 became a typical McMaster campaign. There were beatings, bombings, and torchings.

Hoffa's contingent was a strange coalition of old-line Hoffa men like Johnson and a new breed of young rebel Teamsters who wanted to clean up the union. These reformers pinned their hopes on Jimmy because, both publicly and privately, he had begun talking like a reformer himself.

After July 30, 1975, Jimmy talked no more. He rose early that day at his lakeside summer home, made and received calls about current union events, repaired his grandchildren's toys. Around noon he told his wife Jo he was on his way to meet "Tony Jack and a couple of other guys" and drove off.

Mrs. Hoffa noticed Jimmy was unusually nervous, but thought nothing unusual about the meeting with Giacalone, as Tony Jack had visited the Hoffa home as recently as the previous week. The Hoffa and Giacalone children had grown up together, in the same neighborhood. Jimmy's calendar for that day was marked "T.J. – 2 p.m. – Red Fox."

On the way to the meeting, Hoffa stopped in at an airport limo company in which he had hidden ownership. He had a desk at the company office and frequently worked there. His partner in the limo service, a man named Louis Linteau, had been the go-between who set up that day's meeting after several requests from Giacalone.

Linteau wasn't in. Hoffa talked with two employees, Elmer

Reeves and Merita Crane, telling them he was on his way to the Machus Red Fox restaurant for a meeting. Under hypnosis later, Reeves and Crane recalled Jimmy saying he was to meet with "Tony J," "Tony P," and another man. "Tony P" was Hoffa's standard shorthand for Provenzano.

At 2.30 p.m., Jimmy called his wife and asked if Tony Jack had called. He had not. Louis Linteau claims to have taken a call from Hoffa at 3.30, though one of his employees placed the time closer to 2.30. The 3.30 time would work out better to establish alibis for some of the suspects, leading some authorities to speculate that Linteau knew what was going to happen to Hoffa. During the call, Hoffa complained that Giacalone had stood him up.

Jimmy Hoffa has not spoken to anyone since. His car was found, abandoned but unlocked, on the parking lot of the shopping center that contained the restaurant.

The disappearance created a national sensation and a frenzy of law enforcement activity reminiscent of the days of the Get Hoffa squad. The FBI descended in force on the Red Fox restaurant, checking employees, reservation lists, credit card charges, and even kitchen records to establish the times orders had gone out to patrons' tables. The search turned up six witnesses who had seen Jimmy Hoffa at the Red Fox, or in its parking lot, on July 30 between 2.00 and 2.50 p.m.

One of these witnesses said he had seen Jimmy in a maroon Lincoln or Mercury with three other men, as the car pulled out of the parking lot. Jimmy was leaning forward, yelling at the driver of the car. The driver looked like a newspaper picture the witness had seen of Chuckie O'Brien, Jimmy's "foster son."

Another witness saw – about three-quarters of an hour earlier – a man waiting in a brown or maroon car in the restaurant parking lot. In a lineup the following December, the witness positively identified Salvatore "Sally Bugs" Briguglio as the man she had seen. Sally Bugs was a business agent for Tony Provenzano's Local 560 in New Jersey, but he enjoyed a greater reputation for mob violence than for unionism.

Unlike the other heavies in the Hoffa story, Sal Briguglio did not look the part. He was a small and slender, almost studious-looking character who wore thick glasses. Appearances can be deceiving. A union crony told author Lester Velie, "Sal could kill a man, then sit down and eat a sandwich."

On the day in question, Chuckie O'Brien was driving a maroon Mercury he had borrowed from Joey Giacalone, Tony Jack's son and Chuckie's boyhood pal. Chuckie's own car had been shipped down to his new office in Florida.

The FBI gave the Mercury a thorough going-over. Bloodstains were found on the seat, but the blood proved to have come from a fish, not a deposed union president.

Chuckie explained that he had borrowed the car that morning because a Teamster secretary had asked him to deliver a twenty-four-pound salmon to a union vice-president. He was supposed to be at a meeting in Toronto, but claimed to have missed his flight and thus to have become available for fish deliveries, and perhaps for other errands.

To supplement their own impressions of the Mercury, the FBI men brought along four trained dogs. The dogs had been given clothing of Jimmy's to sniff, and when they sniffed around the Mercury they found, according to their trainer, Jimmy's scent in the car's back seat and trunk. The objection was raised that there was no way of knowing how long the scent might have been in the car. But would there have been any reason for Jimmy Hoffa to be, voluntarily, inside the car's *trunk* at anytime?

The FBI men also found a "single, three-inch brown head hair" in the car's back seat to put under their microscopes. The hair proved to have "characteristics similar to" Jimmy's hair. Chemical tests revealed a tiny bit of blood on the hair, but not enough blood to establish whose body it had flowed from. Further testing at a later date reportedly confirmed traces of Hoffa's blood, hair, and skin in the back seat of Chuckie's borrowed car.

The alibis of the most immediate suspects, with one exception, seemed in good order. Giacalone and Provenzano denied that any meeting with Hoffa had been arranged. Both could account for their time on July 30.

Giacalone's alibi was set in particularly hard stone. He had spent the late morning and afternoon in and around the Southfield Athletic Club, and every minute was duly accounted for, with witnesses supplying conveniently exact details. Giacalone's masseur knew precisely when he had arrived, how long he had napped, and when he had left for a haircut. The barber, whom the impeccably groomed Giacalone had never visited before and with whom he had no appointment, knew exactly when he came and went. During the critical hours of the afternoon, Giacalone was with a lawyer whose records could document the comings and goings of clients.

Provenzano had been playing a game of Greek rummy at his union hall in New Jersey. His companions in the game included Sally Bugs Briguglio and two other men who would become suspects in the disappearance.

While the authorities were looking for Chuckie O'Brien to ask him what his alibi might be, Chuckie was popping up in unexpected places. The night of July 31, the same day the family had reported Jimmy missing, Chuckie showed up at the Hoffa summer house, where the family had gathered. Jim Hoffa quarreled with him about his support of Fitzsimmons and accused him of knowing what had happened to his father. Chuckie left in a hurry.

The next night, Chuckie appeared at the home of a *Detroit Free Press* reporter he knew and planted Giacalone's alibi, saying he had been with Giacalone at the Southfield Athletic Club himself. He later changed this version of events several times. The people Chuckie claimed to have been with during the critical period would not verify his alibi for the FBI.

The following Monday, August 4, Chuckie surfaced at Teamster headquarters in Washington, D.C., to visit Frank Fitzsimmons, who seemed surprised to see him. What the two men talked about is not known. Fitzsimmons sent Chuckie back to Detroit, where the FBI finally interviewed him on August 6, and after which his lawyer reported that the FBI was "satisfied." In fact, Chuckie's shifting alibis caused the FBI to cite his reputation as "a pathological liar who borders on being totally incompetent."

Chuckie later took the Fifth Amendment before a Detroit grand jury. So did Tony Jack. And so did Tony Pro.

Were Giacalone and Provenzano capable of killing the old friend who had done so much to make both of them rich? The two Tonys were certainly not squeamish individuals. Giacalone had been an enforcer for the Detroit Mafia, the man mobs from other cities had to see for permission to operate in Detroit, and the man who punished unwelcome invaders.

In the 1960s, testimony before a U.S. Senate Rackets Committee had identified Giacalone as "king of the streets" in Detroit, the top man in the city's numbers and loansharking action. At the time of Hoffa's disappearance, he was about to go on trial for income tax evasion. He had been arrested fifteen times in earlier years – for gambling, rape, felonious assault, loan-sharking, and armed robbery – but convicted only once, for bribery.

Besides being in the same line of work, the two Tonys were relatives. Tony Jack's wife was Tony Pro's cousin.

Provenzano's name had long been connected with involuntary disappearing acts not unlike Hoffa's. In 1961, the secretary-treasurer of Provenzano's Union City Teamsters Local 560, a man named Anthony Castellito, had shown enough bad judgment to announce that he would run for president of the local against Tony Pro. Castellito disappeared in June of that year.

In 1963, a prosecution witness against Provenzano in the extortion trial that sent him to Lewisburg, an unfortunate named Walter Glockner, was shot to death just before he was to testify.

In 1972, a loan shark associate of Provenzano's named Armand "Cokey" Faugno vanished. The word was that this vanishing act was accomplished with the aid of a tree shredder.

Not that these activities were rare in the world of the Teamsters. Jimmy himself had been indirectly linked to at least one disappearance. In 1955, an Indianapolis attorney named David Probstein vanished after starting a cab company and an insurance agency with Teamster money. Probstein had dealt with Allen Dorfman and with several other close Hoffa associates, and his phone records showed calls to Hoffa and to two of his accountants. Apparently Probstein had made the mistake of imitating his mentors by putting their money to his personal use. They had failed to see the humor.

An apparent break in the Hoffa case came when a convicted murderer held in New Jersey's Trenton State Prison offered to trade information for freedom. Unfortunately for the informant, William Bufalino, who had strangely turned up as the lawyer for all the suspects in the disappearance, claimed to have learned his identity and released his name to the press. The name was Ralph Picardo. Picardo, aka Ralph Birche, had been an important figure in Anthony Provenzano's Local 560, intimately involved in the loansharking, pension fund loan arranging, and collections operations that went on there. Information he provided on loansharking established his credibility by proving to be correct.

Picardo claimed the men who made Jimmy disappear were Sally Bugs Briguglio, his brother Gabriel, who handled sweetheart deals for the Provenzanos through an affiliated local, and Thomas Andretta, a driver for Sal Briguglio and a three-time loser. According to Picardo, his information came from Andretta's brother Steve, who had "stayed in New Jersey to provide an alibi for Tony Pro."

During the investigation into this lead, all the suspects took the Fifth. Steve Andretta was given immunity to force him to testify against the others, but still refused and did sixty-three days in jail for contempt of court. Finally Steve Andretta announced that he would talk.

He appeared before the Detroit grand jury investigating Hoffa's disappearance. Lawyers are not permitted to accompany their clients inside grand jury rooms. Andretta skirted this rule by making a record-setting 1,117 trips outside the room to consult William Bufalino in the hall after each and every question. This method of testimony caused Andretta's appearance before the grand jury to drag out over a six-week period. The jist of this extended testimony, and the secret Andretta had given up two months of freedom to protect? He and Thomas had spent the day in question playing Greek rummy at the union hall with Tony Pro, Sally Bugs, and Gabriel.

Though there were important inconsistencies, the Greek rummy story was at first supported by secretaries, elevator operators, and other Local 560 employees.

As time went by, some of these supporting witnesses became less sure of who, if anybody, had played cards in the union hall that day. In 1977, one of them told author Steven Brill: "He [one of the suspects] told us they were here, but that, just in case we forgot, we'd better not let the cops pressure us into saying we didn't see them, because that would cause us all kinds of problems."

In the meantime, the search for Jimmy, or whatever was left of him, went on. Picardo claimed the body had been shipped to New Jersey in an oil drum and unloaded in a Jersey City garbage dump.

The dump had been owned by Phillip "Brother" Moscato, a friend and business associate of Tony Pro's. Brother's dump had long been suspected as a convenient burial ground for those who had run afoul of Tony Pro and his family. It was thought to be the final resting place of Anthony Castellito, "Cokey" Faugno, and others.

Four unlucky FBI agents spent a week sifting through the foully odoriferous wreckage that littered the forty-seven-acre dump, reaching in some places to a depth of sixty feet. Power shovels were on hand but were not used because of the danger of fire from the methane gas escaping from the rubbish. The search was abandoned before it was completed. No bodies had turned up.

Several investigators pooh-poohed the dump theory as a rotten idea (the agents who searched the dump would doubtless agree), as there were plenty of spots to dispose of a body in Michigan, and the Detroit mobsters were just as adept at body-dumping as their New Jersey cousins.

One FBI lead, based on a tip from two independent informants who were said to be reliable, held that Hoffa's body was shredded, compacted, and then incinerated through the good offices of Central Sanitation Services in Hamtramck, Michigan.

Central Sanitation was owned by two Detroit mobsters, Raffael Quasarano and Pete Vitale, who had a long history of dealing with the Teamsters and who had sided with Fitzsimmons and Rolland McMaster in the struggle for control of Jimmy's Local 299. Quasarano and Vitale also owned a company called Market Vending, which had been a favorite hangout of Frank Fitzsimmons's during his Detroit days, and which had employed one of his sons as sales manager. Through Central Sanitation, Quasarano and Vitale had borrowed $85,000 from a New Jersey bank said to be controlled by Tony Pro, without bothering to pay off the loan.

One of the FBI informants added the juicy tidbit that Frank Fitzsimmons met with Quasarano and Vitale just before Hoffa's disappearance. Fitzsimmons denied this, but could not account for his time when the meeting allegedly occurred, or for an FBI report that he had used a Central Sanitation Services car during a July 25 to 27 trip to Detroit.

FBI agents searched Central Sanitation with the help of sniffing dogs, but found no signs of Jimmy. They opined afterward that too much time had passed for scents to be found.

There were other false alarms. U.S. Senate investigators paid an informant $25,000 for the tip that Hoffa's body could be found in a certain swampy field north of Detroit. They dug up the field without finding anything more interesting than rattlesnake nests.

CBS News followed another tipster to the ocean off Florida, with similarly disappointing results.

In October of 1977, there was a brief flurry of interest in a body found in northeastern Pennsylvania, at first thought to be

Hoffa's. Dental records proved the body had belonged to another victim of the mob's.

Given Jimmy's long association with the transportation industry, perhaps the most fitting theory on his whereabouts is the automotive one. Former mob assassin Charles Crimaldi told his biographer he had definite knowledge that "Hoffa is now a goddamn hubcap." Crimaldi claimed Hoffa's "body was crushed" in a steel compactor for junk cars, then "smelted" to become just another automotive accessory.

This view was corroborated by none other than Chuckie O'Brien. According to author Dan Moldea, Chuckie avowed in front of several witnesses that "Hoffa is now just a fender, being driven around by someone."

The most grotesque Hoffa disappearance story would not surface until the fall of 1989. In this story, Jimmy is neither hubcap nor fender, but an unwilling fixture on a professional football field. From the prison cell where he is defended by the federal government as an officially protected witness, hit man Donald "Tony the Greek" Frankos got in touch with *Playboy* magazine.

Frankos had been spilling the beans on Mafia operations to the feds. He had good reason to know this kind of storytelling was a high-risk business. Because he thought he "was going to be dead pretty soon," he had decided to leave the world his life story as a sort of legacy. He turned over a box of fourteen tapes that described his Mafia career in detail. The most newsworthy tidbit on the tapes was a tale about the death and disposal of Jimmy Hoffa.

Frankos said Jimmy died because he wanted his union back. He wanted it bad enough that he had threatened, during the fight with Tony Pro in Lewisburg, to go to the feds with all the dirt he knew. Obviously, the mob couldn't allow this to happen. Only the Dons who sat at the head of families knew more than Hoffa. Besides, the mob had a much more manageable union boss in Frank Fitzsimmons than it had ever had in Hoffa. There was no reason to put Jimmy back at the head of the Teamsters.

At the time of the disappearance, there were rumors that President Gerald Ford was about to give Jimmy a full pardon. That would have put him back in the union business well ahead of the 1980 date stipulated as a condition of his parole. Jimmy's support among the rank and file would have made him a troublesome adversary.

Frankos says he was originally offered the hit himself. He was summoned by Anthony "Fat Tony" Salerno, a New York underboss who had made his fortune running the numbers game in Harlem. Frankos had killed for Fat Tony's organization before. He was told there was a big-time, $200,000 hit coming down on "a guy in Lewisburg," and paid a retainer for the job. After the meeting, Salerno's "main hitter," an Irishman named John Sullivan, told Frankos the target was Jimmy Hoffa.

For some reason, maybe because of the talk about a presidential pardon, the hit did not come down until four years later. Frankos was busy doing time and was unavailable for the job, but he was given a percentage of the take anyway, for his "consulting" and, presumably, to buy his silence. He says he was visited by the hit team in prison immediately after the killing, and given all the details.

The details were these: Hoffa was hit by two Irish killers, John Sullivan and Jimmy Coonan. The Irishmen traveled to Detroit with Sally Bugs Briguglio. The hit had been opposed by Hoffa's closest friend in the Mafia, Tony Jack Giacalone, but Giacalone was warned off by Salerno and told he would have to cooperate or die himself. Everybody involved knew Hoffa was too smart to expose himself without being lured out by someone he trusted. Giacalone offered the bait. He explained to Jimmy the advantages of settling the long-time grudge with Tony Pro. He said Tony Pro was coming to Detroit for a sit-down. To put Jimmy at ease about the meeting, Chuckie O'Brien was involved.

Like Giacalone, Chuckie was "reluctant" about the hit when it was first proposed to him. He was told he would be killed along with the rest of his family if he did not go along. To sweeten the deal he was also offered a million bucks. "For the rest of his life," Frankos says, "he will be taken care of, as far as money goes." Out of fear or greed or both, according to Frankos, Chuckie sold his "Dad" to the mob.

Frankos says Jimmy left the Red Fox in a car with Chuckie and Sally Bugs, thinking he was on the way to meet Tony Jack and Tony Pro. He was taken to a safe house in Mount Clemens, Michigan. Just as he arrived, Coonan stepped out and shot Jimmy twice in the forehead with a .22 pistol equipped with a silencer. Coonan and Sullivan then carried Jimmy's body into the basement of the house and proceeded to cut it into pieces, using a buzz saw and a meat cleaver.

Frankos describes the dismemberment in gory detail. He had dismembered a few bodies himself and no doubt had a professional interest. Coonan cut off the head and took a lock of hair – which he proudly showed Frankos – "for good luck." He cut the arms and legs into two pieces each, and made three chunks out of the torso. The room was then cleaned up and all the body parts neatly packed into plastic sacks.

An argument ensued about the disposal of the body. The original plan had been to make fenders and hubcaps out of Jimmy, in a metal crusher controlled by the Detroit mob. But Giacalone and his people backed away from this arrangement and said the body was now the New York mob's problem. There were old grudges involved. "Detroit," Frankos explained, "don't like New York." Until a better solution could be found, Jimmy's butchered remains were kept in a freezer in the same room where he was cut apart.

Five months later another Irishman named Joe Sullivan was given the job of finding a more suitable resting place for Jimmy's body. He put it in an oil drum among a bunch of legitimate oil drums and drove it to New Jersey on a Mafia truck. It so happened that a mob-related cement-mixing outfit was then working on the expansion of the New York Giants' stadium in the Meadowlands. Jimmy was entombed in concrete beneath the artificial turf. He rests just in front of section 107 of the stadium, beside the end zone.

Frankos claims Joe Sullivan took him to a Giants game after he was released from prison, and that he and Sullivan toasted Jimmy and speculated about whether he was enjoying the game. This story was reportedly first repeated to the FBI in 1986. So far the artificial turf of the Meadowlands has not been disturbed in a search for Jimmy Hoffa. The FBI has declined comment.

Can Frankos be believed? He does get some of his dates wrong, but after fourteen and more years that may be understandable. Federal investigators have thought enough of his other revelations to make use of them in the course of a number of prosecutions. His story checks out reasonably well against the available evidence and against the main points of previous reconstructions of the crime. He certainly knew and did business with the characters he describes. The stadium construction job was under way at the time he said it was, although an assistant stadium manager has been quoted as saying the area in question was dug up to a depth of four feet in the course of a turf replacement sometime in 1990, and nothing unexpected was found.

The use of an Irish hit team is not an unusual Mafia tactic. The "Irish Mafia" was well established in this country when the Sicilian immigrants arrived, and the two organizations have cooperated with each other ever since, sharing territories through a complex web of unwritten understandings. On New York's West Side, for example, a Mafia operator like Fat Tony Salerno would have to depend on his Irish allegiances to get his business done, because he would be operating on Irish turf. "Freelance hitters" like Frankos, Coonan, and Sullivan hire out not only to Mafia and Irish mobs, but to Israelis, Albanians, Greeks, Puerto Ricans, and Colombians. It is standard practice for a Don in one territory to import the favorite killers of one of his peers in another territory to perform his hits. If Fat Tony Salerno did commission Hoffa's killing, he was probably acting as a subcontractor to another party or parties who wanted the job done.

For a hit as big as Hoffa's, the decision may not have been

made by one man, but by the vote of a coalition of the powerful. Some investigators have suggested the originator of the idea may have been Russell Bufalino. Bufalino controlled a part of the old Vito Genovese family in New Jersey. Tony Pro was one of his captains. Bufalino was thought to be the mob boss with the most to gain from the sweetheart deals that violated Hoffa's Master Freight Agreement, and that Jimmy had vowed to stamp out when he returned to power. He was said to be the main man behind the $500,000 payoff the New Jersey mob reportedly made to President Nixon's aides for Hoffa's parole restrictions. He had been a participant, possibly along with Hoffa, in the Mafia–CIA plots that were in the process of being covered up. Besides all this, if Hoffa regained power and kicked out Tony Pro as he had threatened, Bufalino would lose his main connection to all that lovely Teamster money.

New York undercover cops reported that Bufalino, Tony Pro, and Sally Bugs all sat together at the Vesuvio restaurant in New York five days after the Hoffa disappearance, discussing what the FBI had learned about the case. And long-distance telephone records showed several calls between Bufalino and the owners of Central Sanitation Services in Detroit.

There have always been plenty of suspects in the Hoffa case. The problem is a lack of the kind of hard evidence that brings convictions in a court of law. Police have the witnesses from the Red Fox, but their identification of suspects came after they had seen pictures of the same suspects in the newspapers. It might be proved beyond a reasonable doubt that Jimmy Hoffa had been a passenger at some point in the maroon Mercury driven that day by Chuckie O'Brien, but this in itself would convict no one of kidnapping or murder. Most important, there is no body. The cops on the case find themselves in the frustrating but not unaccustomed position of looking at people they are reasonably sure are guilty, without being able to lay a hand on them.

Still, in roundabout ways, the Hoffa investigation did seem to bring various forms of justice to many of its suspects.

About a year after the Picardo lead, an informant in another prison claimed to have participated in the killing of Anthony Castellito, the man who had aspired to the presidency of Tony Pro's union local, in 1961. The cast this informant named had a familiar ring.

The story was that Tony Pro had contracted with Sal Briguglio and a hulk named Harold "K.O." Konigsberg – an ex-sparring partner of Joe Louis who was known as the "loan shark's loan shark" for his renowned ability to collect on bad debts – to kill and dispose of Castellito.

The FBI could not pursue this development because the statute of limitations on kidnapping had run out. The lead was taken up by New York police because the killing was done in that state, and murder indictments were returned. Tony Pro was finally convicted of the murder of Castellito in 1978 and given a life sentence. He has since died.

Sally Bugs, who had been promoted to secretary-treasurer of Local 560, was deprived of his prison term. On March 21, 1978, he was standing outside a restaurant in New York's Little Italy when two hooded men knocked him down and killed him with five bullets to the head and one to the chest. Government investigators speculated that Sally Bugs was hit to prevent him from trading information on Hoffa for a deal in the Castellito case. Donald Frankos says one of the hit men was Joe Sullivan, the same man he says planted Jimmy Hoffa in the Meadowlands.

Tony Jack Giacalone was convicted of tax fraud and got ten years.

Chuckie got a year for extortion and was subsequently convicted for filing a fraudulent loan application. He also seems to have suffered a certain amount of anxiety. When told Tony Pro was looking for him during the 1976 Teamsters convention in Las Vegas, Chuckie is said to have spent two days hiding under a bed.

On unrelated convictions, Fat Tony Salerno is doing one hundred years; Jimmy Coonan is doing seventy-five; Joe Sullivan seventy-five to life.

Russel Bufalino was given a four-year sentence on an extortion conviction.

The Hoffa case is still open, and with it all the intriguing ties to the death of a President and to four decades of big-time crime. Jimmy's legacy to the Teamsters and to the nation lives on.

Two of the three Teamster presidents since Jimmy have been indicted – Fitzgerald wasn't but his son was – one has done time and one stood trial on charges of embezzling over $700,000 from his local but died before the trial concluded.

The style of Teamster business didn't change any more than the substance. In 1983 Allen Dorfman was gunned down in Chicago, presumably to prevent too much conversation with the law about the three indictments against him.

Long after Jimmy was gone revelations continued about the company he kept. Over a year after the disappearance the contents of FBI tape recordings made between 1961 and 1964 from bugs in the office of Jimmy's good friend Tony Jack Giacalone were finally made public.

Conversations on the tapes reveal that Chuckie's mother and Jimmy's old girlfriend, Sylvia Pagano, now known as Sylvia Paris, had become Tony Jack's mistress, and spied on Jimmy for him. Tony Jack brags of using Sylvia to "control" Hoffa. Sylvia, Tony Jack, and Tony Jack's brother Vito even plotted at one point to rob the Hoffas' Washington apartment, believing Jimmy had a large amount of money stashed there.

The tapes revealed other highly personal matters. Sylvia had apparently lured Josephine Hoffa into an affair with a gangster named Tony Cimini. While Jimmy was out of town, Cimini and Mrs. Hoffa would double-date with Sylvia and Tony Jack.

When Jimmy learned of the affair, he had not dealt with it himself – perhaps because he knew the penalty for unauthorized violence against a Mafia member – but, swallowing his pride, had gone to Detroit mob boss Joseph Zerilli and asked for the old man's help in ending the affair. The request was granted, but in the macho world of the Mafia, Jimmy had undeniably lost face.

The various reconstructions of the Hoffa hit explain *how* Jimmy disappeared. They do not fully explain *why*.

The possibility that Hoffa died because of what he knew about the Kennedy assassination and/or about the CIA plots against Castro opens a disturbing line of speculation. As we now well know, the fact that Hoffa was the victim of an apparent mob hit does not rule out the involvement of other players in his death, some of whom may have been paid for their trouble with U.S. government checks.

A more straightforward answer is that the killers did not want Jimmy back as president of the Teamsters. Using this assumption, the power behind the killing could have been the Fitzsimmons/McMaster faction of the union, or the Provenzano faction of the mob, or both.

Could the killers have believed that Jimmy's promise to clean up the union was sincere? If they did — and if it was — the disappearance of Jimmy Hoffa deprived the world of a great and perhaps inspiring spectacle, and the rank and file members of the world's largest labor union of the best chance they have had to get the Mafia out of their business and off their backs.

Jimmy Hoffa was not the most admirable of men. Even if he did intend to clean up his union, the fact that he had done more than anyone to dirty it cannot be denied. Given what is known of Jimmy, it is difficult to believe his attempted come-back in the union was not motivated more by a drive to reclaim power than an urge to reform. Still, there is some comfort in thinking the best, even of a man like Jimmy Hoffa.

In Lewisburg prison, Jimmy had found a novel way to pass the time. He had taken up reading. He had in fact become a voracious reader, preferring history, sociology, and law. For the first time, he seemed to have become concerned with the way the history books, especially the labor history books, might deal with a man named Hoffa.

During a visit at the prison, Jimmy confided in his son Jim that he was going to take his "place in labor history" when he got back to his Teamsters. He was going to boot the mob out of the union once and for all.

James Riddle Hoffa, tough guy and smart guy, may have finally taken a hard look at his friends.

Postscript

Jimmy has not turned up, but not for lack of rumors of his whereabouts. Giants Stadium remains un-excavated. But the Au Sable River has been searched fruitlessly by those eager to collect a $10,000 reward offered by *Boating* magazine, and a gambling parlor in Gardena, California has been razed (by its new owner, the porno king Larry Flynt) without revealing Jimmy in the rubble.

Meanwhile, there may have been a genuine breakthrough in the case, though the trail may be too cold for it to matter.

Chuckie O'Brien, now 66 and living in Florida, was being interviewed by the FBI as recently as August of 2001. This is probably because the agency had applied recently developed DNA tests to evidence from the borrowed Mercury Chuckie was driving the day Jimmy disappeared, and confirmed a match to the hair they had always suspected came from Jimmy's head.

The Mercury, you may remember, belonged to Joey Giacalone, son of "Tony Jack" Giacalone. Tony Jack died in February 2001 at the age of 82. He was under indictment at the time on a new assortment of racketeering charges. No doubt the FBI would like to talk to him too, but as his lawyer William Bufalino II says, they're "going to have to get into heaven if they want to ask him any more questions." That leaves open the question of whether heaven is a good place to look . . . for either Tony Jack or Jimmy.

3

The Two Kings of the Bahamas

The Murder of Sir Harry Oakes

The wooden harbor ferry, one among a small fleet of converted glass-bottom boats, rocks and sways alongside Prince George's Wharf, Nassau. Every seat is full, and faces show the strain of impatience to get on with the short ride to Paradise Island.

But more tourists are being herded aboard. A young Bahamian exhorts his passengers to make room, and a large American, red-faced with anger, shouts back that the boat's capacity is twenty-six (plainly lettered on a sign) and thirty-eight are already on board. The Bahamian slips the challenge with a joke, keeping his island cool and collecting his fares.

The tourists have disembarked from mammoth cruise ships that await them at the end of the wharf, or from sleek jetliners that come and go roughly every quarter-hour at the crowded international airport at the center of New Providence Island. The charming natural harbor they will cross has sheltered the dreadnoughts of Blackbeard, held slave ships and rum-runners and the booty of shipwreckers moored to its docks. Today the tourists will sun on the manicured sands of the island that rings and protects the harbor from the singular blue of the surrounding Caribbean, the island now known with some acuity as Paradise. Tonight they will make the most of their allotted holidays, in the beguiling perpetual day of the casinos.

Given a certain churlish point of view, the overcrowded ferryboat can seem a metaphor for Nassau itself. Jam-packed with tourists much of the year, the storied downtown Bay

Street section is the kind of jostling, hectic place that can create ambivalent feelings toward one's fellow in the mind of visitor and native alike.

It has not always been so.

The tourist-hustling Bahamas of today is a conscious creation that began to take form decades ago, in the years immediately prior to World War II. The Bahamas of that day was an elegantly languorous British outpost, and the few tourists who came to visit were firmly entrenched members of the idle rich.

Some say the change in the islands can be traced back directly to a single violent night. The night of July 7, 1943.

During the small hours of that night an ugly storm passed over Nassau, whipping the city with high winds and blowing rain. The morning after brought an uglier revelation. Sir Harry Oakes, one of the world's richest men and the Bahamas' leading citizen, was found murdered in his bed. His skull had been fractured by a heavy object with one or more sharp triangular points, leaving four wounds in the vicinity of the left ear, and his body had been partially burned by his killer. Feathers from a pillow clung to the body, fluttering in the breeze of an electric fan.

The body was lying on its back, but blood from the wound toward the back of Oakes's head had run across his face, indicating that he must have been facedown at some point and that someone must have moved the body after the attack. The presence of blisters on the body showed that the sixty-eight-year-old man had been alive when he was set on fire and had lived for a short time afterward.

The fire had not spread much beyond the bed, possibly extinguished by the storm that blew outside a screen door to an upstairs balcony. There were scorch marks and tracked mud on the stairs leading to the second floor bedroom.

There was a smeared handprint on a wall inside the room about four feet from the floor, which appeared to have been made with blood.

The man who made the ghastly discovery was Oakes's best friend, real estate broker Harold Christie, who had stayed the night at Westbourne, one of several residences Oakes maintained on New Providence Island, sleeping two bedrooms down the hall. Oakes and Christie were the only people in the house.

The murder hit the presses billed as the Crime of the Century, and with each new development it seemed more likely to live up to the billing. It had forbidden romance, international intrigue, and a glittering cast of characters worthy of Hollywood fiction. These included a King of England who had given up his throne for "the woman he loved," Mafia over-lords, an international industrialist who doubled as a suspected Nazi spy, and a suave French playboy count standing in as the villain. The Oakes case has long since been displaced as the century's most notorious crime. It remains one of its greatest and most intriguing unsolved mysteries.

At center stage was the storybook figure of Sir Harry Oakes himself.

Harry Oakes was born December 23, 1874, into a locally prominent family in the township of Sangerville, Maine. Small of stature, a daydreamer who kept mostly to himself, young Oakes attended Foxcroft Academy and went on to Bowdoin College and two restless years at Syracuse Medical School.

According to his classmates, Harry dreamed mainly of riches, but was repelled by the idea of making money, as he put it in the idealism of his youth, "off of my fellow man." Business and the professions were tainted, and boring besides. But how else could a young man make his fortune? As Harry mulled the question in his brooding way, along came a gold strike in the Klondike.

For two years Oakes followed the news of the gold rush avidly, finally setting off to join the legions of gold fever victims with the blessings and support of his family. The twenty-three-year-old swore he would return a millionaire. And though it cost him twenty years of incredible hardships, he made the prophecy come true.

The young man learned prospecting and mining as he went. He also learned to live with hunger, isolation, extremes of temperature, and unrewarding, back-breaking labor. Through the years he acquired a toughness and a kind of bitter self-reliance that would not sit well in polite society. The quest took him to the far corners of the world, following the rumors of rich strikes through Alaska, Canada, Australia, New Zealand, the Philippines, the Belgian Congo, Death Valley, and finally back to Alaska and Canada again.

In these travels he developed a well-deserved reputation as a cantankerous little loner, shabby and fanatically hardworking. Partners were sometimes required, and he took these on when necessary and discarded them when not. His only female companionship came with occasional visits to prostitutes in mining shantytowns, followed by Puritanical remorse.

He was once lost with the partner of the moment in a sea storm off Alaska, washing up into the custody of Cossacks on the coast of Siberia. The Cossack captain felt the filthy prospectors were not worth the lead it would take to shoot them, and put them back into their boat. In California, Oakes shared a tiny cave one stormy night with a nest of rattlesnakes. In New Zealand, he once settled long enough to become a wealthy flax farmer, only to catch the fever once again and set off, investing every dime he had in the search for his elusive gold.

The mother lode was Harry's Holy Grail. It awaited him in Canada, at Kirkland Lake, Ontario. The night he staked his claim the temperature reached fifty-two below. Here was his bonanza, beyond doubt, the greater part of it concealed beneath the surface of the lake. Oakes planted himself on the spot and spent eight more hard years – of protracted legal battles, of begging for financing to run the mine, of technical difficulties in getting out the gold – before he could enjoy his find.

But Harry Oakes endured, doing everything on his own and never letting anyone forget it. His Lake Shore Mine made him the richest man in Canada, and, some said at the height of his glory, perhaps the richest man on earth.

He had paid an undeniable price for the distinction.

He had no real friends but a large and growing number of enemies, real and imagined. Somewhere on the road to riches, he had lost the social graces. He had the habit of whistling under his breath during other people's conversation, or of turning his back and walking away in mid-sentence. At elegant dinner parties, he used coarse language and spat the seeds of grapes across the table.

At forty-eight, Oakes met and married a twenty-four-year-old Australian girl during a world cruise. Eunice MacIntyre was said to be everything her husband was not: tall, attractive, gentle, sensitive, and charming. Oakes was devoted to her. Five children came of the marriage.

Oakes had given up his American citizenship and had become a citizen of Canada, purely for business reasons, in 1924. He soon had better business reasons to change countries once again. Taxes were on the rise, and no one in Canada was paying more taxes than Harry Oakes. In the early 1930s, he met Harold Christie in Palm Beach and learned that there were no income taxes in the Bahamas. Oakes developed a sudden interest in the island nation, moving his family there in 1937.

Now a Bahamian, Oakes gave lavishly to charities in London and Nassau, and was made a Baronet in 1939. Sir Harry soon came to own a third of New Providence Island, including several opulent residences, an airline and airfield, and the British Colonial Hotel, a pink memento of old world elegance that still stands as a landmark beside Nassau harbor. His spending created a one-man development boom, boosting wages and employment throughout the island. Within a few short years, his fortune had made him the uncrowned king of the Bahamas, and very little of consequence transpired in the Bahamian capital without his say-so.

One of those who witnessed the dawning of the Oakes age at first hand was Sir Etienne Dupuch, then the editor of *The Nassau Tribune,* and later the newspaper's editor emeritus. The Sir Harry Dupuch remembered was not an entirely likable fellow. "Harry Oakes was Harold Christie's best client. He had one interest: running a tractor. As long as Christie could find something for him to destroy, he knew he had a sale."

Oakes's bulldozer became his favorite island toy. Maurice Kelly, a Nassau chiropractor whose father was Oakes's manager, says, "You can still see Sir Harry's bulldozer tracks around here. That's how I remember him – knocking down trees."

Harry's war on the Bahamian flora was supplanted as a topic of local interest by a larger war. By chance, that war brought the Bahamas another kind of king to join Sir Harry. This was the former Edward VIII of England, now known as the Duke of Windsor, who three and a half years before had given up his throne to marry his Duchess and had created an instant romantic legend in the process.

As a statesman, the Duke had proved to be less than legendary. After some unfortunate actions that made him appear to be pro-German, and after an abortive kidnapping attempt on him by the Nazis, the British Foreign Office apparently decided the best way to keep Windsor out of trouble was to post him to the sleepy and distant Bahamas as Governor.

Each an outcast in his own odd way, the two kings of the Bahamas struck up a sort of friendship, socializing and playing golf together frequently on the course Sir Harry had built.

By the morning of July 8, 1943, as Sir Harry's body still lay undiscovered, times were relatively good in the Bahamas. The far-off war had begun to turn in the Allies' favor, British and American military installations had brought prosperity, and the presence of young Britons, particularly servicemen's wives who were sitting out the war, contributed greatly to the social atmosphere.

News of the murder changed all this, and shocked the island nation as violently as America was shocked by the assassination of John F. Kennedy twenty years later. Though no one, with the possible exception of the murderer or murderers, could know it at the time, the Bahamas had just entered a new era that would change their easygoing character.

This at least is what many who have studied the Oakes case believe, for a number of more or less convincing reasons.

These begin with the strange actions of the Duke of Windsor on that fateful day. On being informed by an aide of the murder, the Royal Governor first attempted to black out the news by using his war powers to declare complete press censorship. This was foiled by Etienne Dupuch, who entirely by coincidence had spoken to Harold Christie by phone and had already created headlines around the world by cabling out the news.

The Duke's next action was less explicable. Instead of relying on the local police or, as the next logical step in a British colony, on Scotland Yard, the Duke took personal control of the investigation by calling in two detectives from the Miami Police Department. The explanation later given was that one of these officers, Captain Edward Melchen, had served as a bodyguard for the Duke during a visit to Miami and the Duke had been impressed with his efficiency. (The Royal Governor, Sir Etienne Dupuch explained, "loved being *salaamed* to a great deal.")

The Duke reportedly told Melchen and his associate Captain James Barker that he wanted them to *confirm the details of a suicide* by a prominent citizen, despite having been well informed that Sir Harry's death was as obvious a case of murder as can be imagined.

As Dupuch later wrote, the Duke "reached a wrong number" by calling Melchen and Barker.

At best, the two Miami cops bungled the case. At worst, they fabricated one piece of evidence and destroyed several others in a failed attempt to frame Sir Harry's son-in-law, Count Marie Alfred Fouquereaux de Marigny.

At the time of his arrest, Freddie de Marigny seemed as likely a suspect as any available. A tall and dashing yachtsman with a reputation as a womanizer, he had been twice divorced and had reached the age of thirty-four when he stole the heart of Sir Harry's eldest daughter Nancy, then seventeen. The two were secretly married the next year.

Freddie was not popular with the more upstanding members of the community. He had shown a tendency to get on in life by marrying money, he flaunted his playboy lifestyle – his racing yacht was named *Concubine,* an outrage to the ever-so-British members of the Nassau Yacht Club – and besides all this he was decidedly French, a native of the island of Mauritius. For a number of other reasons, Freddie was not on good terms with the Oakes family, and he and Sir Harry had quarreled and exchanged mild threats publicly on more than one occasion.

He also happened to have passed by Westbourne at about the time of the murder, taking home two female guests from a dinner party, his wife and other members of the Oakes family having escaped Nassau to spend the summer in cooler climates. Melchen and Barker examined him with a magnifying glass and claimed to find singed hairs on his beard, arms, and hands, presumably from the fire that had burned Sir Harry.

With Freddie de Marigny in jail, the stage was set for one of the most widely covered trials in history. Wire services and newspapers from around the world dispatched their top reporters to Nassau, creating an unanticipated boomlet of economic and social activity in the island colony. Representing the Hearst papers was the mystery writer Erle Stanley Gardner, with a complement of three secretaries to record his words for posterity. The coverage generated by this press corps displaced the Allied invasion of Sicily and the British and American bombardment of German cities as the lead stories in American newspapers.

Nancy Oakes de Marigny was convinced her husband was innocent, and the energies expended by the nineteen-year-old may have been the deciding factor that saved de Marigny's neck. Nancy had read about the exploits of a famous private detective of the day, a man named Raymond Schindler, and she traveled to New York to hire him. Schindler in turn brought in Professor Leonard Keeler, the inventor of the lie detector.

The defense team was headed by two able young Bahamian barristers, Godfrey Higgs and, as his junior, Ernest Callender.

Through the preliminary hearing and the trial, it became clear that some powerful figure or figures in the Bahamas were making a concerted effort to tip the scales of justice against de Marigny. Here are a few of the suspicious developments:

• When arrested, de Marigny asked the police to call his lawyer, Sir Alfred Adderley, then the leading criminal defense specialist in the islands. Instead, Sir Alfred turned up as a special prosecutor at the trial. When confronted by de Marigny, he said no one had called him.

• The Commissioner of Police in the Bahamas, Lieutenant Colonel R. A. Erskine-Lindop, apparently balked at the idea of charging de Marigny and was transferred to Trinidad, preventing him from testifying at the trial. In 1951, Erskine-Lindop told Etienne Dupuch, as Dupuch later reported in the *Tribune*, that "a suspect in the case broke down under his cross-examination." The former police commissioner refused to say who he thought the guilty party was, aside from revealing that he or she continued "to move about in high society."

In an interview with this writer at his Coral Gables home, Dupuch said Erskine-Lindop's transfer was "presumably the decision of the Duke."

• The most damning piece of physical evidence against de Marigny was a fingerprint Captain Barker claimed to have lifted from a Chinese screen that stood beside Sir Harry's bed. This was the first time a fingerprint was introduced into evidence in the Bahamas. With the help of Schindler and Professor Keeler, the defense team reconstructed the photograph of the print, and was able to prove it could not have come from the Chinese screen. It is much more likely to have come from a water glass the Miami detectives handed de Marigny while questioning him at Westbourne.

The defense was also able to demonstrate that Barker, supposedly a fingerprint expert and the head of the Miami police crime lab, either deliberately or through incompetence destroyed or ignored most of the fingerprint evidence at the scene, including the bloody handprint on the wall. Photographs taken of the handprint were mysteriously exposed to light and ruined before they could be seen. Bahamian police were told they could wash off the handprint and clean up other evidence because fingerprints found on this evidence "did not match those of the accused."

• Barker lied about the time de Marigny was first interviewed at Westbourne. This was necessary because, had the actual time been given, it would have been possible for the accused to have touched the Chinese screen the day he was questioned, rather than during the murder. *This lie was corroborated by two Bahamian police officers.*

• Before the trial, a story was current in Nassau that the Bahamian watchman at Lyford Cay, an exclusive development about thirteen miles from Westbourne, had seen a powerboat pull in and let off two strange men the night of the murder. The men had later returned and been carried off by the boat. When the defense team heard the story and went looking for the watchman, they learned he had been "found drowned."

• The two watchmen who would supposedly have seen any suspicious activity at Westbourne the night of the murder – one on the grounds and the other at the adjacent Nassau Country Club – had both disappeared without a trace. This fact was alluded to during the trial proceedings, but the identities of the watchmen and their whereabouts were never revealed.

• Once de Marigny had been found not guilty, the Bahamian authorities showed a surprising lack of interest in pursuing the investigation further. A devoted crime and mystery buff who also happened to be President of the United States, Franklin D. Roosevelt, had followed the case with great interest, expounding his own theories daily to his G-men. Roosevelt offered the services of the FBI to the Duke to find the killer, but the Duke declined.

Raymond Schindler, who had basked in the publicity of the trial and coveted the greater publicity to be had in solving the case, likewise offered his services and the information he had gathered in his already extensive investigation. Again the Duke declined, and his Bahamian police became actively unfriendly to Schindler, shadowing his movements on the island.

Taken together, these circumstances make a fair case that de Marigny was framed, with the knowledge or cooperation of high-ranking Bahamian authorities.

Why? Interviewed at his home near the site of Westbourne on Nassau's Cable Beach, de Marigny's lawyer Ernest Callender saw it this way: "They [Melchen and Barker] were friends of the Duke, and the Duke wanted de Marigny. He hated Freddie."

Perhaps the reasons went beyond personal enmity. Here is another plausible explanation, though one that has never been put before a court of law.

At the same time Sir Harry Oakes was looking at the Bahamas as a place to keep his money, others were looking at the Bahamas as a place to make money. Lots of money.

One of these was Meyer Lansky, the brilliant Mafia "associate" (associate because, as a Jew, he could not be a member) who worked for and with "boss of bosses" Charles "Lucky" Luciano. In Cuba, Lansky had recently demonstrated that casinos and the tourist accommodations that go with them can be excellent sources of cash. His European casinos became so successful he built a factory to manufacture gambling equipment for them.

Lansky had moved into Cuba the same year Oakes moved into the Bahamas, acquiring the gambling concession at the Hotel Nacional in Havana. The war was causing him problems. As he later explained, "There weren't enough boats . . . and at that time you didn't have enough planes . . . you can't live from the Cuban people themselves." The living would have been better in the Bahamas, with its military personnel and its well-heeled British and American war-watchers.

Besides, the toehold in Cuba was proving to be politically slippery. Fulgencio Batista, the strongman Lansky had paid off with a $250,000 bribe, was temporarily losing his grip on the country – he would be defeated in the 1944 election, and would not seize power again until 1952.

Lansky was eager to expand, and looked at the Bahamas as the next logical step for both short- and long-term prospects. The islands were, after all, even closer to the U.S. than Cuba, and on top of that they were a beautiful place to visit. Once the casinos and hotels were ready for them, tourists could be funneled in by the plane- and cruise-boat-load.

The only problem was that casino gambling wasn't legal in the Bahamas. At least not yet.

Similar thoughts must have played through the minds of any number of legitimate Bahamian business men, among them Harold Christie. A tireless promoter of the islands, Christie was always on the lookout for a way to bring economic stability to his country. The Bahamas had historically been subject to repeated boom and bust economic cycles, and there was every reason to believe a bust would follow the boom of World War II activity. Year-round tourism was an out that could provide big income over a long haul, not to mention immense personal wealth for Christie and the rest of the Bahamian power structure.

Given this sentiment among the business community, it could be assumed that legalized casino gambling needed only the support of a few influential persons to become a reality. In fact, the support of only two persons would serve quite nicely: the Duke of Windsor and Sir Harry Oakes.

Legislation was not necessarily required. Casino gambling was prohibited in the Bahamas by the Lotteries and Gaming Act of 1905. However, an extremely exclusive establishment known as the Bahamian Club had operated a small private casino illegally, during the three-month-long "Season," since 1920, and this Act was amended in 1939 to give the Governor authority to exempt certain establishments from the Act as he saw fit. While the intent of the amendment had been to legalize the Bahamian Club, Windsor could have used it to grant other gaming licenses if he thought it prudent to do so.

From today's perspective, one of the most puzzling aspects

of the Oakes case is the character of Harold Christie. By most accounts a kind man who did a lot of good for a lot of people, Christie, who was knighted in 1964 and died ten years later, is remembered with reverence in the Bahamas. His efforts to bring prosperity to his countrymen were tenacious and successful. But with a good deal of digging it is possible to confirm that Christie was involved – with his brother Frank – in the rum-running business during Prohibition. As to Christie's part in the Oakes case, lawyer Callender will only say mildly, "I think Sir Harold knew more than he was telling."

A recent theory of the case names Sir Harold as the murderer. More well-worn theories make him an accessory. He fits into the casino theory through his early connection with illegal booze.

Prohibition in the United States had been a huge boon to the Bahamas, so much so that rum-running had been a leading national industry, much as blockade-running to Confederate ports had been during the American Civil War, and as ship-wrecking and piracy had been in earlier days. Christie was one of a great many Bahamians of his era who indulged in the lucrative trade of sending booze off to Florida in fast boats. Awaiting these shipments on the Florida side was Meyer Lansky, a man who knew the daring young Bahamians well. A story is told that, based on this earlier acquaintance, Lansky approached the now influential Christie with his proposition for Bahamian casinos.

According to this theory, Christie may have been able to convince the Duke that casino gambling and resorts would be good for the Bahamas. They might also be good for the Duke. Sizable quantities of cash – rumor says the payoff to break the ice in the Bahamas came to $1 million – would have been available for those willing to help, and Windsor was constantly in need of money to support his spend-thrift habits. He and his wife were also given to complaining how deadly dull life in the Bahamas could be. A few casino hotels would enliven the social scene immensely.

The stubborn Harry Oakes would not have been so easily convinced.

Why should he be? Could Sir Harry have enjoyed the prospect of thousands of tourists trampling daily across the island he ruled? Probably not. He didn't need money. He didn't seem the sort to share the good things of his life with strangers. He himself owned the staid old British Colonial Hotel – having reportedly bought it to take revenge on a maitre d' who had given him a bad seat because of his grubby clothes – and was perfectly happy to watch it sit largely unoccupied during the nine-month-long off-season. Presented with a proposition for modern resort hotels and casinos in his neighborhood, Sir Harry would in all likelihood have told the proposer where to go and what to do when there.

Following the theory, this resistance to progress was Sir Harry's death warrant. A tale often told is that Sir Harry was done in on a boat during an attempted reconciliation with Lansky's men, then taken back to Westbourne with Harold Christie – who had not expected violence – riding along in a state of panic.

If true, this would explain why Captain Edward Sears, the Superintendent of Police and a well-respected officer, testified at the trial that he had seen Harold Christie on the passenger side of the front seat of a station wagon in downtown Nassau on the night of the murder.

Sears had known Christie all his life. The place he said he saw Christie is directly on the route between Westbourne and Prince George's Wharf, where an incoming boat could have been moored. Christie owned a station wagon and had it with him at Westbourne, but vehemently denied having left Westbourne during the night of the murder.

It would also explain why the body had been moved and why mud had been tracked on the stairs. The fire may have been started to burn down the house and cover up the crime, or may have been meant only to mutilate the body as a gruesome warning to the uncooperative.

Whether or not we accept this version of events in all its particulars, certain later developments lend support to the casino theory.

If Sir Harry was the dam holding back the flood of tourists, the floodgates opened in the years following his death. In 1937, a peak prewar year for tourism, the Bahamas attracted 34,000 visitors. In 1984, 2,325,250 people came and went. Among Caribbean nations, the Bahamas is far and away the most successful marketer of tourism.

Certainly this startling growth in the key Bahamian industry has to do with a great deal more than the death of Sir Harry Oakes. It involves the hard work of Sir Harold Christie, after him of Sir Stafford Sands, and of many others since. But casinos are an undeniably important factor. And so is the switch in strategy from attempts to attract the few available Harry Oakeses of the world to attempts to attract anybody and everybody who can afford a cut-rate package fare.

Though it took twenty years, casinos did come to the Bahamas, and when they did Meyer Lansky's people came with them. The Duke of Windsor had left the scene in May of 1945, resigning before his term as governor was up. Perhaps because of the uproar over Oakes's death, no serious push was made for legalization until the early 1950s. When Castro came to power in Cuba in 1959, the need for Bahamian casinos became acute.

By 1962, the Mafia had given up on its efforts – some of them in cooperation with the CIA – to overthrow or kill Castro, and the pressure in the Bahamas was turned up several notches. The pressure brought results in 1963, after generous "consultancy" fees were paid to high-ranking Bahamians by an American businessman and convicted mail-fraud practitioner named Wallace Groves.

Once the dice were rolling in the new casino at the Lucayan Beach Hotel in Freeport, FBI agents followed with interest the movements of one Dusty Peters, as he made regular deliveries of large amounts of cash from the first Bahamian casino to a man waiting in Florida. The waiting man was Meyer Lansky.

In Miami, Captain Barker had been shot dead by his own son some years earlier during a domestic argument. Investigations indicated Barker, who had become a drug addict, had been in the pay of the local mobsters for an undetermined number of years before his death.

American press coverage of mob involvement in Bahamian casinos was the straw that broke the back of white minority rule in Nassau. Prime Minister Lynden Pindling's Progressive Labor Party came to power January 10, 1967, and has held power ever since.

Over time, the PLP's pledge to clean up corruption has developed an empty ring. In December 1984, a special Commission of Inquiry appointed to investigate the involvement of government officials in drug trafficking reported that "corruption must have reached to a senior level of government." Serious allegations of influence-peddling were aired about the Prime Minister and several of his cabinet ministers, and some of the alleged payoffs involved subsidiaries and consultants of Resorts International, the company that operates the casino just across the picturesque harbor from Nassau.

If Sir Harry did die so that casino gambling could live, his death was followed by a final insult. The Ambassador Beach Hotel and Casino was erected on the site of Westbourne. The casino has since moved into larger quarters just down Cable Beach.

The casino-tourism connection is by no means the only explanation for the murder of Sir Harry Oakes. There are several other theories tracking with the available evidence in varying degrees.

One proposes a simple robbery-murder, because Sir Harry was rumored to have been hoarding gold. This theory was given a boost in the 1950s when a family living on Great Exuma, one of the Bahamian out islands, began making purchases with gold coins. The family said the coins had been found in a cave. One of the family members was said to have worked in the Oakes household at one time. Bahamian police investigated but could prove no connection between the family's windfall and the Oakes murder.

A less straightforward theory has the added spice of espionage. Sir Harry was an acquaintance of another man of enormous wealth, a Swedish industrialist named Axel Wenner-Gren who maintained a large estate called Shangri-La on Paradise Island, which was known in those pretourism days by the more prosaic name of Hog Island.

Wenner-Gren owned the Electrolux Company, which made vacuum cleaners and appliances, and the Bofors Munition Works, which made guns. Though he professed neutrality, he was widely rumored to be a Nazi spy. Both American and British intelligence were greatly interested in his movements, especially when he set off in his 320-foot yacht *Southern Cross,* which had been owned by Howard Hughes and was said to be the largest private yacht in the world. It was also the best equipped with sophisticated radio equipment and with arms, which Wenner-Gren claimed to carry for demonstration purposes.

Wenner-Gren had a lot of connections. He was a good friend of Hermann Goering and Mussolini. And the Duke of Windsor, who was a frequent guest and traveler on *Southern Cross* in the days before Wenner-Gren was blacklisted by the British and American governments and thus prevented from entering the Bahamas.

The Swede established a bank in Mexico, the Banco de Continental, and was pursuing other investments in that country. Allied intelligence thought this bank might be useful in deals for petroleum and arms, two commodities the Nazis needed badly.

Wenner-Gren needed the bank for personal deals, as most of his cash had been frozen by the Allied governments. Among the bank's customers were a number of prominent Bahamians, among them Wenner-Gren's friends Sir Harry Oakes, Harold Christie, and the Duke of Windsor. Wenner-Gren was said to be helping these friends circumvent wartime currency regulations by moving funds around for them, and Sir Harry was said to be interested in the Mexican investment schemes.

Perhaps Sir Harry was killed to prevent his moving his fortune out of the Bahamas and into Mexico. Perhaps he knew too much about an espionage operation. Perhaps, as American intelligence people once believed, Wenner-Gren was plotting to control the economy of Mexico, using his friends' money and his connections to the pro-Fascist General Maximino Camacho, brother of the Mexican President. Perhaps Oakes paid for his involvement with his life. These and other lines of speculation have been drawn between the activities of the enigmatic Swede and the murder, but with only the aid of sketchy, and circumstantial, evidence.

Another theory finds its appeal in the occult. Because the fire and the feathers suggest ritual murder, some have divined the thrillingly sinister presence of black magic in the Oakes case.

In the Bahamas, the practice of magic is called Obeah. Like voodoo, Obeah has its roots in African shamanism, well mixed with later acquired bits of Christian teachings. But unlike voodoo, Obeah is not a religion. It is not practiced by organized groups but by individuals who sell their services to clients.

For those who believe, Obeah can cure a sickness, protect a crop from theft or harm, bring success in love or business. It can even kill. But Obeah does not kill with a blunt instrument against the skull; it kills by magic from afar, sometimes aided by poison from close range. And the use of Obeah would presuppose a motive – sexual jealousy, revenge for mistreatment of some kind – that is not known to exist.

Obeah is practiced by black Bahamians, and Sir Harry had done more to improve the lot of black Bahamians than any other white man of his time. Some turn the black magic formula around and have Sir Harry killed by white racists who disapproved of his raising the wages and expectations of blacks and who attempted to cover their tracks by seeming to have used Obeah.

None of these interesting theories is supported by the weight of evidence, albeit circumstantial, that supports the casino argument. And none explains so neatly the desperate need to frame Alfred de Marigny and to cover up any other explanations of the crime.

A recent solution to the Oakes mystery was provided by author Charles Higham, in his biography of the Duchess of Windsor. Higham mixes a little black magic with some hard information from declassified documents and a lot of supposition about the actions of Sir Harold Christie.

Higham says Harold killed Harry, because Harry was about to call in some large IOU's and ruin Harold financially. According to Higham, Oakes was mad because Christie had cut him out of a major real estate deal. The actual killing was done by a hit man-witch doctor who belonged to the Brujeria sect, and who was imported for the assignment from south Florida. Higham says the head wounds were caused by a fishing spear, and that the pattern of the wounds and the use of feathers and small fires were typical of the ritual killings practiced by the sect. He goes into great detail in his reconstruction of the crime, apparently relying heavily on his own imagination. He thinks the hit man was really a hit dwarf, thus explaining the bloody handprint four feet from the floor.

According to Higham, the Duke was forced to run his cover-up operation and to frame de Marigny not because of the involvement of American gangsters, but because racial tensions on the island were high – there had been recent rioting – and the ritual aspects of the evidence strongly suggested the guilty party was a black man. To maintain peace, the Duke needed a white man as a fall guy and de Marigny was handy and conveniently unpopular.

The Christie-as-killer theory is given credibility by Higham's use of recently declassified FBI documents that suggest the Nassau police knew Sir Harold was guilty all along and, for some reason, never pursued him. Perhaps this explains Commissioner Erskine-Lindop's tantalizing report of a confessed killer who continued "to move about in high society." Interestingly, Sir Harold fits as snugly as a killer in the casino theory as he does in Higham's reconstruction.

Who killed Sir Harry Oakes? Each passing year makes it less likely that there will ever be a conclusive answer. Whoever swung the fatal instrument, the force that killed Harry Oakes was almost surely greed, the same force that bought and paid for his golden island in the sun.

At various periods of their long and fascinating history, Bahamians have lived by piracy, by blockade-running, by ship-wrecking, by bootlegging. Now they live by the relatively innocent trade of tourism. By packing them in to Paradise. By showing them, if only for a few hard-earned days, an enchanted kingdom that anyone's money can buy.

Postscript

Not much has come to light about the Oakes case, but a great deal of fun has been had with it. One recent book claimed the Duchess of Windsor was "genetically" a man. (Reviewer Peter Kurth felt the book "shouldn't be critiqued so much as held at a distance with tongs.")

The case has spawned at least two TV movies, a mini series, and a stage play. The play posits that the Duke and Duchess framed Freddie de Marigny to protect the real killer, Harold Christie, because Christie could've spilled the beans about their money-laundering for the Nazis. In the play, the Duchess has sex with Freddie because she wants to "sleep with the condemned man."

De Marigny wrote his own book about the business. He pegs Harold Christie as the killer too, and says he was framed to cover up the money shipments to Mexico.

In an interview with *Maclean's*, de Marigny quoted an old Chinese maxim: "Never avenge yourself. Sit on your doorstep and one day you will see the corpse of your enemy go by."

"All the corpses," he concluded, " have gone by."

4

The Dumb Blonde
Who Knew Too Much

The Death of Marilyn Monroe

"Being a sex symbol is a heavy load to carry,
especially when one is tired, hurt, and bewildered."

Clara Bow

"It's all make believe, isn't it?"

Marilyn Monroe

In the world she moved through, nobody who mattered used
their real names. The names they used were made up for them,
like magical incantations. But she was never sure of her real
name, so even by the standards of this world of make-believe,
she was an insubstantial creature. The actress the world knows
as Marilyn Monroe created herself anew each day. What she
created was a dream, a myth, the closest thing our times have
summoned to a love goddess in the flesh. The death that came
to her had all the scope of emotive possibilities she had brought
to every day in life. From one perspective, it was squalid,
pointless, and pitiable. From another, it was of itself a myth, an
epic role in a drama involving the most potent names and
players of her age.

Sometime in the night of August 4, 1962, Marilyn Monroe
slipped away into the ultimate unreality, riding a massive dose
of Nembutal and chloral hydrate. The Chief Medical Examiner
of Los Angeles County made a hedging call on the cause of

death – "*probable* suicide." Other investigators, with considerable evidence but no hard proof, are still calling it murder.

Murder, accident, or suicide, Marilyn's death is a mystery today not because of differing interpretations of the facts, but because this mistress of make-believe had been playing in a real and dangerous world, and the monarchs of that world were powerful enough to rewrite the script of her last hours.

In life and death, Marilyn embodied a supremely surreal and ambiguous version of the all-American success story. Raised in orphanages and foster homes, she became the Queen of Hollywood, using her talent and her body in equal measure to ascend from one imagined tier to the next. By the end she had achieved everything any starry-eyed bit player could dream of, and along the way she had bedded a president, married a sports legend and a literary giant, and captured the adulation of the world more completely than any actress of any time. She could be in turns a bitch and a baby, cunning and helpless, the goddess of sexual promise and the ghost of oblivion. She was a woman who could move, in the same afternoon, from a trembling mess of insecurity and self-doubt into an absolute master of her art. No one before or since has put more electricity and magic onto a piece of film.

The baby girl born at Los Angeles General Hospital at 9.30 a.m. on June 1, 1926, was named Norma Jean Baker. The first name was inspired by the actress Norma Talmadge. The last was a convenience, borrowed from her mother's departed second husband. Though the matter has been endlessly researched, the identity of Marilyn's real father has never been firmly established. There are several candidates, the leading one a man named Gifford, who worked with her mother. The search for a father would become one of the themes of Norma Jean's strange life. A number of surrogates – in fantasy, Clark Gable was a favorite – would fill and abandon the role.

The child who would be Marilyn had little more in the way of a mother. At the time of her daughter's birth, Gladys Pearl Baker Mortenson was a delicately beautiful woman in her mid-twenties, working as a negative cutter at Consolidated Film Industries. She had two other children – a boy and a girl – who were living in the custody of her first husband's family.

Norma Jean spent her first eight years with foster families while her mother worked, visiting the child on weekends. In 1934, mother and daughter lived in the same household for a few months – the longest period they would spend together during Norma Jean's childhood – until Gladys suffered the first of many mental collapses and entered the same state hospital in which her own mother had died. The mother of Marilyn Monroe would spent most of the rest of her days in institutions, diagnosed – like her parents and brother before her – as a paranoid schizophrenic.

At nine, Norma Jean entered an orphanage and slept by a window overlooking the RKO studios. Beginning at eleven, she migrated from foster homes to guardians. Biographers have charted a total of twelve different households, not including the orphanage, inhabited by young Norma Jean before her marriage at sixteen. This upbringing did little to build a stable personality. After her transformation into movie stardom, Marilyn would milk the poor-orphan story for all it was worth with writers and studio publicists. Her accounts included an attempted smothering by her grandmother and no fewer than ten episodes of rape or molestation, beginning at age six. Even allowing for her exaggerations and self-contradictions, there is no doubt that Marilyn's childhood was a perfect breeding ground for insecurity and loneliness.

Norma Jean's first marriage, to a twenty-one-year-old former high school hero named Jim Dougherty, was more or less arranged by her guardian of the moment, who was moving out of state and preferred not to take the teenage girl along. In later years, Jim would remember the marriage more fondly than Marilyn. However happily it may have begun, the marriage was doomed when Jim shipped out with the merchant marine and the head of his luscious young bride was turned toward a career in modeling. With every stunning photograph, with every line of agent's hype and every leer from ad executives and movie producers, Norma Jean moved closer to rebirth as Marilyn.

The official incarnation happened while Norma Jean was working as a contract player for 20th Century-Fox in 1946. Ben Lyon, the Fox casting director, borrowed the name Marilyn from an actress he admired named Marilyn Miller. Marilyn herself contributed Monroe – it was the maiden name of her grandmother.

Her first screen appearance came the following year, at the age of twenty-one. Marilyn briefly rowed a canoe in an insipid movie starring a team of mules and titled *Scudda Hoo! Scudda Hay!* The infamously jiggling Monroe walk had its debut in a bit part in a Marx Brothers movie called *Love Happy* (1949), causing Groucho to evaluate the young starlet as "Mae West, Theda Bara, and Bo Peep all rolled into one." The importance of these early cameos was that Marilyn's uncanny ability to make love to a camera lens was being noticed by the men who owned the cameras. She was not, by Hollywood standards, an exceptionally beautiful woman. She was an exceptionally photogenic woman, and that was all that mattered. Remembering his first session with Marilyn in an early screen test, veteran cinematographer Leon Shamroy says, "I got a cold chill. This girl had something I hadn't seen since silent pictures. She had a kind of fantastic beauty . . . she got sex on a piece of film."

She also knew how to use sex on a casting couch, and her talents in this line contributed as much to her early successes as her undeniable screen presence. One advantageous relationship was with the seventy-year-old Joseph Schenck, the head of production at Fox and one of the founders of the company. Another was with a powerful agent named Johnny Hyde. Marilyn minced no words in describing her attitude at this stage of her career: "I spent a lot of time on my knees." There were genuine love affairs to go with the affairs of business, and a good deal of near-pathological abandon. By the end of her life, Marilyn may have undergone as many as fourteen abortions.

Hampered by the studios' unfortunate choices of vehicles to showcase her talents, the on-screen Marilyn remained more a sexpot than a major star until her twentieth picture, *Gentlemen Prefer Blondes* (1953). A succession of movie classics followed, among them *The Seven Year Itch* (1955), *Bus Stop* (1956), and *Some Like It Hot* (1959).

She was the movie star she had dreamed of being, lived to be. More than that, she had become a marvelous, if difficult, actress who worked long and seriously at her craft. She built these powers by a force of will, but the one thing she could never build was a complete and secure human being to occupy Marilyn's – or Norma Jean's – celebrated body. Take the time to sift through the recollections of those who knew her, and one word of description will occur more frequently than any other. The word is not "sex" – though the person described packaged and sold sex more powerfully than anyone. The word is "child." Marilyn Monroe was a child, sometimes petulant and obnoxious, sometimes spontaneous and effervescent and living to charm and please, but more times than anything, afraid. Afraid of being unloved and alone.

Though lacking in formal education, this child-woman was not the dumb blonde she played in the movies. The saber wit and the insights into character were not created by the scriptwriters. One example. An attempt is made to blackmail the studio because Marilyn's nude image has been discovered on a cheesecake calendar, which will make millions for its publishers but which was shot years before when Norma Jean needed the fifty bucks she was paid for the session. The time is the prudish early 1950s, but Marilyn skates through the thin ice to an enormous publicity advantage with a crowded press conference.

Reporter: Is it true you didn't have *anything* on when these pictures were taken?

Marilyn: We had the radio on.

In January of 1954, just as she ascended to the heights of stardom, Marilyn married another star who had been longer and even more widely adored. He was Joltin' Joe DiMaggio, the Yankee Clipper, one of the greatest baseball players ever to swing a bat and the man who had held America in his grip during the entire summer of 1941, hitting in fifty-six straight games. The courtship had made good copy for a year and a half. The marriage lasted nine months. Joltin' Joe, it seemed, wanted a wife more than a movie star. Still, Joe could "hit homes runs" in bed; but more than that, he was something Marilyn couldn't find in Hollywood. He was "genuine" and he loved her as a woman. He would reemerge as a friend and protector in the last year of her life, and he would be the guardian of her violated body at the end.

In the summer of 1956, a second star from an entirely different constellation joined the goddess of love in marriage. Arthur Miller was – with Tennessee Williams – one of the two great living playwrights in America. For Marilyn, who desperately wanted to be taken seriously as an actress, the oh so serious playwright held all the fascination of the one who supplies the deathless words for the one who speaks them. In the media, it was the wedding of the Beauty and the Brain, the Egghead and the Hourglass. It proved to be a storybook romance that could not survive a prolonged reading by the eyes of the real world. After many difficulties, the divorce came at the beginning of 1961.

There was, or at least there may have been, another "marriage." This marriage – if real – would have been the second, before DiMaggio and after Jim Dougherty. Though undocumented, this marriage is of great interest to those who believe Marilyn Monroe was murdered, for it was to the man who has maintained a single-minded crusade to expose the murder to the world, a man named Robert Slatzer. Slatzer is a writer and producer who met Marilyn in the summer of 1946, when he was a young fan-magazine reporter and she was the struggling model and would-be starlet Norma Jean Mortenson. Slatzer has subsequently claimed that he and Marilyn fell in love and were married in an alcoholic haze in Tijuana, on

October 4, 1952. According to his account, the young couple lived together as man and wife "about three-days," until they were strong-armed by Darryl F. Zanuck – the head of 20th Century-Fox and Marilyn's boss at the time – into annulling the marriage and having all records of it destroyed.

Monroe's biographers are divided on the marriage story. It is well established that Robert Slatzer and Marilyn were certainly good friends, and that their friendship extended from the late 1940s until her death in 1962. In any case, Slatzer's credibility is a crucial issue in the murder story, as much of the first-hand evidence in the case comes either directly from him or from his long and determined legwork.

To accompany the confirmed and could-be husbands there is a Homeric list of confirmed and could-be lovers. Marilyn could be ambivalent about how much she personally enjoyed the sex act, but there is no doubt she enjoyed attracting men. "If fifteen men were in the room with her," said one Hollywood publicist, "each would be convinced he was the one she'd be waiting for after the others left." Through personal magnetism, compulsion, or both, she raised the art of seduction to a new level. Not too surprisingly, a vast number of the men who had speaking acquaintances with her have claimed at one time or another to have shared her bed. But for our purposes the most interesting of the lovers are those who could not afford to brag. Of these there are two more interesting than all: the President of the United States and his brother, the Attorney General.

Some accounts trace the origin of Marilyn's affair with John F. Kennedy to the early 1950s, when Kennedy was a rising star in the U.S. Senate and Marilyn was an established sex symbol in Hollywood. Other sources say the romance began just before Kennedy received his party's nomination for president in 1960. Whenever it may have started, the affair – judging by the independent testimony of several who witnessed it first-hand – seems to have reached its peak in the early, heady days of the Kennedy presidency, through the offices – and in the beachfront Santa Monica home – of the President's brother-in-law, actor

Peter Lawford. The timing of the coupling is significant. Marilyn was at the end of a marriage and in a downward spiral both professionally and personally, due to heavy drug abuse and the endless drain of her own insecurities. John Kennedy was very much married and the most powerful man in the world. As a security risk, the unstable Marilyn was as risky as they come.

Not that John Kennedy was above taking risks where sexual adventure was concerned. The list of *his* confirmed and could-be liaisons rivals Marilyn's in its proportions. For Kennedy – and his brother Robert – the indiscretions may have seemed a sort of family tradition. "Dad," JFK revealed to Clare Boothe Luce, "told all the boys to get laid as often as possible." Joe Kennedy had taken his own advice. He himself had reportedly enjoyed Hollywood girlfriends in his heyday, the most famous being Gloria Swanson.

Robert Kennedy's fling with Marilyn is less well documented than his brother's, and its beginnings are no less difficult to trace. There are those who claim Robert was the first Kennedy to date Monroe. At least one first-hand account, however, suggests that Robert's affair began as the President's was ending – in the summer and fall of 1961. The inference has been drawn that the younger Kennedy was enlisted to soften the blow of the end of the President's dalliance, and that he, like so many others, found Marilyn's temptations impossible to resist. However and whenever it started, this affair appears to have continued until just prior to Marilyn's death in August of 1962. At least from Marilyn's viewpoint, there was an important difference between the ways the two brothers conducted their affairs. From what she reportedly told others, it seems the love goddess took Robert Kennedy's attentions more seriously than John's. Speaking of the President, she could be lighthearted: "I think I made his back feel better" and "I made it with the Prez." Of the Attorney General: "Bobby Kennedy promised to marry me."

Again, the timing relative to Marilyn's state of mind is important. Her life, never securely anchored, was becoming increasingly unraveled as the decade of the 1950s wore into the 1960s. Her attempted "suicides" – some or all of which were accidental overdoses – had recurred perhaps a dozen times, with increasing frequency in later years. Her tendency to keep whole, and enormously expensive, film production ensembles awaiting her appearance for hours and even days had increased to the point that she had been fired from her last film, *Something's Got to Give,* on June 8, 1962, after showing up on the set only twelve times during thirty-three scheduled shooting days. Marilyn's last day before the cameras had been June 1, her thirty-sixth birthday. Her psychiatrist had noted an alarming disintegration beginning in the summer of 1961, including "severe depressive" reactions, suicidal tendencies, increased drug use, and random promiscuity. She may have been a goddess, but she was not a goddess to be trusted with anybody's secrets. And the Attorney General of the United States may have trusted her with the most important secrets that he knew.

The source for this intriguing possibility is Robert Slatzer. Slatzer was one of a number of friends in whom Marilyn confided about her affairs with the Kennedy brothers, but he appears to be the only one she told about Robert Kennedy's weakness for dangerously indiscreet pillow talk. Slatzer says Marilyn told him Bobby had become annoyed when she forgot things he had told her during previous visits, and that she had resorted – unbeknownst to the Attorney General – to making notes of their conversations in a red diary. Ten days before she died, Marilyn showed Slatzer the diary, as they sat on a beach at Point Dume, north of Malibu on the Pacific Coast Highway. Most of the entries, Slatzer says, began with "Bobby told me." He remembers entries about Kennedy's war with Jimmy Hoffa and the Mafia, with Kennedy swearing to "put that SOB behind bars." But most chillingly, he remembers an entry that read, "Bobby told me he was going to have . . . Castro murdered."

The Kennedy administration's bungling attempts to kill Fidel Castro – through the strangely combined efforts of the CIA, anti-Castro Cubans, and the American Mafia – first came to light during U.S. Senate hearings in the mid 1970s, and have since become common knowledge. But in 1962, a revelation of this kind would have been the most dangerous political fiasco imaginable. It could certainly have done critical damage to the administration; it could feasibly have started a nuclear confrontation; it could even cause the assassination of the President of the United States – which, as a matter of fact, it may well have.

According to Slatzer, Marilyn not only knew these state secrets, she was prepared to tell the world about them. He says she talked of plans to call a press conference and "blow the lid off this whole damn thing," revealing her affairs with the two Kennedys and the broken "promises that had been made to her." The date allegedly mentioned for the press conference was Monday, August 6, 1962 – the day after she was pronounced dead. Slatzer says he asked if Marilyn had told anyone else of her plans for the press conference and she replied that she had told "a few people." He claims to have warned her that what she knew was "like having a walking time bomb," but that she said she "didn't care at this point . . . these people had used her . . . and she was going to . . . tell the real story."

Some confirmation of Slatzer's story comes from Peter Lawford's ex-wife Deborah Gould. Gould has said that – years after the fact – Lawford broke down and offered a tearful account of the end of Marilyn's life. Taken as a whole, Lawford's "confession" raises as many questions as it answers. But in this case Lawford's alleged account echoes Slatzer's: Marilyn tells Lawford, "I've been used . . . thrown from one man to another . . . and I'm going public with everything." If Marilyn wanted word of this threat to get back to the Kennedys, she could have chosen no better vehicle than Peter Lawford.

There is no record that Marilyn notified anyone in the media about plans for a press conference. The fact remains that the mere suggestion of such an ultimatum could have been an extremely dangerous gambit. It appears Marilyn was desperate enough to play this card in hopes that it would force Robert

Kennedy to contact her. She had told several friends that Robert had abruptly ended the affair, and no longer called her or returned her phone calls. He had gone so far, she said, as to disconnect the private number he had given her, and the Justice Department operators refused to put her calls to the main switchboard through. Marilyn's frequent calls to Justice during July of 1962 are documented on her phone records. The last call for which records are available was placed July 30, the Monday before her death.

Marilyn's reasons for calling Robert Kennedy may have gone beyond the sting of the spurned lover. In late June, she told an interviewer, "A woman must have to love a man with all her heart to have his child . . . especially when she's not married to him. And when a man leaves a woman when she tells him she's going to have his baby, when he doesn't marry her, that must hurt a woman very much, deep down inside." Between late June and early July, she told several friends that she had lost a baby, without specifying abortion or miscarriage. To some friends she confided that the father had been John Kennedy, to others, Robert. At least two sources have reported that there was an abortion, performed in Tijuana by an American doctor. Depending on which authority you trust, this may have been the fourteenth abortion of Marilyn's life, an especially sad count for a child-woman who spent her final interviews talking about how much she wanted a child of her own. During the same period, Marilyn told several friends – to universal disbelief – that she and the Attorney General would someday be married.

In the available accounts of these last scenes of her life, there is another word that crops up frequently in descriptions of Marilyn. The word is scared. One long-time friend, Arthur James, recalls that Marilyn was "frightened stiff." Slatzer says she told him that "because of circumstances that led all the way to Washington," she was "scared for her life." James and others say she became convinced that she was being watched, that her phones were bugged, and that she resorted to making personal calls from a phone booth in a park near her home, lugging pocketfuls of change for this purpose.

Marilyn may have had paranoid tendencies, but in this instance she was very much in tune with the real world. She was right about the phones. She was right about being watched. In fact her whole home was bugged, and so was Peter Lawford's home, where she had rendezvoused with her two most powerful lovers. The bugging was not being done by the government.

Though she almost surely did not know it, the recording devices and the sinister people behind them may have been precisely the reason Robert Kennedy had become incommunicado. Kennedy was in the fifth year of a personal war against organized crime in general and Teamsters Union President Jimmy Hoffa in particular. The struggle had been joined when Kennedy was Chief Counsel to the McClellan Committee in the U.S. Senate, and carried on, with unprecedented force, when he became Attorney General. Hoffa was convinced Robert Kennedy had used the attack on his union as a stepping stone to national power for himself and his brother, and in a sense he was right. The union boss and his mob friends hated both of the elder Kennedy brothers enough to want them dead – and were reportedly not above saying so, among themselves – but they especially hated Bobby.

In the course of the struggle, Robert Kennedy had created a special "Get Hoffa" strike force in the Justice Department, with the FBI, the IRS, and the government itself aligned on his side. But Jimmy Hoffa and his Mafia allies were not without their own resources and their own considerable army of foot soldiers. Hoffa knew the Kennedys were vulnerable because of their womanizing. When he learned of the amorous dance of John and Robert and Marilyn Monroe – by one account the information came to him as early as 1957 – he must have rubbed his hands in glee.

The ideal weapon for this phase of the war on Kennedy happened to be a human being who happened to already be on

Hoffa's payroll – the man acknowledged by his peers to be the best wiretapper in the world, one Bernard Bates Spindel. Spindel had learned the basics of his trade in the U.S. Army Signal Corps and in army intelligence during World War II. One of the ironies of his remarkable career is that he could easily have served on the Kennedy side in the bugging wars: as a young man he applied for a job with the CIA but was rejected. Though he is said to have worked both sides of the fence thereafter, Bernie Spindel spent the bulk of the rest of his days beating the government spooks at their own game. Spindel had been taping Robert Kennedy for his client Jimmy Hoffa since at least the late 1950s. According to Hollywood-based private eye Fred Otash, Spindel got the Marilyn Monroe assignment in the summer of 1961.

Otash has said Hoffa summoned him and Spindel to a meeting in Florida that summer. Hoffa wanted "to develop a derogatory profile of Jack and Bobby Kennedy and their relationships with Marilyn Monroe and with any other woman. The strategy . . . was to use electronic devices." The first target was Peter Lawford's home, where bugs were placed not only on the phone lines but "in the carpets . . . under chandeliers and in ceiling fixtures." Otash says the tapes from the Lawford bugging contained conversations between both Kennedys and Marilyn, and phone conversation to arrange rendezvous between both Kennedys and Marilyn, and both Kennedys and other women.

Another private detective who worked on the assignment, John Danoff, has been more graphic in his description of the tapes from the Lawford house: it "was cuddly talk and taking off their clothes and the sex act in the bed – you could hear the springs squeaking and so on."

If this was good stuff, maybe better stuff could be had at Marilyn's home, the modest Spanish-style house in Brentwood in which she spent the last months of her life. Marilyn's friend Arthur James says he was asked in the spring of 1962 to get Marilyn out of the house so that "people could come in there and bug . . . for the purpose of getting evidence on Bobby Kennedy." James says he turned the request down, and never told Marilyn about it. The house was bugged anyway. Examination in later years turned up indications of eavesdropping devices both on the phones and on the premises.

Despite all these frightening developments, there are indications Marilyn had rebounded to some extent from her depressions during her last few days. The studio, with reluctance but with little choice in the matter, had rehired her on *Something's Got to Give,* and shooting was set to resume before the end of 1962. She was negotiating on other film projects, giving interviews, enjoying setting up and landscaping the Brentwood house, the first home she had bought and lived in on her own. She had set several appointments for the week that would follow her death. Though never a model of stability, she did not appear to be a person who was contemplating suicide.

The Brentwood household included a housekeeper-companion, a sixty-year-old woman named Eunice Murray, who had been installed by Marilyn's psychiatrist, Dr. Ralph Greenson. Mrs. Murray, who seems to have had some experience dealing with psychiatric patients, came on the scene after Marilyn had alienated a succession of nurses. It was Mrs. Murray who had found the Brentwood house for Marilyn to buy, and Mrs. Murray who brought her own son-in-law into the household as a salaried handyman. The housekeeper and the handyman were two of many links between the film star and the psychiatrist. During her final summer, Marilyn saw Dr. Greenson in his professional capacity as often as twice a day. She also relied on him increasingly for advice and moral support, spent a great deal of time in his home, and became close to his children. Marilyn came to depend on Greenson so heavily that some of her friends observed that the doctor was, in effect, running her life. It was a pattern she had lived through before with her acting coaches, and if it troubled her there is only one indication that she may have been trying to change it: a report that she made inquiries about replacing Mrs. Murray with a housekeeper of her own choosing at the end of July, just before she died.

As it happens, Mrs. Murray has become the enigma within the riddle of the Marilyn Monroe case. Her evidence is critical, because, according to the officially accepted version of events, she was the only other person in the house when Marilyn died. But beginning with her first statements to police that night, and stretching almost to the present day, her accounts have been so abstruse, ever-changing, and self-contradictory that they may be interpreted in any number of vastly different ways. In the impossible event that any party or parties were ever put on trial for the murder of Marilyn Monroe, one can imagine Mrs. Murray in the role of witness for either the defense or the prosecution, depending on the story she chooses to tell on that particular day. It is hard to escape the conclusion that this kindly and soft-spoken old lady is either impossibly befuddled or is doggedly hiding a dangerous truth.

Mrs. Murray is not alone in her capacity for confusion about the last hours of Marilyn's life. In fact, virtually all of the small number of people who spent extended periods of time with Marilyn that weekend have shown an alarming tendency to forget or to offer contradictory stories, so much so that their testimony would seem highly suspicious even if there were no other reason to doubt the official suicide verdict. And there are plenty of other reasons.

Given all the fuzzy recollections, it is impossible to reconstruct with any certainty the last two days Marilyn Monroe spent on this earth. There are a few documented facts. One is that Robert Kennedy was in California that weekend. With his wife and four children in tow, he was to address the American Bar Association meeting in San Francisco, staying at the ranch of a lawyer named John Bates, about sixty miles south of the city. Marilyn knew Kennedy was coming, and was still desperately trying to contact him. Her phone records for the four days she lived in August were mysteriously confiscated, but an enterprising reporter established that she made several calls to the

San Francisco hotel where the Bar Association had reserved rooms for Kennedy, and that the calls were not returned. Bit by bit, evidence has emerged that Kennedy left the San Francisco area to visit Marilyn that weekend. His host John Bates has steadfastly insisted that this could not have happened. A number of other witnesses, including Los Angeles police, claim otherwise.

For her part, Marilyn spent the early hours of Friday shopping for plants to landscape her yard. She visited her doctor and her psychiatrist. No one has clearly established what she did that night. One of the questionable sources for Marilyn's activities that weekend, her press aide Pat Newcomb – who later worked for and was close to the Kennedys – has said she and Marilyn dined at one of their favorite Santa Monica restaurants that evening, but that she could not recall the name or location of the restaurant.

At dawn on Saturday, August 4, Marilyn's friend and self-described "sleeping-pill buddy" Jeanne Carmen received a phone call from Marilyn, speaking in "a frightened voice . . . and very tired – she said she had not slept the entire night" and complaining about "'phone call after phone call after phone call' with some woman . . . saying, 'you tramp . . . leave Bobby alone or you're going to be in deep trouble.'" During this call and twice later in the day, Marilyn asked Carmen to come over and "bring a bag of pills" but Carmen was busy and couldn't comply.

Marilyn made a number of other phone calls during the morning – one to her friend and masseur Ralph Roberts, making a tentative plan for dinner at her home that evening. At one point Mrs. Murray's son-in-law Norman Jeffries, Jr. encountered Marilyn while working on the kitchen floor. She was wrapped in a bath towel, looking "desperately sick" as though "she must have taken a lot of dope . . . or was scared out of her mind. I had never seen her look that way before." Late in the morning, Marilyn's hairdresser Agnes Flanagan visited and observed that Marilyn was "terribly, terribly depressed" at the delivery, via messenger, of a stuffed toy tiger. The significance of the tiger has never been explained.

The afternoon is a mystery about which very little clear information is available. The only reported event with several sources to support it is a visit by Robert Kennedy to Marilyn's home. If Kennedy did visit, it would not have been the first time. Jeanne Carmen says she was once at Marilyn's when Kennedy arrived, and Marilyn, fresh out of a bath and dressed in a bathrobe "jumped into his arms" and "kissed him openly, which was out of character for her."

A private investigator working for Robert Slatzer reports that a neighbor of Marilyn's was hosting a bridge game on the afternoon of August 4, and that the ladies at the game – understandably interested in the comings and goings at the home of their famous neighbor – observed Robert Kennedy arrive in the company of another man "carrying what resembled a doctor's bag." A daughter of one of the women at the game (the woman is deceased) has repeated the story, adding that the hostess was harassed for weeks by men warning her "to keep her mouth shut." Robert Kennedy himself allegedly testified in a deposition – no record of which is available – that he did visit Marilyn's home that afternoon escorted by a doctor, who injected the distraught actress with a tranquilizer to calm her down. Mrs. Murray, having denied over the course of twenty-three years that Kennedy had been in Marilyn's home that Saturday, finally admitted on camera in a 1985 BBC documentary that the Attorney General had been there during the afternoon, though she offered no details. Peter Lawford's ex-wife Deborah Gould says Lawford told her Kennedy went to Marilyn's that Saturday to tell her once and for all that the affair was over, and the confrontation left her "very very distraught and depressed." A neighbor of Lawford's says he saw Robert Kennedy arrive by car at Lawford's home during the afternoon.

Marilyn's psychiatrist, Ralph Greenson, fills in the story as of about 4.30 or 5.00 p.m. Dr. Greenson has said Marilyn called him in an anxious state, seeming "depressed and somewhat drugged." He went to her house, spending "about two and half hours" there. According to his carefully worded account, she told him she had been having affairs with "extremely important men in government . . . at the highest level," and that she had expected to be with one of these men that evening, but had been disappointed. At around 6.30 p.m., the masseur Ralph Roberts called to confirm the dinner plans. Roberts recognized Dr. Greenson's voice, as it told him Marilyn was not home. Joe DiMaggio's son Joe Jr. tried to call twice, reaching Mrs. Murray, who said Marilyn was out. The press aide Pat Newcomb had spent the night in the house and had been on the scene all day. According to Greenson, Marilyn now became angry with Newcomb, and he asked Newcomb to leave.

There is an interesting sidelight to this seemingly minor incident. One source – a friend of Newcomb's who also knew Marilyn – has said that Pat Newcomb, a bright and attractive young woman, was herself "deeply in love with Bobby Kennedy." Marilyn considered the younger Newcomb a rival as well as a friend, and had been jealous of her in the past. Newcomb, who was sequestered in the Kennedy compound at Hyannis Port immediately after Marilyn's death and who subsequently became a Kennedy employee, has long refused comment on the Kennedys' relationships with Marilyn.

Though Marilyn "seemed somewhat depressed," Greenson had seen her "many, many times in a much worse condition." He had a dinner engagement, and, according to his account, he judged that Marilyn was sufficiently recovered that he could return to his home around 7.15, asking Mrs. Murray to stay the night as a precaution. At about 7.40 p.m., Greenson says, Marilyn called him to report that she had talked to young DiMaggio. She sounded in better spirits.

The Kennedys' brother-in-law, Peter Lawford, gave a number of differing accounts of the night Marilyn died to a number of different people. In all of them, he claims to have had a phone conversation with Marilyn at about this time, in which she turned down his invitation to come to dinner at his home. The dinner party may have been the gathering Marilyn had hoped to attend with Robert Kennedy that night. By this time, she was in no shape to go.

As far as anyone knows for certain, the only person on the scene with Marilyn at this point was Mrs. Murray. Of the many stories she has told of the fatal night, this is essentially the original – the one repeated in the first police reports:

At around 8.00 p.m., Marilyn says good night and, taking one of her two phones with its long cord in with her, closes her bedroom door.

Mrs. Murray tidies up about the house and goes to her own room. At about 3.30 a.m., for some reason – perhaps alerted by a "sixth sense," as Dr. Greenson somewhat mystically referred to it – Mrs. Murray arises and notices that Marilyn's light is still on and that the phone cord is still under her door. The phone is normally disconnected at night. Mrs. Murray is too timid to knock and risk awakening Marilyn, but alarmed enough to call Dr. Greenson. He tells her to knock on the locked door, and she does. There is no response. He tells her he is on the way and instructs her to call Dr. Hyman Engleberg, Marilyn's personal physician. As she awaits the doctors' arrival, Mrs. Murray goes to the front of the house and uses a fireplace poker to pull back the curtains and peek in. She sees Marilyn lying nude on the bed. At about 3.35 a.m., Greenson – who lives nearby – arrives, breaks the bedroom window, and enters the room. Marilyn is lying face down with the phone clutched "fiercely" in her right hand. Greenson realizes immediately that she is dead. Dr. Engleberg arrives about five minutes later. The police are finally called at 4.25 a.m.

On the face of it, the story almost makes sense, though it certainly has its queer touches. For one, it has Mrs. Murray awakening a psychiatrist in the middle of the night before she makes any effort on her own to find out if anything is really wrong. Odder still, it shows us two doctors – who knew their obligations in what was clearly a coroner's case – waiting, inexplicably, almost an hour to report the death of their most famous patient. There are other serious discrepancies that are not so immediately apparent. One is that Mrs. Murray could not, as she claimed, have first been alarmed by the light under Marilyn's bedroom door. The house had newly installed white wool carpeting that brushed firmly enough against the bottom of the door to make it difficult to close. No light showed through.

This early account of Marilyn's death is not, as it may seem, stranger than fiction. It *is* fiction.

The first cop on the scene had immediate misgivings about the story he was told. The belated call to the police had been placed by Dr. Engleberg. It had been taken by the Watch Commander on the West Los Angeles desk, a Sergeant named Jack Clemmons. Given that the death of Marilyn Monroe had been reported, Clemmons was curious enough to make the run to the scene himself. Clemmons was a tough-minded and experienced cop. Ironically, he was also a friend of Marilyn's ex-husband Jim Dougherty, who became a policeman years after his divorce from his famous first wife.

The doctors showed Clemmons a Nembutal bottle among the fifteen bottles of medication cluttering Marilyn's bedside table. The bottle was empty and had its top in place. Its label came from the San Vicente Pharmacy in Brentwood, and indicated a prescription from Dr. Engleberg, filled on Friday, August 3. Engleberg told Clemmons the bottle had contained fifty capsules when full. No suicide note was in evidence.

Perhaps more significantly, no water glass was in evidence either, and the water in the adjoining bathroom was turned off because of work on the plumbing system. People who knew Marilyn well have said she could not bear to swallow even one pill without water. Swallowing fifty pills without water was out of the question. It has been noted that photographs of the room show what appears to be a Mexican-style ceramic jug on the floor that could have held water. Apparently no one thought to see if it did, or ask if it was used for that purpose.

Clemmons had an "uneasy feeling" about the behavior of the

doctors and of Mrs. Murray. There was something about the death scene itself he couldn't buy. It was too pretty, too arranged, to jibe with the death throes by overdose in his experience: "It looked like the whole thing had been staged." Marilyn's body was in rigor mortis. By Clemmons's experienced guess, she had not died during the early hours of that morning, but may have been dead as long as eight hours. He did not like the fact that Mrs. Murray was busying herself by doing laundry and packing boxes when he arrived, or that her son-in-law had already been called to repair the broken bedroom window. Most of all, he did not like the time sequences he was given.

Though his concerns did not find their way into the final version of his written report, Clemmons has insisted that Mrs. Murray told him she first became alarmed about Marilyn "immediately after midnight." He says the two doctors were present when she made this statement, and *did not disagree*. Clemmons's impression was that Drs. Greenson and Engleberg had been on the scene themselves since around midnight, and he remembers questioning the doctors "very pointedly" about why they had waited not one hour but four to call the police. He got no satisfactory reply. When Sergeant Clemmons went off duty that Sunday morning and turned the case over to other officers, he was highly suspicious. By the time the official suicide verdict was returned, he was convinced that Marilyn Monroe had been murdered. He remains adamantly convinced today, though his refusal to accept the official line in the case cost him his job with the Los Angeles police.

Twenty-three years after the fact, Mrs. Murray told the BBC interviewer that it had indeed been "around midnight" when she first became concerned about Marilyn. In this version of her story, she says she did wait until 3.30 a.m to call Dr. Greenson. Why did she wait so long? She can't remember.

In fact there were hours of frantic activity – beginning well before midnight – in Marilyn's house that night that Mrs. Murray can't remember. It was about 11.00 p.m. – perhaps even slightly earlier – when Marilyn's press agent Arthur Jacobs's enjoyment of a Henry Mancini concert was interrupted by an urgent message. Jacobs's widow Natalie, who accompanied him to the Hollywood Bowl that night, remembers: "About three-quarters of the way through the concert someone came to our box and he said, 'Arthur, come quickly . . . Marilyn is dead, or she's on the point of death.'" Mrs. Jacobs believes the message came from Pat Newcomb, an employee in her husband's firm. She says Jacobs dropped her off at their home, and she saw nothing of him for two days thereafter. In her phrase, "he had to fudge the press."

Presumably one of the things Jacobs had to fudge was the possibility that Marilyn did not die at home after all. In the early hours of the morning she left the premises for an ambulance ride. The ambulance story first surfaced during a District Attorney's review of the case in 1982, and has since been confirmed by writers and reporters. The ambulance driver has been identified as one Ken Hunter, and the attendant as Murray Liebowitz. The ambulance belonged to Schaefer Ambulance, the largest private company of its kind in L.A. at the time. Hunter and Liebowitz, who has since changed his name, have confirmed the call at Marilyn's house, but have been mysteriously reluctant to talk about it. The owner of Schaefer Ambulance, Walter Schaefer, has not. Schaefer insisted Marilyn was alive, but in a coma – apparently suffering from a drug overdose – when she was picked up and taken to Santa Monica Hospital. The time has been reported as 2.00 a.m. Schaefer believes Marilyn died at the hospital. An obvious problem with this opinion is that, if the time report is correct, Marilyn was found in rigor mortis just two and one half hours later. Rigor mortis takes from four to six hours to set in.

Records of the ambulance company are only kept for five years, and have been destroyed. Hospital records for the period are likewise not available, and no one has been located who worked at the hospital in 1962 and who remembers treating Marilyn Monroe that night. It is of course possible that she was treated but, lacking makeup, not recognized, and possible that she died en route to the hospital. The autopsy records no evidence of medical attempts to resuscitate her from an overdose. Still, it seems incredible that Schaefer and his two employees could be mistaken about so memorable an emergency call. And the case for an attempt to save a dying Marilyn was reinforced by Mrs. Murray, whose on-again, off-again memory recollected during a 1985 version of her story of a late night visit by an unidentified doctor while Marilyn was still alive.

What was happening at Marilyn's house between the time someone – Pat Newcomb? – sent Arthur Jacobs the message that Marilyn was dead or dying around 11.00 p.m. and someone called for an ambulance, perhaps about 2.00 a.m.? And if she did ride to the hospital, who took her body home? It wasn't Schaefer: Marilyn's trip in the ambulance was one-way. It would have been no mean feat to make a corpse vanish from an emergency room. Standard procedure in such a case would be for the Medical Examiner to be called and to officially release the body only after an autopsy. A clever manipulation – or the wave of some powerful hand – would have been required to bypass the system.

With each new revelation in the case, the scene at Marilyn's house grows more crowded. One of her lawyers, Milton "Mickey" Rudin, reportedly appears at around 4.00 a.m., calling Peter Lawford's agent on the phone and telling him Marilyn is dead.

Peter Lawford himself appears. According to his ex-wife Deborah Gould, he shows up to purge the house of any evidence of contact with the Kennedys. He even finds and destroys, in the story as Gould reports it, a suicide note. Several of Lawford's later accounts of the evening feature a distress call from a slurry-voiced Marilyn telling him to "say goodbye to Jack, and say goodbye to yourself, because you're a nice guy." Two of his dinner guests have confirmed that there was some discussion about whether Lawford should go to Marilyn's and check on her. Judging by the statements of the guests, his trip to the house happened sometime after 11.00 p.m.

Private detectives and their operatives troop in and out. Fred Otash recalls that Lawford – unaware that he is hiring one of the men who have been bugging his home – bursts into his office around 3.00 a.m., "completely disoriented and in a state of shock . . . saying that Marilyn Monroe was dead, that Bobby Kennedy was there, and that he was spirited out of town by some airplane, that they [Marilyn and Robert Kennedy] had got in a big fight that evening, that he'd like to have . . . someone go out to the house and pick up any and all information . . . regarding any involvement between Marilyn Monroe and the Kennedys."

And all of the actors on this crowded stage play out their parts for at least five hours – and probably more – before anyone feels safe enough to call the police and tell them Marilyn Monroe is dead. No wonder Marilyn's body was already in rigor mortis – indicating she had died at least four to six hours earlier – when Sergeant Clemmons arrived and found only the two doctors and Mrs. Murray on the scene.

Where is the leading man? There is no proof that Robert Kennedy was back at Marilyn's house the night she died, but there are several reports that place him at Peter Lawford's house, only minutes away. Police sources have said Kennedy was seen at the Beverly Hilton during the afternoon, was at Lawford's house that night, and broke a dinner date with Marilyn. An enterprising photographer named Billy Woodfield ran down a lead to the owner of an air charter company often used by Lawford and his guests. Woodfield says the charter man showed him logs indicating that Kennedy had been picked up by helicopter at Lawford's house around 2.00 a.m. Sunday morning, and flown to Los Angeles International. Neighbors were awakened by the sound of the helicopter. Another report, from Deborah Gould, confirms Woodfield's story. She says Lawford told her Kennedy left by helicopter during the night, going back to his accommodations near San Francisco.

few pill bottles, and a high concentration of drugs in the body would be expected. There would be no incriminating needle marks. And there would be no obvious residue remaining in the colon because the drug would have been administered in liquid form.

Aside from the forensic evidence, the death-by-enema theory is supported by a thoroughly odd remark attributed to Peter Lawford. Asked by ex-wife Deborah Gould exactly how Marilyn had died, he allegedly replied, "Marilyn took her last big enema."

Noguchi has written that the absence of pill residue in the stomach did not surprise him in the least. In the belly of a pill addict like Marilyn, he says, pills would be familiar visitors and would be rapidly "dumped" into the intestinal tract, just as familiar food is easily digested, while exotic food causes indigestion. Other reputable coroners – including those interviewed for this book – have disagreed, saying that such a massive dose of pills should leave some telltale residue behind.

The high level of barbiturates found in Marilyn's liver does suggest that drugs were taken over a period of hours, rather than in one dose, and could offer some explanation for the lack of residue in her stomach. At the same time, the liver concentration does not negate the fatal-dose-by-enema theory. No doubt Marilyn had been taking pills over a period of hours, as was her habit. A fatal dose administered into the colon on top of her self-administered oral dosages would reach the liver through "portal circulation" – entering the blood vessels directly from the large intestine – rather than through the usual digestive process.

The enema explanation and other forensic theories in the case remain theories not because of anything Dr. Noguchi said or did, but because of an incredible slip-up in another part of the coroner's office.

Noguchi made the following notation at the bottom of his autopsy report:

"Unembalmed blood is taken for alcohol and barbiturate

examination. Liver, kidney, *stomach and contents,* urine and *intestine* are saved for further toxicological study." [My emphasis].

Standard procedure, then and now. But in Marilyn Monroe's case, standard procedure went out the window. The blood and the liver were tested, revealing a blood level of 8.0 mg% chloral hydrate and a liver containing 13.0 mg% pentobarbital (Nembutal), "both well above fatal dosages." But the stomach and its contents, the intestine, the other organs, and tissue samples taken for microscopic analysis *somehow disappeared* and were never tested. Noguchi, who has nothing to do with this aspect of the examination, has speculated that the toxicology department may have *assumed* suicide because of the blood analysis and the empty pill bottles. If so, the assumption has fed the flames of conspiracy theories, and with good reason. A thorough analysis of the stomach, its contents, and the intestine could have shed more light on the crucial question of whether the fatal drugs entered Marilyn's body through her mouth or through some other avenue.

Elsewhere in the coroner's office toiled a deputy coroner named Lionel Grandison, who happened to be the man who signed Marilyn's death certificate, and who surfaced years later to provide one of the more bizarre sideshows in the case. Robert Slatzer stumbled across Grandison – by this time a radio engineer – while appearing on a program at a Los Angeles radio station in 1978. Slatzer was eager to talk with Grandison, and in the course of the recorded interview, Grandison made a number of startling allegations. He claimed to have seen, among Marilyn's personal possessions, the red diary Marilyn had told Slatzer about. Grandison said he skimmed the diary and saw references to the President, the Attorney General, and Fidel Castro. The diary subsequently disappeared, as did other things of Marilyn's, particularly a scribbled note Grandison assumed was a suicide note. He claimed there were numerous bruises on Marilyn's body that were not mentioned in the autopsy report. He said he had to be forced to sign the death certificate, for he did not agree with the suicide ruling. And he topped his story off with the revelation that there were necrophiliacs in and about the coroner's office who had taken liberties with Marilyn's corpse.

The necrophilia tale, together with the discovery that he had done six months on a forgery rap, damaged Grandison's credibility on more salient points. His allegations remain unproved.

If Grandison's story was manufactured, what did happen to the red diary? One of the private detectives hired by Peter Lawford to destroy evidence at Marilyn's house may have just missed it. He reported entering the house, with the help of a police contact, at around 9.00 a.m. Sunday morning, just four and a half hours after the police were first called to the scene. His brief search revealed a filing cabinet in the garden room that had been jimmied. Marilyn apparently used the filing cabinet to hold valuable papers. She had recently had the lock on it changed. A friend of Joe DiMaggio's has said that when Joe went to the house later Sunday, he was looking for "what he referred to as a book." He didn't find it. The book and other personal papers were long gone. The implication is intriguing: Lawford's clean-up team *was not the only one at work*. Whoever rifled the filing cabinet must have done it either before the police were called, or while there were still police officers in the house.

At the coroner's office, the fine line between bad judgment and deliberate cover-up is difficult to distinguish. At the police department, the line appears to have been blatantly crossed. The Police Chief at the time was William Parker. The head of the Intelligence Division was Captain James Hamilton. Both men were friends and admirers of Robert Kennedy. Parker reportedly made the amazing statement during the investigation that he expected to be named FBI Director when Robert Kennedy became President. Robert Kennedy had alluded to Hamilton as "my friend" in the foreword to his book *The Enemy Within,* and later recommended him for the job of Chief of Security with the National Football League.

Very early on in the investigation, Chief Parker took the unprecedented step of yanking the Monroe case from Homicide and making it the exclusive domain of the Intelligence Division. Thereafter, in the words of Parker's successor Tom Reddin, nobody outside intelligence "knew a bloody thing about what was going on." A file that ran to hundreds of pages was reportedly developed on the case, but only a few innocuous fragments from the file exist – so far as is known – today. When former Los Angeles mayor Sam Yorty asked to see the Monroe file, he was told it could not be found. Reddin has said that the only justification possible for making the Monroe case a secret Intelligence Division operation would be "a national security problem."

No doubt the police file contained much information that could make the Marilyn Monroe case less a mystery than it is today. Like so much of the material on the John F. Kennedy assassination, it has been withheld from public view by a few individuals who have decided for the rest of us that ignorance is preferable to unpalatable truths. Again like the Kennedy assassination, the difficult business of learning the truth has been left to private citizens – to writers, researchers, and investigators – whose collective efforts have pieced together much of what is known about the case today.

One of the most visible of these citizens is a private detective with the colorful name of Milo Speriglio. Speriglio is Director and Chief of Nick Harris Detectives in Los Angeles and a public figure in his own right who has, among other things, run unsuccessfully for mayor of the city. In 1972, Speriglio accepted Robert Slatzer as a client. In so doing, he joined Slatzer's crusade to prove to the world that Marilyn was murdered, a crusade that continues to the present day.

Speriglio has written two books on the case himself, is at work on a film and a third book, and is periodically featured in splashy tabloid articles with headlines like "Marilyn Was Murdered by the Kennedys." Despite all their efforts, Speriglio and his client Slatzer have produced no conclusive proof that

Marilyn was killed. They have, however, filled in a great deal of the story that would otherwise be unknown, and have provided some chilling suggestions in the process.

Perhaps the most chilling is the possibility that Marilyn's murder may have been recorded on audio tape. It is well established that clandestine recording devices were in place at her home at the time. Speriglio claims to have been contacted, in August of 1982, by an informant who, twenty years before, had been in the employ of ace wiretapper Bernie Spindel, the man who bugged Marilyn and the Kennedys for Jimmy Hoffa. The informant provided Speriglio with technical tidbits about the bugging of Marilyn's home, including the band frequency used and the pioneering hardware Spindel brought to his assignment – bugs smaller than matchbooks with VOX, or voice-activated, capabilities that turned on the recorders only when audible sounds were present.

The informant had not actually heard the tapes himself, but heard them described by an associate Speriglio calls Mr. M, who supposedly still had, as of 1982, a copy of the tapes in his possession. According to the informant, Mr. M had described what he took to be the tape of the murder, with Marilyn being "slapped around." Speriglio, who at first accepted this account and repeated it in his first book, now believes that the slapping was not the murder but an earlier event. He remains convinced that the murder tape once existed – and may still exist.

In checking out the story, Speriglio says he made contact with a newspaper reporter who in turn located Mr. M – identified as a "well-respected" Washington attorney with offices in the Watergate complex and a former associate of Bernie Spindel's. M denied having the tapes and would not admit having heard them.

Speriglio also claims to know of a phone call – likewise recorded by a bug – to Marilyn's house the night she died. The call came from San Francisco (the operator's voice is heard) and the caller asks an unknown party, "Is she dead yet?" Since the Kennedy party was in San Francisco at the time, Speriglio speculates that the caller may have been a Kennedy aide, and the call may have occurred sometime after Marilyn was put in the ambulance en route to the hospital.

These reports are hearsay, and, pending the discovery of the tapes themselves, they should be weighed accordingly. Still, there were bugs in Marilyn's house – and on her phone – the night she died. If the bugs were active, they presumably produced tapes. Where are those tapes? And if we could play them back today, what would we hear?

In addition to the copy supposedly possessed by Mr. M, Speriglio believes other copies of the tapes were once held by Bernie Spindel's widow, by Jimmy Hoffa, and by the New York County District Attorney, who carried off a collection of bugging tapes during a raid of Bernie Spindel's home in 1966. Hoffa's "foster son" and associate Chuck O'Brien has confirmed that Hoffa had tapes of the Kennedys and Marilyn.

There may have been still another copy. Researchers for a 1985 BBC documentary discovered that the tapes were a potential time bomb placed dead center in Robert Kennedy's career path. In 1968, when Kennedy was the most promising Democratic candidate for President, a right-wing Republican group hired a journalist named Ralph De Toledano to find the rumored Marilyn–Kennedy tapes. According to De Toledano, an investigator was hired, who reported back that the tapes could be had – through an unnamed ex-policeman – for $59,000. The Republican group agreed to the deal on June 4, 1968, but requested "a couple of days" to raise the money. That night, as he celebrated his California primary victory at the Hotel Ambassador in Los Angeles, Robert Kennedy was fatally shot. (As a final irony, the autopsy on Robert Kennedy – which would also become a matter of controversy – was performed by Dr. Thomas Noguchi.) The plan to buy the tapes was dropped. De Toledano says he is certain the tapes would have been used against Kennedy if he had lived to be nominated for the presidency.

Interviewed for this book, Speriglio says he is still "positive" Marilyn was murdered, but less sure anything will ever be done

about it. The authorities are "not planning to do a damn thing
. . . One of the best things they could have gotten was the tapes,
if they wanted to prove what really happened, and they never
made an effort." The detective claims to have given an L.A.
District Attorney specific information on where a copy of the
tapes could be found, and "he never went after it."

Speriglio's latest theory is that two men – he says he knows
who they were – murdered Marilyn on orders from Chicago
mob boss Sam Giancana. Giancana's private army was involved
in the CIA–Mafia plots to kill Fidel Castro – the same plots we
are told Marilyn had documented in her red diary and threatened to reveal in a press conference. The gangster shared with
John Kennedy a sexual involvement with starlet Judith
Campbell. And his organization had reportedly done Kennedy a
favor – either by request or gratuitously – by suppressing information on the President's alleged involvement with another
starlet, Judy Meredith, as recently as the spring of 1961. He had
even bragged that his machine delivered Illinois to Kennedy in
the 1960 election. Marilyn spent the last full weekend of her
life, stoned and disorderly, at the Cal-Neva Lodge, a mob
hangout on the Nevada border in which Giancana once had an
interest. Could she have said or done something that made her a
target? Could Giancana have wanted her dead because of her
threat to talk about the top-secret Cuban plots?

Giancana and his henchmen were active players in the
Hollywood power game. For that matter, their successors still
are. If they killed Marilyn, it would not have been the first time
real blood has been spilled in the land of make-believe to serve
the purposes of their secret society.

The mob was a partner with the Kennedy administration in
Cuba, but a bitter enemy at home, due to Robert Kennedy's
unrelenting attacks on organized crime. Because of this two-
edged relationship, Speriglio finds it difficult to choose between
two motives in his mob-killed-Marilyn theory: "to embarrass
the Kennedys . . . or as a favor to them, we've never been able
to put that together."

Speriglio's theory echoes that of one of the case's original investigators. The late Frank Hronek was a Los Angeles DA's investigator in 1962. According to his family, he suspected that Sam Giancana and his associate Johnny Roselli – another link in the CIA–Cuba connection – were involved in Marilyn's death. Hronek also mentioned his suspicions of the CIA's involvement in either the death or the cover-up. Hronek's report file, like the police file, has mysteriously disappeared.

In 1982, due largely to the efforts of Slatzer, Speriglio, and others who had joined the cause, the Monroe case was reopened by the Los Angeles District Attorney's office. A great deal of new information came to light – the ambulance ride, details of the cover-up, etc. – but despite these intriguing developments the case was dropped with the conclusion that "no further criminal investigation appears required."

Many disagree. John Miner, the Deputy District Auorney who stood beside Dr. Noguchi during the autopsy, has never been comfortable with the suicide ruling. This may be particularly significant, because Miner appears to have information on Marilyn that is possessed by no one else. During the original investigation, Miner conducted a four-hour interview with Dr. Greenson, Marilyn's psychiatrist. Speaking with a guarantee of confidentiality, Greenson opened up to Miner, told him the reasons he did not believe Marilyn was a suicide, and played a forty-minute tape of Marilyn talking, presumably to prove his point. The tape was not a recording of a psychiatric session, but a statement Marilyn had specially recorded on her own for her psychiatrist to hear and to keep. According to Miner, Greenson (who died in 1979) later destroyed the recording.

Miner has steadfastly refused to tell anyone what the psychiatrist told him, and continued to honor his twenty-seven-year-old promise when interviewed for this book. A crucial question, of course, is whether Greenson offered any reason to believe Marilyn was murdered. Refusing direct comment, Miner points out that any information he had from Greenson was "a product of either single or . . . double hearsay . . . it's not admissible in court, it's not valid for any purpose legally." He did, he says, write a memo about the Greenson interview to the coroner and the Chief Deputy District Attorney that included a phrase he remembers as, "I believe I can say definitely that it was not suicide." After writing the memo, Miner worried that he would be called before a grand jury, and might be cited for contempt for refusing to answer questions on ethical grounds. There was no grand jury. Not surprisingly, the memo has disappeared.

Caught off guard by a phone call from a reporter, Greenson himself may have suggested some of what he revealed to Miner. The reporter had his recorder running. The resulting tape exposes an exasperated Dr. Greenson saying, "I can't explain myself or defend myself without revealing things that I don't want to reveal . . . It's a terrible position to be in . . . because I can't tell the whole story." Greenson ends the conversation with a few cryptic words of advice: "Listen . . . talk to Bobby Kennedy."

No one can talk to Bobby Kennedy now. Or to Dr. Greenson, Peter Lawford, Sam Giancana, Police Chief Parker, and others of the major players in the drama. All are dead. It is still a safe bet that there are people who live today with secrets that could reveal the truth in the case. And there still remains the macabre possibility that the last few moments of Marilyn's life may be recorded on a tape that may someday be played for the world to hear. The red diary – if it still exists – would be a fascinating find, but would likely prove nothing as far as the cause of death is concerned. The key to the question of whether Marilyn was murdered is in the bungled autopsy: if she swallowed a fatal dose of pills, she was probably a suicide or the victim of an accidental overdose; if she didn't swallow the fatal dose – and the evidence suggests that she did not – her death was caused by someone else. The key to the questions of how and why she was killed is on the hidden tapes and in the hidden thoughts of her killers and their silent accomplices.

In her last interview with *Life* magazine, published days before her death, Marilyn Monroe unknowingly delivered an epitaph for herself as fitting as any other: "I now live in my work." She was a brilliant performer, and she is best remembered in the images of that vast and all-forgiving screen of unreality that were her gift to the world. The story of the real Marilyn, the abandoned and vulnerable child who played with a powerful fire and was burned, is perhaps too painful and too full of disillusion to live in our memories for long.

Postscript

Milo Speriglio died in 2000 at the age of 62. He remained convinced that Marilyn was the victim of a mob hit because of what she knew.

Michael Selsman, one of Marilyn's PR agents, has said he doesn't buy the murder story. He didn't like Marilyn much, calling her "cold, imperious and arrogant." He thinks Marilyn just OD'd. But he does confirm that she had affairs with both Kennedys, and that she had an abortion six weeks before she died, unsure which of the Kennedy brothers had been the father.

Meanwhile, Marilyn books have become a sub-genre in the publishing industry. Various authors have rehashed the Kennedy affair stories; one has maintained there were no Kennedy affairs and claimed psychiatrist Dr. Greenson and housekeeper Mrs. Murray were the culprits (if this were true there would have been no need for the massive and well documented cover-up); and lawsuits have flown back and forth among the writers.

As recently as the spring of 2000, John Miner was still making public appeals to have Marilyn's body exhumed so that current forensic techniques could be applied. It hasn't happened.

And the telltale tapes have not been found or heard.

5

Napoleon's Demise

The Murder of Serge Rubinstein

When a cop starts work on a homicide, the social set with which he most desires acquaintance is, quite naturally, the victim's circle of enemies. Who could have wanted this guy dead bad enough to kill him? That is the question. But when the dead guy was Serge Rubinstein, the answer could – and did – fill volumes.

There were quite literally thousands of people, on at least four continents, who loathed the sound of Serge Rubinstein's name and had good reason to celebrate the news of his demise. He was a scoundrel of monstrous, even historic, proportions. Serge achieved this eminence not by practicing mass murder or political tyranny, but by an inspired capacity to cheat and to swindle. The scale of his wrongdoing and the brilliance and flair he brought to it made him a fascinating rascal – at least until the day one was numbered among the victims of his scams, and fascination would turn to hate.

Had Serge hired a ghostwriter to script out his last scene, it could hardly have been more jam-packed with the trappings of the archetypal murder mystery. At 8.00 a.m. on January 27, 1955, a reserved, distinguished, and impeccably clad English butler slips soundlessly down the hall of his Russian emigrant master's five-story home on upper Fifth Avenue in Manhattan. He raps on a massive bedroom door to awaken his employer, than enters with an unaccustomed sense of foreboding. The room is in disarray. The master of the house is not in his satin-canopied bed. Instead, he is supine on the rich, wall-to-wall green carpet, dressed in silk pajamas of midnight blue and trussed like an animal for slaughter. His hands and feet are bound with curtain cord, and his mouth is covered with a gag of two-inch adhesive tape. His face displays the bruises of a beating. He is quite dead.

A few feet from the corpse, among the room's nineteen pieces of furniture and fifteen paintings, the deceased stares down upon himself from a poster-sized photograph, taken at a costume ball. He wears the outfit he had loved the best, the imperial uniform of Napoleon.

The body the butler gazed upon was not a physically imposing specimen. Serge had lived to the age of forty-six. He had been relatively small – about five feet seven – and pleasant-looking in a chubby way, with an engaging grin, lively green-gray eyes, a boyish enthusiasm, and a squeaky voice that squeaked higher when excited.

But like his hero Napoleon, Serge Rubinstein was a powerful little package. The man who had occupied the body in the silk pajamas had been worth – give or take a few farthings – around ten million bucks American. Consider that these are 1955 bucks, and you have a corpse that has unwillingly turned loose of a very healthy financial statement. Few if any of the gains that built this fortune had not been ill-gotten in one way or another. It was not that Serge was incapable of making money by earning it, it was just more fun the other way.

Serge's fun had included dazzling financial maneuvers that crippled huge companies and brought the currency of entire nations to the verge of collapse. As an influence manipulator, he had bought and sold the services of powerful politicians and business barons, leaving a broad wake of shattered reputations and ruined careers. And as a Casanova, charm and money served him well. He maintained virtual harems of the loveliest young women New York could offer, and the turnover rate among his favorites was high. All these remarkably successful endeavors were undertaken without apology and with only one end in view: the greater enrichment and glory of Serge Rubinstein.

To be fair, Serge was only practicing his own variations of the lessons he had learned as a pup in Mother Russia. His father Dmitri, in the family's ancestral city of St. Petersburg had been banker and financial advisor to Czar Nicholas II and the mad monk Rasputin, moving in some of the most decadent circles of the century. The opulent lifestyle of the Rubinsteins was disrupted by the Russian Revolution, and the family fled their homeland in 1918.

The story that has come to us of young Serge's exodus from Russia could hardly be more picturesque and romantic, even with the quibbling qualification that it is Serge's own, and that veracity was not his strong suit. Here is little Serge, ten years old, standing before an anxious father Rubinstein as a king's ransom in rubles, rubies, diamonds, emeralds, and sapphires is pinned and sewn into his small fur coat, his knickers, and his underwear. The brave boy is tucked into a troika and slides off across the frozen Gulf of Finland, the Bolsheviks hot on his well-heeled heels. Four months later, the lad is reunited with his family in Stockholm.

As his fifteenth birthday approaches, he is in Vienna. Offered his choice of birthday presents, he chooses psychoanalysis by Freud's disciple Dr. Alfred Adler. Why? He fears an inferiority complex. After two or three sessions, the revered head doctor sends him packing, with the judgment, as Serge reports it, that a "cure" would leave the young man "just ordinary. The way you are now, you'll be driven by ambition and desires." Whether these words are Dr. Adler's or Serge's, they are certainly on target as a description of their subject.

Father Dmitri never recovered what the Revolution had cost him, and died a bankrupt in the Balkans. Determined not to share this fate, Serge settled on Cambridge as he neared college age, with a clear eye to the proper connections for a moneyed future. There was a problem. He was fluent in Russian, English, French, Swedish, and German, but he had no Latin, and Latin was required. Locking himself in a London boarding house with a Latin dictionary and an assortment of ancient Roman texts, Serge conquered the language, entered Cambridge and conquered that, too, graduating with honors in two years.

It was at Cambridge that Serge made one of his most long-standing enemies, his own elder brother Andre. It seems Andre financed Serge's education and was never repaid for it. He later claimed the younger sibling had stolen several million dollars from him, sued for it, and pursued this suit and others during the balance of his lifetime.

It was also at Cambridge, again according to the hero of the story, that Serge was informed by no less a figure than his Economics professor John Maynard Keynes that he was destined to be "one of the world's great financial figures." This description too was right on target, if taken with a twist.

At the tender age of twenty-three, the prodigy found himself in Paris, installed as manager of a small bank called the Banque Franco-Asiatique. Serge first surrounded himself with White Russian émigré pals in positions of authority, and proceeded to set up his first major killing. The main distinguishing feature of the bank was that it served as the French financial agent for Chiang Kai-shek's China. It did not escape Serge's notice that the Chinese had defaulted on a bond issue floated by the bank. When the apparently worthless bonds were nearing maturity, he quietly scooped up a million dollars worth of them for $25,000. As manager of the bank, he then dutifully pointed out to the Chinese that their credit depended upon the prompt payment of interest on a more recently issued series of bonds. When the million dollar payment on the new bonds was forwarded, what could the bank manager do but turn the payment over to the owner of the old, defaulted bonds? "I had the bonds," Serge explained in all candor, "and I had the money. I just paid myself off." A million was pocketed, and a well-deserved reputation was born.

While playing banker, Serge similarly discovered a chain of restaurants holding the franc equivalent of $450,000 in cash, with controlling interest available because of the circumstances for a mere $60,000. Using $60,000 he had borrowed without formalities from his depositors, Serge bought up the restaurants and made use of their assets in a series of speculations on the international money market. One result was that the value of the franc fluctuated wildly, and the French government took enough offense to deport M. Rubinstein. The deportation was the final result of a three-year effort to rid France of Serge, who saw the whole affair in purely personal terms. According to Serge, he was kicked out solely because of the French Premier's small-minded view of his close relationship with the Premier's mistress, who happened to be a marchioness.

At twenty-seven, Serge departed for England and larger conquests. He had already gained control of a British mining company with the alluring name of the Chosen Corporation. The once reputable company, which owned gold mines in Korea, had fallen on hard times. It is said that these hard times were in fact promoted if not created by Serge himself. Using information provided by a paid informer, Serge reportedly leaked to the press the story that one of Chosen's directors was dealing illegally in its stock. The subsequent scandal forced a normally solid stock price into the bargain basement. And when a deal was proposed through which the accused director would sell Serge 173,000 shares of Chosen to raise his legal expenses, the young and no doubt softhearted bank manager could not refuse. He responded not with cash but with a bookkeeping entry representing a deposit in his bank. Serge got the stock, and the unfortunate director went off to Wormwood Scrubs prison without a cent of Serge's money.

The new stockholder then set himself up in the Savoy Hotel in London, entertained England's power elite as time allowed, installed his own team at Chosen, and bought up another 150,000 shares in another deal that cost him nothing. The Korean mining properties thus falling into Serge's ready hands were worth around $6 million.

Off to Japan, in company of a Hungarian lovely who liked to

be called Countess Natasha. It was time to cash in. Serge sold
the Korean mines to a conglomerate headed by Japan's Prince
Ito – selling out all other Chosen stockholders in the process –
and hid the proceeds in a bunch of paper corporations. The proceeds amounted to about $3.5 million in yen, but the Japanese
were disturbingly paranoid over letting that much of their currency out of their country in 1937. Serge was able to convert all
but about a million and a half to British sterling. The rest he
contrived to smuggle out in the obis worn by Japanese women
around their waists. When the illegally removed yen was
dumped on Western money markets, the Japanese currency took
an immediate nosedive, losing a third of its value. Serge had
added a second national government to his long and prodigiously growing census of enemies.

The remaining Chosen stockholders filed suit four years later
when they finally learned the truth, and after a five-year struggle
settled out of court for a fraction of the value of the company's
former assets. Serge was by this time no stranger to lawsuits,
and had a formidable army of lawyers to defend him. The set-
tlement left him with a profit close to $2 million for his labors
with the mining company.

The Chosen Corporation lawsuit was an early study in
Serge's ingenious methods of money management. Documents
filed in the suit revealed that Chosen's assets had mysteriously
disappeared in the process of being switched back and forth
between four Delaware companies, four New York companies,
three Texas companies, four British companies, and one
Japanese company. The trail was too complex to follow. The
only conclusion was that somehow a shell game that started
with $6 million had ended in a vanishing act.

By this time Serge Rubinstein was living in the United States.
He had entered the country, in 1938, by virtue of a miraculous
transformation. Once a Russian named Rubinstein, he had
become a Portuguese named Serge Manuel Rubinstein de
Ronello, and the passport he presented described him accordingly. Serge placidly explained to the astonished immigration

officers that the matter was simple, if somewhat embarrassing: he was really, well, a love child. His Russian mother had somehow taken as a lover a Portuguese nobleman named de Ronello, and he was himself the result of the union. Later reports revealed that the passport had been obtained in Shanghai for $2,000. To many, the poor-bastard story exposed the depths to which Serge was willing to stoop to achieve his own ends. His brother Andre, already involved in a plethora of legal entanglements with Serge, was offended enough to add another suit for defamation of their mother's character.

Never one to rest on his laurels, Serge immediately set out making money and enemies in his adopted country. He had been loosed into his element, a major player in the Wall Street major leagues. Wall Street was not ready. What is known today by the antiseptic term "insider trading" was known in Serge's day as swindling. If swindling can be raised to an art form, Serge was Michelangelo.

When the Brooklyn Manhattan Transit Company and its subways were about to be taken over by the city, Serge had the news in advance from a company official who happened to be in personal financial trouble. The deal required approval by ninety percent of the shareholders, who were to be bought out at $20 a share. Dissenters would get $148 a share. Given this tidbit of knowledge, Serge surreptitiously bought up about forty percent of the company and netted a quick $800,000. When Western Union merged with Postal Telegraph, a similar stunt added another couple of million to Serge's bank balance. In one series of manipulations of an oil company stock, he cleared a cool three million. The government tried to nail him on the oil deal, but Serge's lawyers prevailed. Unlike today's insider traders Serge was remarkably candid about his line of work, telling no less a personage than an SEC investigator, "I never speculate unless the elements of speculation have been removed, and I turn the wheels, or the man who turns the wheels is on my payroll." To this end, he employed a swarm of informers, bought or effectively blackmailed major executives, looted assets or juggled stock prices, and hid the proceeds in the maze of corporate mirrors under his control.

The oil company deal is illustrative of Serge's Byzantine approach to profit taking. The stock in question was that of Panhandle Producing & Refining Company, which made aviation gasoline, a hot item during World War II. After Serge allegedly spread false information to inflate the stock's price and then took a killing by selling short, outraged Panhandle stockholders sued him for $5 million. The complainants knew they had been robbed, but soon discovered how difficult it could be to prove they had been robbed by Serge Rubinstein. This is because Serge controlled Panhandle through Midway Victory Oil, which was owned by Victory Oil, which was owned by Norfolk International, which was owned by Norfolk Equities, which was owned by British American Equities, which was owned by the shell of Chosen Corporation. When *Fortune* magazine tried to chart the Rubinstein empire after his death, the result looked more than anything like the web of a demented spider, hoarding more than forty flies. Seven countries were represented on the chart through a system of color coding.

Serge's success both bred and fed off power. Considering that he was so recent an arrival, his power base in the United States was astonishing. On the eve of his wedding in 1941, he dined at the Roosevelt White House. At the wedding reception in Washington's Shoreham Hotel, nine ambassadors, a near quorum of senators and congressmen, and a gaggle of movie moguls and Wall Street magnates were on hand to pay court to the happy couple.

Given Serge's apparent motive in the marriage, the turnout for the wedding is especially ironic. Serge wanted to avoid the draft. Try as he might, he could not see the army or the war effort as an appropriate showcase for his talents. He poured the same energies into draft dodging that he had into his more profitable ventures. He fathered two children. He bought an aircraft company to make himself indispensable to an American victory. In the course of this maneuver, he involved the president of the aircraft company in conspiracy and got him sent to jail. He bribed and cajoled. He got his draft classification changed a total of fifteen times. Sometime during this struggle he made a rare mistake, claiming that he had supported six people during the year 1940 on an income of just over $11,000. This led to his eventual conviction, in 1947, for draft evasion. It was his one and only fall on criminal charges. He did two years in Lewisburg Federal Penitentiary and paid a $50,000 fine. While he was in the pen, his wife – a former model named Laurette Kilborn – divorced him for roughing her up.

A conviction for draft dodging was a serious stigma at the time, and the ex-con Serge found it increasingly difficult to make deals in the light of day. He responded by becoming even more surreptitious in his operations, frequently employing financial agents to keep his identity concealed. One of his favorites in this stage of his career was a stockbroker with the memorable name of Stanley T. Stanley. If the name sounds made up, that is because it was. Stanley's original name was Ruziewicz. Born in Warsaw and educated in the best European schools, he claimed to hold a doctorate from the University of Geneva and to have been, among other things, Vice-Consul of Portugal in Warsaw and manager of the Bank of Warsaw in Berlin. Reportedly an old school pal of Rubinstein's, Stanley turned up in New York after the war and became an instant hit on Wall Street with Serge as his major account. While Serge was cooling his heels in Lewisburg, Stanley was quietly buying up close to 200,000 shares of Boeing Airplane Company on his behalf, using corporate fronts to represent his buyer. Thus one of the country's most notorious draft dodgers came to own a massive interest in one of the country's biggest defense contractors, with a paper value that approached $15 million.

At the time of his murder, Serge was in the midst of a typically complicated, and typically underhanded, deal. It may be significant to the murder case because it is the deal in which Serge appears to have acquired his last set of enemies from the financial community. The prize was Stanwell Oil & Gas, a

Toronto company Serge viewed as a base of operations in Canada's booming oil industry. Stanwell had some valuable wells and leases in Alberta, and showed its assets as about $2 million. The company was controlled by a promoter named Lee Brooks, also known as Leon Bookbinder, who was an estimable wheeler-dealer in his own right. In 1953, Brooks let it be known that he would part with a large portion of his Stanwell stock.

Shortly thereafter, Stanley T. Stanley approached the president of a company called Blair Holding Corporation, one Virgil Dardi, with a plan to acquire Stanwell Oil. Stanley represented an undisclosed "client" who would act through a Swiss bank called Bank Hofmann. The client turned out to be Norfolk Insurance, said to be a Panamanian corporation headquartered in Havana, Cuba. Subsequent investigations found no such corporation registered in Panama, and no phone number for such a company in Havana. Real corporation or not, Norfolk was one of the many "corporate" flies in Serge's tangled web.

Virgil Dardi swore he had no idea the notorious Serge Rubinstein was involved in the deal. But Serge himself reportedly surfaced with a sales agreement for Lee Brooks to sign, and Brooks then backed off from the negotiations. Brooks was later reassured that Serge was nowhere near the deal, and one-half of a complex two-part exchange of stock and money was done. As part of the arrangement, a new board of directors took over at Stanwell. The new president of the company was a Texas oilman who was a close associate of Serge's. Other directors included Serge's accountant and a stockholder in one of his other companies. Serge controlled three of the five seats on the new Stanwell board.

Before the second part of the Stanwell deal could be done, Serge discovered that stock put up by the Blair company in the exchange had been vastly overvalued. Lee Brooks discovered the same thing, but before he could stop the deal the Rubinstein-controlled board of directors made the stock transfer anyway. Serge then hit his partner the Blair company with a lawsuit for "fraud and deceit," claiming well over a million dollars for his new company Stanwell, and effectively squeezing Blair out of the deal altogether. Lawsuits flew from all sides, and as a part of the fallout Virgil Dardi lost his job at Blair and was sued by his former company for conspiring with Rubinstein. Though Serge was clearly holding the cards, and was in fact working to parlay his Stanwell plunder into an empire centering on another Canadian company called Trans-Era Oils, the matter remained legally unresolved the day his body was found by the butler. The whole affair had been classic Serge Rubinstein: with a minimum investment but a maximum of ruthlessness and cunning, he had stolen a $2 million company and enlisted a new regiment of enemies in the process.

Because the intricate undersides of Serge's deals were hidden from public view, it is impossible to say what exactly he left behind in the way of ruined fortunes, plundered companies, and shattered reputations. Often the key players in a Rubinstein operation had little idea who the other players were or what the game plan was. In the Stanwell deal, for example, Serge had employed at least one other agent besides Stanley T. Stanley to work a completely different angle, unbeknownst to Mr. Stanley. During the last year of Serge's life, several bizarre – and still unexplained – episodes did become a part of the public record.

The month of August 1954 was a particularly strenuous one for the busy financier. At mid-month, Serge was beaten up by two men who attacked him in the street. He either couldn't or wouldn't identify the men to the police, and the reason for the attack was never established. On August 18, a rock wrapped with a threatening message – the contents of the message were not reported – was thrown through the window of the Rubinstein home. During the same month three men were arrested for allegedly making a $535,000 extortion attempt on Serge. Only one of the men, an Emanuel Lester, born with the name Lieberman, was indicted. Lester, incidentally, was out on bail but said to be on the West Coast at the time of Serge's murder.

On another occasion, astonished citizens observed Serge

chasing an unidentified man down the street while waving a large amount of money at him. The man took refuge in a phone booth, and Serge reportedly barged into the booth and hurled fluttering handfuls of bills upon his not-so-unfortunate victim's head. The amount of the flung currency was said to be in the vicinity of $20,000. The story goes that Serge had offered the man a bribe, which he had the audacity to refuse. Whether this is true, or whether Serge was simply throwing money at an unknown problem, the event does show a certain desperation on the part of a normally cool and calculating character.

Understandably, the aspect of the case that sold the most newspapers had nothing to do with these mysterious reports, nor with the complexities of Serge's financial schemes. It had to do with Serge's sex life. On January 13, 1955, Serge made the gossip columns by arriving at a gala New Year's Eve White Russian Ball at the Ambassador Hotel as the escort of not one but seven beautiful young women. The flamboyance was less a grandstanding gesture than a glimpse into Serge's daily, or nightly, life. According to police, he maintained a running stable of at least half a dozen women at a time. It was his habit to hand out keys to his Fifth Avenue mansion to this circle of favorites – so that he would not be troubled to go to the door when they came to visit – and to change the locks when the favorites became rejects and were replaced. This discovery especially interested the cops. It meant that at least six people, and any number of other people who knew them well enough to borrow or steal their keys, could walk into Serge's home unannounced at any time of the day or night. In the weeks following the murder, newspaper and magazine photographers worked over-time snapping pictures of the alluring stream of models, actresses, singers, and secretaries who found their way in and out of the offices of the Manhattan East detective division. Snapshots of Serge and his girlfriends were secured and splashed across spreads on the case. The pictures revealed little besides Serge's happy enjoyment of variety and his preferences in female companionship: all pretty, mostly in their twenties, and taller than himself – he is typically shown standing to around the nose level of the girl at his side.

The love-nest angle gave rise to interesting questions. Could one of the rejects have taken her ouster from the harem personally? Could a jealous spouse or boyfriend have exercised his territorial imperative? The fifty detectives assigned to the case were diligent at the onerous task of interrogating a legion of attractive young women – about half of the one thousand interviews held in the investigation fell into this category. Numerous leads were developed, but each was followed into thin air.

The very first lead was the young woman who appears to have been the last person – aside from the killer or killers – to see Serge Rubinstein alive. This was Estelle Gardner, a pretty brunette in her early twenties, who was a cosmetics saleswoman and sometime model. Estelle had been Serge's dinner date at Nino's LaRue, a pricey, dinner-jackets-only restaurant on East Fifty-eighth Street. The proprietor and the headwaiter confirmed that the couple had been on the premises from 9.30 p.m. until shortly before 1.00 a.m. Serge left his companion at the table on several occasions to make phone calls, at least two of them to Patricia Wray, another girlfriend who was a secretary at one of his companies. When Estelle and Serge left, two men who had been sitting nearby were observed following them from the restaurant. In hindsight, it seemed to the restaurant staff that these men had been keeping an eye on the couple all evening.

A cab was hailed. The cabdriver remembered Serge because he had to lend him a quarter so Serge could tip the doorman. The cabbie took his fares to Serge's home at 814 Fifth Avenue and watched them go inside. Estelle joined Serge for a nightcap and left in another cab at about 1.30 a.m. At about 2.30 a.m., Serge made one last call to Patricia Wray, trying to convince her to come over for a late-night visit. Patricia was asleep when the call came and remembered little about it, except that she declined the invitation. No one would hear from Serge Rubinstein again.

At 8.00 a.m., the butler entered Serge's room and made the grim discovery. He alerted the handyman, who had just arrived for work, and the police were called. The other people in the house were Serge's seventy-eight-year-old mother Stella, who lived with her son despite his earlier assault on her character before the immigration authorities, his eighty-two-year-old aunt Eugenia Forrester, a cook, and two maids. Serge's bedroom was on the third floor of the five floor home. Mrs. Forrester's room was immediately above Serge's on the fourth floor, while his mother slept on the fifth floor, where Serge also maintained an office.

The cops found twelve different fingerprints in the room, including latents on the adhesive tape that covered the victim's mouth, but were unable to connect the prints to any suspects. Though valuables were virtually everywhere, the only thing missing from the room was Serge's wallet. Nothing appeared to be missing from the rest of the house, and robbery was thus ruled out. A single glove and an empty woman's purse were found, but turned out to have been left by Patricia Wray during a visit months before. Because escape from the rear of the house was deemed to be virtually impossible, and no signs of forced entry were found, it was assumed the killer or killers had walked in through the front door. Had Serge let them in, or had they admitted themselves? No one could supply an answer.

The most productive clue was left behind by Serge himself. Six loose-leaf notebooks reportedly contained the names and phone numbers of as many as two thousand girlfriends, business associates, politicians, informers, pimps, and other high and low-lifes. Because of the way Serge had done business, the notebooks amounted to a ready-made list of suspects. The problem was the list was too long. The notebooks supplied the cops with interview material for months to come. The contents were not released to the public.

The time of death was estimated at between 2.30 and 5.00 a.m. After the autopsy, Chief Medical Examiner Milton Helpern said the cause of death was "manual strangulation." He found abrasions, but no clear fingermarks, on Serge's throat.

The two elderly ladies in the house confused the situation by offering ambiguous recollections. They had attended an opera at the Met and returned home around midnight. Mrs. Rubinstein recalled hearing the voices of men arguing in her son's room during the night. She thought little about this because Serge frequently entertained guests in the early hours, but did call down to her son, receiving no reply. She told reporters the argument took place at 1.00 a.m. – before Serge was home – but told police it happened "sometime before daylight." It may be noteworthy that Serge's mother had been in ill health and suffered from impaired hearing. Both she and Serge's aunt reported sighting a mysterious "woman in brown" moving through the house during the night, and this report caused great excitement until the police deduced that the "woman" was really either the butler or an ambulance attendant, and that the sighting must have taken place not during the night but the following morning, after the body was found.

Stanley T. Stanley offered his own intriguing but, as it turned out, unhelpful theory of the crime. He arrived on the scene while Serge's carpets were still being trampled by a horde of reporters and policemen, and announced to anyone who would listen that the murder was obviously "a mob job – a syndicate job." Why a mob job? Stanley did not elaborate, beyond confirming the obvious point that his late associate had "many business enemies." Shortly thereafter, Stanley inquired about obtaining a pistol permit. Within four months, he was dead himself at the age of fifty. The cause was reported as a heart attack.

Interviews with Serge's associates established that he was involved in business meetings until about 7:30 p.m. the evening before his death. The scene was the Madison Avenue office of Trans-Era Oils, the international company Serge coveted and in which he already had secured a foothold. He had acquired three percent of the stock and managed to install Stanley T. Stanley as chairman and add two of his other pals to the board of directors.

One of the subjects of Serge's last business conference was the ongoing struggle over Stanwell Oil & Gas, a key piece in a game plan that included the takeover of Trans-Era and other companies. The Stanwell Oil & Gas connection led police to Lee Brooks, a highly visible adversary of Serge's ever since Rubinstein had effectively stolen the Stanwell company from him the year before.

Himself no slouch as a big-time financial manipulator, Mr. Brooks was located in Jewish Memorial Hospital, where he had gone the day before the murder for surgical treatment of a slipped disk. He readily confirmed that he was no friend of Serge's, but was not prepared to take any credit for killing him. The Brooks connection grew more interesting when it was revealed that Brooks had twice been questioned in connection with the unsolved murder of a textile executive named Albert E. Langford in 1945. The explanation at the time was that Brooks had been involved in a business deal with Langford. When questioned in the Rubinstein investigation, Brooks reportedly denied any involvement with Langford. Beyond the fact that he was one among the multitude who may have had good reason to want Serge dead, no definite links were established between Brooks and the killing.

The investigation seemed to grind along with unpromising monotony until mid-February, with name after name checked off in Serge's address books. Then the news came that an informer had tired of cooling his heels in a jail cell and dropped a bombshell that seemed to solve the case. The informer had heard about a plan to kidnap Serge Rubinstein. The cops followed this lead to a small-time, fifty-year-old hood named Herman Scholz, who worked as a car-for-hire chauffeur to and from floating crap games. Scholz was a little man – the newspapers kept describing him as "jockey-sized" – with a long criminal record and big plans. When detectives tailed him to the house in Queens where he lived with his wife and her parents, they found a modest arsenal hidden in the cellar. There was a Thompson submachine gun, a .45 automatic, a .32 revolver, a

.38 revolver, a blackjack, a switchblade, and a stock of ammunition. They also found a small library of afternoon newspapers containing every detail then known about the Rubinstein murder, and, reportedly, a quantity of curtain cord and adhesive tape, the same devices that had been used to bind Serge. Things looked bad for Herman Scholz. But after questioning him for twelve hours straight, police and prosecutors decided he made a better material witness than a suspect.

Scholz's story was that he had hatched a plan to kidnap Serge maybe one or two years before, but had dropped it when one confederate chickened out and another went to jail on a burglary rap. About three months before the murder, he regained interest in the kidnap plan and began casing the Rubinstein home from the front seat of the second-hand Cadillac convertible he used professionally. The guns, Scholz said, had nothing to do with Serge. They were laid away for use in the robbery of two banks, another plan of his that never came to fruition. The newspaper clippings were saved only to prove to his associates what a golden opportunity they had let slip through their fingers.

Apparently Scholz had a good alibi for the night of the murder. For this or some other reason, the prosecutors in the Rubinstein case became convinced that his only connection with the murder was that he had been too loose-lipped about his kidnap plan, and someone else had beat him to it. Assistant District Attorney Alexander Herman theorized that the Scholz plan had inspired "certain members of the underworld who in our very definite opinion committed this murder." This became the bungled snatch theory of the case. In the Assistant District Attorney's words, "it was kidnap for ransom that went wrong."

The public statements from the DA's office had the "we know who they are" ring that suggests an imminent arrest. But the arrest never came. If Herman Scholz did name the names of any kidnappers, there must not have been enough of a case to seek indictments.

The bungled snatch idea was the first and only official explanation of the death of Serge Rubinstein. It came three weeks after his murder, and nothing better has surfaced in the ensuing thirty-five years. Perhaps the theory never became more than a theory because of its one glaring weakness: why would anyone setting out to kidnap a man for ransom strangle him to death without even removing him from his own house? Manual strangulation is a deliberate act, not something that happens by accident. Serge was securely bound and gagged. He was under the complete control of his killers and wasn't about to go anywhere on his own steam. Whoever strangled him did it because he or she wanted him dead.

If Serge's murder is forever unsolved, the cops who worked it can hardly be blamed. It was an impossible case from the beginning, and it was the victim himself who made it that way. Cunning as he was, there was a built-in and fatal flaw in the conduct of his business. When his time ran out, he left behind too many deadly enemies, and far too many answers to the question "Who could have wanted this guy dead?"

Postscript

There have been no developments of note in the Rubinstein case, not too surprising since the trails are so many and so cold.

But I did recently come across the eulogy delivered by Serge's rabbi at his funeral. One can hardly avoid sympathetic feelings for the rabbi, who must have struggled mightily in his efforts not to speak ill of the dead. The rabbi, obviously an honest man, called Serge a "psychopathic personality." But he did go on to say, searching for a positive remembrance, that Serge had always been kind to his mother.

No doubt he had never heard of the time when it became expedient for Serge to falsely claim his father was a Portuguese and little Serge himself the product of Mama's infidelity.

Oh well, the rabbi tried.

6

Sunny in Darkness

The Trials of Claus von Bülow

"The very rich are different from you and I," F. Scott Fitzgerald said to Hemingway.

"Yes," Hemingway said, "they have more money."

This is the story of people who had more money than anyone could ever use. It could just as easily have been a fairy tale, for it has princes and princesses and glittering soirees, and the charmed existences of those who live as far from cares as any in this world. Instead it is a tale of greed. Of lust and betrayal and vengeance and, perhaps, attempted murder. The princess in this story sleeps under the spell of an evil potion, a sleep from which all the princes in the world will never wake her.

Martha "Sunny" von Bülow has lain in a coma since December 21, 1980. A radio plays softly in her nursing home room, and there is a vase of freesias, fragrant and freshly cut. So far as anyone knows, she has never heard the radio or smelled the flowers. So far as anyone knows she has no thoughts, no memories, no dreams. Except for the purely mechanical functions that keep her breathing and circulate her blood, her brain appears to have died.

The pale figure on the bed is the shell of a woman who was once a striking beauty, but who possessed a great deal more than good looks. In her day, Sunny von Bülow was the most dazzling – and the richest – of the East Coast debutantes, the bride in a storybook marriage to an Austrian prince, the pampered heiress to a $75 million fortune. To the world at large, she is now no more than a very famous victim.

What, and who, put Sunny into darkness? It is a question that has been examined through the course of two lengthy criminal trials and several lawsuits. No one has been found guilty of harming Sunny von Bülow. But the courts, as Oliver Wendell Holmes reminds us, dispense law, not justice. There are many who believe the sleeping beauty in the hospital bed is half alive today only because a would-be murderer botched his job. Perhaps just as many believe Sunny, whether by intention or accident, brought the damage on herself.

These well-divided opinions spring from the nature of the case, a case in which the character of the victim became as important as the hard evidence. What you believe about Sunny von Bülow has a great deal to do with whether you believe her husband tried to kill her.

Sunny's father was good at finding oil and gas. His name was George Crawford. The empire he built began in the gas fields of western Pennsylvania and extended throughout the Midwest, into Oklahoma and Texas, and down into Mexico and Colombia. At the age of sixty-six, George Crawford turned his attentions from empire building and settled into marriage with a lovely twenty-eight-year-old redhead named Annie Laurie Warmack, who was heir to a respectable fortune of her own, resulting from her own father's knack for making and selling shoes. George Crawford died in 1935, when his daughter was three years old.

Sunny was raised by her mother and maternal grandmother. She quite literally had everything money could buy. Spoiled is too ordinary a word to describe her upbringing. Sunny Crawford was surrounded by money, sheltered by money, conditioned by everything she knew to exist only in the rarefied atmosphere of the ultra rich. Sunny never lived in a house that was not fully staffed with servants. When she needed a ball gown, she traveled with mother and grandmother to Paris, and was the first to wear the latest creation of Dior. When Sunny summered, she summered in Europe, with a Rolls and a chauffeur and the watchful attentions of mother and grandmother accompanying her on the passage. She attended the Chapin school and St. Timothy's, but skipped college. A career was not one of the things she needed. When Sunny came out into society, she did it at the most lavish party of the year, at Tamberlane, her mother's estate in Greenwich. There were crystal chandeliers hanging from the trees. The Lester Lanin orchestra played, and guests walked down a flight of fifty steps to the pool and poolhouse with its display of exotic game, under canopies specially matched to the ice-blue curtains that adorned the Georgian manor for this occasion only. Sunny wore a Dior gown with eighty yards of tulle and two diamond bows.

With all this power at her command, one might expect Sunny to have grown into a worldly, if not overbearing, young woman. The opposite was true: for all her wealth and beauty, Sunny is described by friends of the period as exceptionally vulnerable, passive, and pathologically shy. She was serious and good-hearted. She made up for her lack of formal education by devouring books voraciously. The idea of a social encounter gave her hives. Still she dated, but asked her dates to sit with her at the edge of the party, as far from the crowd as possible. When her affections for one young beau – a Russian translator of noble but impecunious heritage – seemed serious, mother whisked her off to an Austrian resort called Schloss Mittersill.

The owners of this resort had the good sense to employ a staff of titled but unwealthy European bluebloods to attract untitled but super-wealthy Europeans and Americans as paying guests. The tennis pro at the resort was right out of the pages of *Cinderella:* twenty years old, blond, athletic, devilishly handsome, and a genuine, certifiable prince. His name was Alfie von Auersperg. Prince Alfie's family had lost its money and its property to the Communists in World War II. His job at Schloss Mittersill put him in the perfect position to recoup the family lifestyle by meeting and marrying money. Enter Sunny Crawford. The love came at first sight. The marriage came, over the objections of Sunny's mother, on July 20, 1957. Sunny was twenty-three years old.

The Prince proved to have a roving eye, but the marriage lasted eight years and produced a little prince and princess. The daughter was named after Sunny's mother – Annie Laurie – and would go by the nickname Ala. The son was named Alexander. The young couple acquired another member of the household who would play a central part in this story, a wiry and severe German woman named Maria Shrallhammer, Sunny's personal maid. In 1965, long after it became clear that Alfie was more interested in big-game hunting and romantic conquests than in family life, Sunny took the children and settled near her mother in New York, obtaining a divorce a few months later. Maria moved to America with her mistress.

During the latter days of her marriage to Alfie, Sunny had traveled to London. There, mutual friends introduced her to a dashing barrister and boulevardier named Claus Bülow, who worked as a sort of international troubleshooter for the billionaire J. Paul Getty, and traveled in Europe's loftiest social circles. Sunny and Claus hit it off instantly. They were married thirteen months after Sunny's divorce from Alfie, on June 6, 1966.

Claus was forty at the time, to Sunny's thirty-four. He lacked Alfie's bloodline, but made-up for it with a deep and intriguing character. Well educated and urbane, Claus was the perfect sophisticate, with a slashing wit and an abiding love of money and all that it could buy. He was in a complete sense a self-made man: even his name was made up.

Several versions of Claus's life story have appeared in print. A broad-brush version of the story goes like this:

When Claus was born in Copenhagen, Denmark, in 1926, his name was Claus Cecil Borberg. His father was a playwright and drama critic named Svend Borberg, who was accused of being a Nazi collaborator during World War II. His mother sprang from a prominent and well-off Danish family. Her father had been Minister of Justice and a leading businessman and financier. Young Claus was raised by his mother and grandfather, after his parents divorced when he was still a young child. Perhaps because of his social aspirations, he chose as a young man to take his mother's family name, Bülow, and – after marrying into the Crawford fortune – gave the name an added ring of importance by transforming it to von Bülow. Claus has claimed he has the right to the "von" through a patent of nobility granted to his mother's family, and has told friends he added it only upon Sunny's insistence.

Claus's early education came in elite Danish and Swiss schools. During World War II, his Bülow family connections helped him escape to London, where his mother was waiting out the war. According to his story, he became, at age nineteen, the youngest man ever to take a law degree at Cambridge. He attended the Sorbonne in Paris, returned to London and worked briefly as a banker, then settled in as barrister in the distinguished chambers of Lord Hailsham. By his mid-twenties, Bülow was well established in London society, throwing lavish parties in his Belgrave Square apartment and jet-setting to the poshest European resorts. His London running buddies included some notorious characters. One was Stephen Ward, the man who ran the call-girl operation that became infamous in the Profumo scandal. Another good friend was Lord "Lucky" Lucan, who disappeared after allegedly murdering the family nanny and attempting to murder his estranged wife in 1974.

In 1959, at age thirty-three, Claus left the practice of law to accept a job offer from J. Paul Getty, perhaps the world's richest man. He worked as chief executive assistant to Getty, putting together deals for Getty Oil around the globe. Getty would not set foot on an airplane. Claus would, and when he did he carried Getty's proxy and a considerable accumulation of financial, legal, and diplomatic skills.

Claus appears to be one of those people who create no neutral impressions. He is certainly a smart man, with a broad self-awareness and a sophisticated view of the world. He cannot help, he says, being a "melancholy Dane." He knows that to some he seems pompous, cold, and full of pretension. To others, he is warm and witty, companionable, even "cozy." His conversation is delivered in a plummy upper-crust accent, laced with gossip, anecdote, and literary allusion. With his chilly demeanor and his outdated mannerisms, von Bülow could pass for an overdressed and overeducated funeral director. Perhaps this is why he inspires the juiciest of rumors. One held that his sexual preference leaned toward sadism, and that his London quarters included a well-stocked torture room. Another, based on a joke originated by his jet-set friends, was that he enjoyed necrophilia. "Dado [Allessandro] Ruspoli called him a necrophiliac," an old acquaintance told a reporter, "and then everyone wanted him for dinner."

Whatever the truth about Claus, one thing was indisputable: when Sunny became Sunny von Bülow, he became fantastically rich. He had never been poor, but with Sunny's money he could indulge his most refined and most expensive tastes. He stayed on with Getty for two years as a consultant, but gave up that job to become a full-time husband. According to Claus, he did this because Sunny objected to his traveling. It was a career move he would bitterly regret.

The couple moved into Sunny's massive New York apartment, on Fifth Avenue at Seventy-seventh Street. Claus set about redecorating the place with eighteenth-century furniture. He also took the opportunity to redo his Belgrave Square apartment in London, and the couple gave and were given lavish entertainments on both sides of the Atlantic. The von Bülows' first and only child, born in 1967, was a daughter named Cosima. The choice of names seemed strange to those who knew their music history: another Cosima von Bülow created one of the greatest scandals of the nineteenth century by carrying on a blatant affair with Richard Wagner under the nose of her husband, the conductor Hans von Bülow.

Given their position in society, the von Bülows could hardly do without a second home outside New York. They focused on Newport, Rhode Island, a traditional summering place for the great and moneyed families. Sunny's mother, who had become

Mrs. Russell Aitken, already maintained a stately residence there. After some shopping, Claus and Sunny bought Clarendon Court, a twenty-room stone mansion overlooking the Atlantic, and just down the street from the Aitkens. The house was built in 1904. It had been displayed to America as the set for the 1956 Grace Kelly and Frank Sinatra movie *High Society*. The von Bülows spent a reported $1 million reworking the grounds, and more remodeling and redecorating the house with art and antiques. In the end they had created a showplace that put the other great houses of Newport to shame. Acquaintances of the time saw Claus and Sunny as a happy couple. They traveled widely, entertained regularly, and, with Claus taking the lead, quickly established themselves in the important functions, clubs, and charities of Newport society.

The happy period was short-lived. By the mid to late 1970s, serious issues were threatening the marriage. A pall had fallen over the couple's once charmed lives. To their Newport peers, the magnificent Clarendon Court began to have the feel of a mausoleum or a sickroom. At her own entertainments, which became ever fewer and further between, Sunny wore a frozen smile. At other social occasions, she bolted without explanation. Claus had grown tired of the idle life and wanted to reestablish his business career; Sunny wanted him underfoot. Sunny seemed to slip further back into reclusiveness. Her supporters blame Claus, saying he consciously isolated Sunny from her friends. On his side, the argument goes that Sunny simply lost interest in society, and Claus was left to go alone or make excuses. The ever-so-sociable von Bülow was reduced to putting himself to sleep in front of the television. Claus began to complain to friends that Sunny was drinking heavily. Then there was the matter of sex, or more precisely, the matter of no sex. Claus claimed that Sunny had broken off sexual relations with him shortly after Cosima's birth, telling him that he could take his sexual pleasures anywhere he pleased so long as he was discreet. Sunny, according to the testimony of a psychiatrist, mentioned a shorter but nonetheless substantial period of celibacy. She said she and Claus had not had sex in five years.

In 1978, at age fifty-two, Claus made a connection that would ease his suffering. He met Alexandra Isles, a dark-haired, fawn-eyed, delicately beautiful daughter of an old Danish acquaintance. Alexandra was thirty-two, a divorcee and the single parent of a young son. She was no stranger to the upper echelons of New York society; she had attended the same schools as Sunny and had been married to a prominent investment banker. While Claus's grandfather had been Minister of Justice in Denmark, Alexandra's had been Foreign Minister. A sometime actress, she had appeared on the vampire-infested TV soap opera *Dark Shadows*. Claus discreetly courted Alexandra, and they began an affair in earnest in early 1979. According to Alexandra, Claus declared his love and said he wanted to marry her as soon as he could loose himself from Sunny. Alexandra gave Claus what amounted to a deadline: if he was not available for marriage by the end of 1979, she might look elsewhere.

Alexandra was apparently not Claus's only distraction from his marital problems. Pretrial investigations reportedly indicated he was a client of an alleged prostitute named Leslie Baxter, for sex, drugs, or both.

During the same period, Claus took other steps to dissociate himself from Sunny. He began to look for business opportunities. Using Sunny's money, he invested in Broadway shows. The first was *Deathtrap,* the story of a man who plots a perfect murder. The second was a musical called *Carmelina*. Claus also made investments in art, and started looking for a job in earnest. He found one with the financier Mark Millard, who was an energy specialist and appreciated Claus's international experience with Getty Oil. Claus told Millard that because of his wife's objections he would only be available for part-time employment. Still, Millard was impressed with the effort he put in and the results he achieved.

There can be little doubt that the von Bülows' marriage was in a precarious state in late 1979. Sunny herself talked about it. She told her son Alexander that "she felt she was restraining"

Claus because he felt strongly about having a job and "she wanted him to be at home with her." In December of 1979, she remarked to her daughter Ala that a divorce might be imminent because Claus was becoming "very nervous" and "it was becoming very difficult to live around the man."

Nevertheless, Sunny was extremely generous to her husband when she chose to make out a new will that month. According to testimony, Claus was to receive roughly $14 million in the event of her death – about the same amount given to each of the three children – the New York apartment, the Newport home, and all jewelry, furs, and household articles. Almost as important to a power-conscious socialite, Claus was given control over decisions involving charitable trusts, and thus the potential to wield an enormous influence in his milieu.

As she considered the details of her will, Sunny was only days away from a crisis that would bring her to death's door. The von Bülows spent Christmas of 1979 at Clarendon Court. In the early evening on December 26, Sunny was having an after-dinner eggnog with the family when her son, then twenty years old, noticed that she appeared to rapidly weaken and her speech began to slur. Her voice trailed off to nothing. Claus was not in the room at the time, and the young man helped his mother to her bedroom. Sunny's personal maid, Maria Shrallhammer, went in to check on her at about 8.00 p.m. She reported that Sunny appeared to be asleep, and that Claus was in the bedroom, still awake and fully dressed.

At about 9.30 the next morning, according to Maria's story, Claus approached her and told her Mrs. von Bülow had a sore throat and would be spending the day in bed; Maria's services would not be needed. Claus was not speaking to an ordinary servant, but to a formidable adversary. Maria had been at Sunny's side for more than twenty years. She had spent more time with Sunny than either of her husbands or any of her children. Sunny was, quite literally, Maria's life work, and her devotion was complete. She says she went to Sunny's bedroom door and listened. She heard Sunny moaning, knocked, and got no reply. Despite Claus's instructions, she entered the room. On one of the twins beds, Sunny appeared to be sleeping. On the other, Claus was reading a newspaper. Sunny was usually a light sleeper, awakened by the opening of the door. Maria was alarmed. She called Sunny's name but got no response. She took Sunny's arm, found it limp and cold, and shook it, yelling, "Madam, wake up!" No response. According to Maria, Claus showed no concern.

Maria says she told Claus that Sunny was unconscious, but he replied that she was only sleeping. He explained that Sunny had not slept in two nights, and needed the rest. She pleaded with him to call a doctor, but he repeated that Sunny was only sleeping and should not be disturbed.

Thoroughly upset, Maria went back to her ironing. After about half an hour, she returned to the bedroom and tried again to awaken Sunny, with the same results. She again asked Claus to call a doctor or Sunny's mother. This time, she says, he told her Sunny had drunk too much the night before and needed to sleep it off. Maria, who maintains that her mistress was not a heavy drinker, did not buy this story. These strange confrontations apparently went on at intervals throughout the morning, with Claus von Bülow stretched out beside his unconscious wife and an increasingly agitated personal maid popping in and out of the room.

Sometime early in the afternoon, after Maria had finally threatened to call a doctor on her own, von Bülow called a local doctor named Janis Gailitis who had seen Sunny for minor ailments. Maria says she overheard Claus telling the doctor his wife had a serious alcohol problem and had had "one of those nights," and left the room in disgust. Before doing so, she heard Claus tell the doctor that Sunny had been up during the day and that he had given her a drink of soda. He says the doctor told him that given the two nights of insomnia, there was no need for serious concern. He should keep an eye on Sunny's breathing and call back if there was any change. Toward evening Sunny's breathing pattern changed into what both sides have described as "a kind of rattle." Claus called the doctor in a panic, and at about the time the doctor arrived Sunny stopped breathing. She had no pulse. Gailitis cleared her throat of vomit and started mouth-to-mouth. Then he gave her a pericardial punch and worked to get her heart beating. When her pulse and breathing resumed, an emergency crew took Sunny to Newport Hospital. She had come within minutes of dying.

Changing the bedsheets, Maria says she found a puddle of urine where Sunny had been lying. She concluded that her mistress had not gotten up during the day at all, and that von Bülow had lied to the doctor.

At the hospital emergency room, the routine blood tests were performed on the still-unconscious Sunny. No alcohol or barbiturates were found. The most significant finding seemed to be that Sunny's blood sugar was low – at 41 milligrams per 100 milliliters. A normal reading would be between 70 and 110 mg. Sunny was given glucose, and her blood sugar was tested again about three hours later. The level was not higher, as would be expected after the glucose injections, but *lower:* this time it was 20 mg. Something appeared to be consuming Sunny's blood sugar. A reasonable conclusion would be that there was an unusually high level of insulin in her body. Insulin is, of course, the medication given diabetics to control blood sugar levels. It is a naturally occurring hormone produced in the pancreas. Because it is a natural substance and difficult to trace, insulin can be – and has been – used as a means of murder. For that matter, it has also been used as a means of suicide. About five hours after Sunny was admitted to the hospital, she was tested for insulin. The result showed 72 mg., a high but not extremely high level. Insulin levels vary widely in a normal individual, ranging anywhere from 15 to 100 mg. The glucose injections were continued, and Sunny's insulin level the next morning was down to 54 mg. Because Sunny had been receiving glucose for five hours before her insulin was first tested, it seemed reasonable to speculate that her insulin level may have been much higher earlier in the crisis.

Sunny regained consciousness during the day of December 28, and appeared to make a full recovery. The cause of the crisis was a mystery. Sunny was eventually diagnosed as a reactive hypoglycemic, a person whose body produces too much insulin when too much sugar is consumed. According to her family, Sunny did not take the diagnosis seriously, and continued to eat sweets as she pleased.

Another person who did not accept the diagnosis was Maria Shrallhammer. From her viewpoint, Claus's behavior during Sunny's crisis had been outrageous and unforgivable. She blamed Mr. von Bülow for what had happened to Mrs. von Bülow, and told both of Sunny's older children, Alexander and Ala, of her suspicions. These suspicions were communicated to Mrs. Aitken, who in turn made it clear to Claus that she expected him to call a doctor anytime Sunny had so much as a hangnail. Claus responded by addressing a letter to Dr. Gailitis, in which he stated his case and asked the doctor for an opinion, "preferably in writing," on whether he had been remiss in his response to Sunny's illness. Gailitis wrote a letter stating that Sunny's deterioration was unpredictable and that Claus, by calling a doctor, had saved her life.

Oddly, while these communications flowed back and forth, no one talked to Sunny. At the least, her family and her servant suspected her husband of gross negligence. At the most, they suspected him of attempted murder. Why did they keep silent? Maria has said she did not think it was appropriate for her to interfere in the marriage. Alexander has said that you do not accuse someone of attempted murder without proof. But in the light of subsequent events, the fact that no one warned or questioned Sunny creates a mystery within a mystery.

In February of 1980, at the New York apartment, Sunny rang Maria for breakfast and gave her a breakfast order. But when the breakfast was brought in, according to Maria, Sunny was too weak to sit up. She couldn't even see the breakfast tray, and was barely able to talk. Maria says she told Claus about this, and he replied that Sunny had the flu and had eaten a greasy hamburger the night before. Sunny's long-time doctor was called but gave only a telephone consultation over what appeared to be a case of the flu. Sunny recovered within a few hours.

Maria remained vigilant. During the same month, she uncovered an object that would become a premier exhibit in the case. Maria has said that she was cleaning a walk-in closet in the New York apartment, a closet that Claus and Sunny shared. A piece of luggage that Claus used to carry personal items between the two homes in New York and Rhode Island was open. Inside it, Maria spotted a little black bag. It was an un-remarkable bag, a small item about six inches long with a zipper running around the top. It had once held a calculator. Without knowing why she did it, Maria says, she picked up the bag and unzipped it. Inside were pill bottles, the kind that came from the drug store. There were pills, but there was also a bottle that held a white powder, and another that held a yellow paste. One of the labels was made out to someone named Leslie Baxter, a name Maria had never heard before.

Maria took the bag to Ala, and the two of them took samples from the bottles. These samples were given to Sunny's family doctor, Richard Stock, who had them analyzed. The pills were Valium. The yellow paste was Valium. The white powder was the sedative secobarbital. The strange thing was the form the drugs were in: sedatives are not available to the general public in paste and powder form.

Maria returned the black bag to its place in Claus's luggage. From this point forward the little black bag and the man who carried it were under scrutiny.

In April 1980, Sunny had another episode of illness. Her speech was slurred and her body movements became uncoordi-nated. Claus was not at home, so Maria called Mrs. Aitken, who called Dr. Stock. The doctor put Sunny in the hospital, and it was here that the reactive hypoglycemia diagnosis was delivered. Reactive hypoglycemia is a relatively common illness that can make its victims weak and dizzy. It is controlled by the avoidance of sweets and liquor, and is not considered life-threatening. Except in the rarest of circumstances, it does not put people into comas.

Because of Claus's earlier confrontations with Sunny's mother, the question of who was responsible for Sunny's health had become a territorial issue. When Claus learned Maria had called Mrs. Aitken, he appeared to be angry. He spoke to Sunny, and shortly afterward Sunny called Maria in and told her she was never to call Mrs. Aitken without prior approval.

In May the family and its entourage traveled to Austria for Ala's wedding to a ski equipment magnate named Frank Kneissl. Sunny appeared to be in good health and spirits. That same spring, Claus resumed his affair with Alexandra Isles. During the summer, without telling Sunny, he took an apartment of his own in New York. Sunny later learned about the apartment from a friend, but whether she confronted Claus about it is unknown. The affair with Alexandra was rocky, with Claus repeating his intention to leave Sunny and then doing nothing about it. In November Alexandra took a job in Washington without telling Claus. He tracked her down there and offered to call Sunny and ask for a divorce while Alexandra listened in. Alexandra claims she told him such news should be communicated face to face.

During the Thanksgiving holiday of 1980, Sunny told her son Alexander that she had decided to divorce Claus. He says that when he asked why, she replied the reason was "too horrible to tell." She did not elaborate. Maria claims to have spotted the little black bag again during the same weekend, this time in a white canvas sack Claus had packed to take to Newport. She looked inside. She testified that she found the pill bottles again, but with them she found something new: a glass vial holding a clear liquid, with a label marked "Insulin." Beside the vial were several needles and a syringe. Maria showed her find to Alexander. "Insulin," she asked, "what for insulin?" It seems a good question. Still, no one put the question to Sunny.

The syringes and needles were not a great surprise, because Maria had seen similar objects before. She knew that Claus had once been in the habit of injecting himself with vitamin shots, and that he had also given injections to Sunny. Once, during a family vacation to Majorca, Maria remembered the children using the syringes as water guns.

One week later, on December 1, 1980, Claus knocked on Maria's door around 10.00 in the evening. Sunny had been suffering from a headache all day and, as was her habit, had been taking heavy doses of aspirin. Now, Claus said, she had fallen and hit her head. Maria ran to Sunny's room and found her bleeding profusely from a cut on the back of her head. There was blood on the pillow, the bed, and the carpet. Sunny was conscious and talking, but her speech was too slurred to understand. Claus called the emergency number and Sunny was rushed to the nearest hospital. She remained for six days, under treatment for aspirin toxicity. Her blood sugar levels were normal. According to Dr. Stock, Claus approached him during Sunny's hospital stay and confessed that he was contemplating a divorce. He wanted to know if the doctor thought Sunny was strong enough to withstand the experience. Stock said he thought she was.

At about this time, Maria wrote a letter to a friend in Germany, detailing the traumas of the past year and her suspicions about Claus. She described an unhappy household where there were no parties, no social life, and the husband had a girlfriend. Still, she said, "Mrs. trusts her husband blindly and is totally dependent."

"Bülow and I," she wrote, "are at daggers' points."

On December 19, the family packed up to spend a pre-Christmas weekend in Newport. They planned to return to New York to celebrate Christmas itself with the Aitkens. Maria had planned to go to Newport, but says Claus told her he felt she was tired and should take the weekend off. Claus has said Maria did not usually accompany the family on weekends. As she was taking luggage down to the elevator, Maria spotted the little black bag. She says she opened it, saw the insulin bottle and the syringes and needles, and put it back where she had found it.

She said goodbye to Sunny, who seemed happy and well. It was the last time she would ever see her mistress conscious.

Sunny spent most of the day Saturday, December 20, decorating the Clarendon Court Christmas tree. Ala was in Europe. The family members gathered at the Newport house were Sunny, Claus, Alexander, who was home from college, and Cosima, then thirteen. After dinner, Sunny had a large bowl of ice cream with caramel sauce. She complained of a headache but otherwise seemed in good spirits. The group went to see the movie *Nine to Five* at a local theater. According to Alexander, Claus approached him while Sunny was dressing for the show and told him how unhappy he was at being unable to have a full-time job. He felt "like a gigolo" and was afraid people thought of him as living off Sunny. His stepson claims this was the second time Claus had confided these feelings. The first time was the night of Sunny's first coma, almost a year before.

After the movie, Sunny and the two children were talking in the library while Claus worked in his study, which was off the master bedroom. Sunny went to her bedroom and returned in a dressing gown, carrying a glass of something Alexander thought was ginger ale. During the conversation, Alexander noticed that his mother's speech had begun to slur. When Claus came into the room, Sunny asked him for a cup of chicken soup and he fixed it for her. While she was waiting for the soup, her voice became so weak that Alexander couldn't hear it. Claus brought the soup and returned to his study. Sunny drank the soup, but then seemed to weaken very quickly. She tried to stand up and staggered. Alexander asked her if she had taken any sleeping pills and she said no. Despite her protests, Alexander picked her up and carried her to her bedroom. Alexander went to tell Claus that his mother was ill, then returned and helped tuck her into bed. Before Alexander left the bedroom, Sunny asked him to open the windows. She had always preferred sleeping in a cold room. This night was especially cold: the wind chill factor was below zero.

Claus says he awoke at around 5.30 the next morning. The

couple owned four Labrador retrievers who slept in the room with them. Sometimes the dogs snored, and Sunny and Claus had taken to wearing ear plugs to shut out the noise. Claus let out the dogs, showered, read the paper, and went for a walk. Sunny appeared to be still sleeping. At about 11.00 a.m., Alexander observed his stepfather walking back from the ocean with the dogs. He seemed surprised that Sunny was not up, and went to check on her. He quickly returned and signaled Alexander to come with him. Sunny was lying on her bathroom floor. Her mouth was bleeding from a cut on her lip, and her nightgown was pulled up around her waist. She was in a puddle of urine. Claus established that she was breathing and rushed to call the emergency number. Alexander felt how cold his mother was and put a throw rug over her.

Sunny was taken again to the emergency room at Newport Hospital. She went into cardiac arrest almost immediately and was resuscitated. Her body temperature was only 81.6 degrees, and her pulse below 40. The standard blood tests were taken. Her body was not examined for needle marks. As soon as Sunny stabilized, she was moved into intensive care and given glucose injections. This was because the first blood tests had showed an extremely low blood sugar reading of 29 mg. Small amounts of barbiturates were found, but no alcohol or aspirin. Dr. Gerhard Meier, the attending physician, ordered an insulin test and found a level that was extremely high: 216 mg, compared to the normal range of 15 to 100 mg. Sunny's doctors concluded that she must have received exogenous insulin – insulin from outside the body. The next day Sunny was still in the coma from which she has never recovered. She was moved to a hospital in Boston that specializes in deep coma care, and from there to a hospital in New York.

For Sunny's family, this was the point at which suspicions about Claus were transformed into convictions. It was too late to be of any use to Sunny. Alex and Ala attended a meeting with Mrs. Aitken and her husband, and Morris Gurley, a long-time family trust officer and advisor. Gurley suggested that the group retain a lawyer to conduct a discreet investigation, and recommended Richard Kuh, the former District Attorney of Manhattan. Kuh began his investigation in early January of 1981. In the meantime, there were discussions about taking Sunny off the life-support equipment that was then keeping her alive, and Claus seemed to Alex and Ala a bit too eager to take this fatal step.

Alexander had looked for the little black bag of drugs at Clarendon Court, but had found his stepfather's closet locked. This was unusual. When this was reported to Richard Kuh, he dispatched Alexander back to Clarendon Court in the company of a private detective named Eddie Lambert. A locksmith was hired, but his services turned out to be unnecessary, since a key to the locked bedroom closet was found in Claus's desk. A search of the closet revealed a metal box, and inside the box was the little black bag. There would later be uncertainty about what was in the bag, because no record was made of its contents and no photographs were taken. The initial report was that the bag held several bottles of pills, other drugs in liquid and powder form, one syringe, and three needles. Two of the needles were still in their plastic sleeves, but one of them appeared to have been used.

The issue of the bag's contents was further confused when the two men gathered up samples of pills from Sunny's bedside table and bathroom, from Claus's pockets and bathroom, and dumped them in the bag with the other drugs. Dr. Stock had the drugs said to have come from the bag analyzed, and the liquid and powder turned out to be Valium. But the most damning piece of evidence was the used needle. Laboratory analysis of the needle showed that it had been in contact with Valium, amobarbital, and a high concentration of insulin.

The case against Claus seemed clear. Kuh took his evidence to the authorities. In the meantime Claus, by all appearances unaware that the family was moving against him, got on with life. In mid-February of 1981, less than two months after his wife was hospitalized and just after the doctors had pronounced her coma irreversible, he took a vacation to the Bahamas with Alexandra Isles and her son. He told his stepchildren he was going to New Orleans on business. He took another trip with Alexandra the next month, this time to Florida. Von Bülow's first inkling that he was under suspicion seems to have come in an interview with Rhode Island police in April. In July he was indicted on charges of attempting to murder Sunny.

Thus began one of the most widely reported and controversial legal spectacles of our time. Newport society in particular and the media-watching public in general became divided into pro-Claus and anti-Claus camps. There was a determined set of Claus groupies; there was an army of reporters sniffing at every lead; and, for those who couldn't personally attend the Newport circus, there was the eye of the television camera in the court-room, bringing news snippets of the action to every armchair in America. After the dust had settled on the pretrial legal maneu-vering, the trial itself opened in Newport on January 11, 1982. Claus was charged with causing both of Sunny's comas: the brief one in December of 1979, and the final one in December 1980.

Claus had expensive legal help: a politically connected Rhode Island insider named John Sheehan, and a big-name New Yorker, Herald Price Fahringer, who had defended pornogra-pher Larry Flynt and other notables. The chief prosecutor was a thirty-four year old Assistant Attorney General named Stephen Famiglietti. At first glance this lineup had the look of many another rich man's trial, an encounter where the defense has the resources to outspend, outgun, and outwait the state. But in the event the formal prosecution team benefited from a second team behind the scenes, armed with all the resources of Sunny's family and of its hired gun Richard Kuh.

The state's case was circumstantial and relied on complex medical testimony. No one had seen Claus inject Sunny with insulin, but it seemed clear he had the motive, the means, and the opportunity. From there it was simply a matter of who the jury would believe. Maria told her story convincingly. By all accounts, the maid was the deadliest witness against her power-ful employer. Alexander's testimony corroborated Maria's, and added the discovery of the dirty needle. Morris Gurley, the trust officer, laid out all that Claus had to gain from the will Sunny wrote just before the first coma. And Alexandra Isles gave a captivating account of the affair and of her ultimatum giving Claus a deadline concurrent with the first coma.

These witnesses stirred the emotions, but it was the doctors who tied the ribbon of medical opinion around the prosecution's package. A small parade of MD's repeated that the only possi-ble cause of both of Sunny's comas was exogenous insulin. In addition to the doctors who had actually treated Sunny, the state brought in Dr. George Cahill, a Harvard Medical School pro-fessor considered the world's leading authority on blood sugar.

In the face of all this, the defense seemed uncertain where and how to attack the prosecution's case. No serious challenge was mounted to the proposition that the only possible cause of Sunny's comas was injection with insulin. A medical expert was presented to offer other scenarios, but even he concluded that insulin could not be ruled out.

Could Sunny have injected herself with insulin? The defense suggested this by bringing on a surprise witness named Joy O'Neill, an exercise instructor who claimed to have given Sunny private exercise classes five times a week for four years, and to have been as close to Sunny as a sister. Ms. O'Neill testified that Sunny had once suggested insulin injections as a way of losing weight, and had further recommended injections of vitamin B and Valium. This appeared to be exactly the kind of testimony Claus needed. But the prosecution poked holes in Ms. O'Neill's credi-bility by introducing evidence that she barely knew Sunny and had only rarely given exercise classes to her. A great deal more would be said about Sunny's familiarity with drugs, but not in time to help Claus at his first trial. The defense brought on other witnesses to try to establish that Sunny was suicidal and/or addicted to drugs, but none of them, as it turned out, offered much more in the way of credibility than Joy O'Neill.

On March 16, 1982, the jury brought in a verdict of guilty on both counts. Claus would be sentenced to ten years on the first count and twenty years on the second. Had he been a man without wealth and connections this might have been the end of the story. He was fifty-six years old, and hardly the type to thrive in prison. As it was, Claus would never spend a day behind bars. He posted $1 million bond, and began working on his appeal.

The appeal was orchestrated by a high-profile Harvard Law professor named Alan Dershowitz, who enjoyed a well-deserved reputation for brilliant appeals strategies. Claus had been given the generous financial support of his old associate J. Paul Getty, Jr., so price would be no object. Dershowitz enlisted an enormous crew of law students, who were divided into teams charged with the investigation of different aspects of the appeal. In effect, Claus now had the Harvard Law School on his side. The effort paid off handsomely.

Technically, all that mattered in the appeal were points of legal procedure during the first trial. But the investigation unearthed disturbing questions of guilt and innocence. There were, certainly, legal and constitutional issues. To what extent may private citizens investigate a crime and provide the state with evidence – the little black bag, the test results on the needle – gathered outside the boundaries of official police inquiries? Can a private attorney – Richard Kuh – conduct an investigation later used by the prosecution, and then claim his notes on the investigation are protected from the eyes of the defense by attorney-client privilege, as he did in Claus's first trial? Normally, information gathered by the prosecution must be shared with the defense.

One issue raised by the unofficial Kuh investigation was the handling of the evidence. The appeals researchers discovered that Alexander had told one story about the contents of the little black bag when it was found in the closet at Clarendon Court, and the private investigator who was with him had told a story that differed in one important regard. According to one story, there was a prescription bottle in the bag made out to Claus von Bülow. According to the other story, there was not. If there was a prescription bottle made out to Claus, a much stronger argument may be made that the bag belonged to and was being used by Claus. In fact, pretrial testimony suggested that there may have been a prescription bottle made out to Sunny inside the little black bag. The issue was further confused by the fact that other pill bottles found elsewhere in the house during the search were put in the bag for safekeeping. No record was made of what was originally in the bag. No pictures or fingerprints were taken, as would have been standard procedure in an official police investigation.

A good deal of new information came to light about Sunny's alleged use of drugs and alcohol. If Sunny regularly injected herself with drugs, the case against Claus was obviously weakened. Even during the first trial, there had been indications that Sunny may not have been a model of stability. She was said to have been addicted to laxatives since her teenage years, and to have consumed enormous quantities of aspirin. Saying that they felt guilty about Claus's conviction, several old acquaintances came forward during the appeals process to paint an entirely new picture of the poor little rich girl they had known. The most famous of these was the writer Truman Capote. In an interview with *People* magazine, and later with Claus's lawyers, Capote claimed that he had first met Sunny in the early 1950s, and that she had tried to show him how to inject himself. In the late 1970s, according to Capote, Sunny told him about her experiments with Demerol, amphetamines, and Quaaludes, and sent him a book called *Recreational Drugs*. Capote also described Sunny as "deep into drinking." Other revelations about Sunny centered on the drinking problem. Claus's new lawyers would claim that Sunny's family, and her faithful servant Maria, had done an exceptional job of shielding Sunny's nasty habits from public scrutiny.

A bizarre sideshow to this aspect of the case was provided by a young man named David Marriott, a trained mortician who

seemed to have connections in the drug world. Marriott contacted Claus and his lawyers with a story that, if true, would
have been most useful to the defense. He said he had been a
courier of drugs to Sunny's son Alexander, that Alexander had
told him that some of the drugs were given to his mother, and
that Sunny herself had once accepted delivery of one of
Alexander's drug packages at Clarendon Court. Marriott's allegations were supported by none other than a respected parish
priest who said he had met Alexander in Marriott's company
and that Marriott had told him the drug tales during counseling
sessions. Marriott reveled in the attention he received as a result
of his story, held his own press conferences, and dined lavishly
during interviews at great expense to the nation's news organizations. Later Marriott recanted the affidavits he had given,
saying Claus had paid him for them. Claus's lawyers had in fact
paid Marriott's expenses, lost wages, and investigatory fees
after looking into the legality of doing so. The priest who had
given a supporting affidavit, and who appeared to be under
some pressure from Marriott, was eventually charged with
perjury.

By far the most important discovery of the appeals research
team concerned what was, in effect, the "murder weapon" in the
von Bülow case: the dirty needle in the little black bag. Experts
who had not been contacted in the course of the first trial opined
that the needle had not been injected into anyone. If it had been,
test results on the needle should have mentioned the presence of
blood and tissue. They didn't. Besides, the needle had showed
an encrustation of drugs on its *outside* surface. A needle that had
been injected, the new defense experts said, would have been
effectively wiped clean of drugs as it was pushed into and pulled
from the body. To the defense team, the fact that drugs appeared
on the outside of the needle provided an intriguing suggestion
that Claus von Bülow may have been framed by someone who
dipped the famous needle into a solution. Finally, a defense
expert showed that a test of needle washings containing amobarbital and Valium – the two other drugs reported to be on the

needle besides insulin – can produce a false positive for insulin. It thus appeared possible that there may have been no insulin on the needle in the first place.

The defense team went on to question the laboratory results of Sunny's insulin levels during the second, and lasting, coma. They had been reported at the first trial as an alarming 216 mg. %. In fact, according to the defense, this reading was only one of four vastly different readings recorded during testing. Defense experts said that the variances recorded in the tests were not within acceptable limits.

The Supreme Court of Rhode Island decided to reverse Claus's conviction on two legal grounds. One was the fact that the privileged information gathered in Richard Kuh's investigation was used selectively, to help convict the defendant. The other was that the Rhode Island police did not produce a search warrant before sending the pills found in the little black bag for testing. The prosecution asked the U.S. Supreme Court to review the decision, but it declined.

Rhode Island now had the option of retrying Claus. By this time there was a new Attorney General in Rhode Island, an ex-nun named Arlene Violet whose tough reputation and law and order attitudes had earned her the media nickname "Attila the Nun." Violet, her prosecutors, and the police investigators who had worked the case remained convinced that Claus was guilty. Besides, there was a good deal of political hay to be made in a second showcase trial. Claus would be tried again.

The second trial opened on April 25, 1985, this time in Providence. There were new faces among the cast of characters. Alan Dershowitz was there to consult on defense strategies behind the scenes. The new point man on Claus's legal team was Thomas Puccio, a wise-mouthed, street-smart lawyer who had earned a reputation as a prosecutor in the Abscam trials. The prosecution team was led by a thirty-year-old Assistant Attorney General named Marc DeSisto.

Claus and Sunny's daughter Cosima, then eighteen, was more visible than she had been in the first trial. By siding with her father and believing him innocent, Cosima had created a breach in the family. She was bitterly alienated from Alexander, Ala, and Sunny's relatives.

Another high-profile player on center stage was Claus's new girlfriend. Alexandra had left the scene after the first trial. Her replacement was Andrea Reynolds, a Hungarian-born, world-class socialite who had abandoned her third husband to take up with Claus. Andrea was smart and tough and made a powerful ally for Claus, taking over the management of what was in effect the public relations side of the spectacle. And spectacle it was. If the first trial was a media circus, the second trial was the Greatest Show on Earth. Highlights from the first trial had been shown on TV in the form of news stories. The second trial was broadcast live on cable television, and followed across America with no less avidity than *The Young and the Restless*. A sea of reporters engulfed Providence. There were hangers-on and trial freaks and weirdos of every description. It was easy to forget the quiet and immutable fact that had started all the excitement: Sunny von Bülow was lying in a coma and would never wake up.

Defendants generally have a better shot at a second trial that follows an appeal. The defense has seen the prosecution's cards: contradictions can be exploited and a stronger case can be prepared; witnesses may disappear or suffer faulty memories; passions may cool. In Claus's case the passions and the witnesses were still around, but there can be no doubt that his prospects were much brighter at the opening of the second trial. The luxuries of money and time had allowed his new defense team to construct a completely different version of events than was heard in the first trial.

The prosecution's case was basically a replay. Maria again told her story convincingly. But this time the defense could plant a seed of doubt about Maria's testimony. Access to the notes Richard Kuh had taken in his investigation had provided what seemed to be a glaring contradiction. Kuh's notes on his first interview with Maria do not say that Maria mentioned finding insulin in the little black bag. The Kuh interview happened in early January 1981, just six weeks after Maria says she first found the insulin, and yet she apparently did not mention it to Richard Kuh. By the time of the first trial, after insulin had been identified as the "weapon" used on Sunny, Maria was unshakably certain that she had seen insulin in the bag. Her explanation for this lapse was that she had not realized the significance of the insulin when she first spoke to Richard Kuh. The Kuh notes allowed the defense to poke similar holes in Alexander's story. The circumstantial case against Claus remained strong, but now there was an element of doubt about the best witnesses against him.

The prosecution's medical arguments were likewise weakened by the new information the defense brought to the table. Dr. Gailitis – the first doctor to see Sunny at the time of the first coma – caused a flap by announcing that he had never believed the first coma was caused by insulin. He claimed to have been kept from saying so at the first trial by prosecutors who "rehearsed" him through his testimony. The first coma, Gailitis now said, was in his opinion caused by lack of oxygen following the aspiration of vomit. But the real damage came when the defense took its turn at presenting witnesses. The decision had been made to present a case based solely on the medical evidence.

Sunny's instability was discussed. A toxicologist testified that the aspirin overdose she suffered three weeks before the last coma came as a result of swallowing at least sixty-five aspirin during a half-hour period. Jurors heard experts say that a needle that had been injected wouldn't show encrustations on the outside; that the high insulin reading at the time of the last coma was an invalid test result; that the indication of insulin on the needle could have been a false positive; and finally, that the comas attributed to exogenous insulin could just as feasibly have been caused by some combination of drugs, alcohol, and exposure – the open windows, with a wind chill factor below zero, and an unconscious woman lying uncovered on a bathroom floor.

A reasonable doubt is all that is required for an acquittal. The central assumption of the state's case against Claus was that he tried to kill his wife by giving her injections of insulin, and the defense's answer had been surprisingly simple: Insulin? What insulin? There were some breaks for the defense – the judge ruled that the jury would not hear the testimony of trust officer Morris Gurley, and thus would never know about the $14 million Claus stood to inherit if Sunny died – but the prosecution's case was fundamentally as strong as it had been at the first trial. The difference was that a juror at the second trial would have to overcome new and nagging questions: What if Maria was lying about the little black bag? What if someone framed Claus by dipping the needle in insulin? What if Sunny's comas weren't caused by insulin at all? Claus von Bülow was found innocent on both counts.

Claus walked from the courtroom a free man, still married to the comatose Sunny and still a beneficiary of her will. But too much money was involved for the story to have ended there. Alexander and Ala filed suit against their stepfather for $56 million, hoping to prove in civil court what they could not prove in a criminal trial. Claus countersued Alexander for $20 million, and Cosima, claiming she had been effectively disinherited by the family for siding with her father, brought her own suit for $22 million. The flurry of suits were not settled until 1988 when, according to Newport gossip, the widower of Sunny's mother refused to pay any more lawyers' bills. In the settlement, Claus agreed to give up all claims to Sunny's estate on the condition that Cosima would inherit the same amount as the other two children. Taking her mother's and her grandmother's money into account, Cosima can look forward to an inheritance that could come to $60 million.

Alexander and Ala have gone on to found a victim's rights organization and a coma foundation. A painful irony of their lives is that their father, Prince Alfred von Auerspergs is also lying in an irreversible coma as a result of an auto accident in 1983. At last report, the Auerspergs were still estranged from their half-sister Cosima. Claus is living in his accustomed style in London, where the furniture and art he had collected during the heady early days of his marriage to Sunny was recently auctioned at Sotheby's for $11.5 million.

As far as the law is concerned, Claus von Bülow is an innocent man. But those who follow the case are no less divided in their opinions now than they were at the beginning of the first trial. For every person who believes he is innocent, perhaps even the victim of a frame-up, there is another who will tell you Claus is a free man today only because of the legal niceties his money could afford.

There is another view of Claus that emerged during a dramatic moment of his second trial. His former lover, Alexandra Isles, had taken herself conspicuously out of the prosecution's reach. After well-publicized efforts to locate her, and just at the moment of conclusion of the prosecution's case, the former soap opera actress made an entrance from her hiding place in Ireland as full of drama as any Hollywood creation. Her testimony tracked along the lines of the first trial, with one notable exception. Alexandra recounted a telephone conversation she had with Claus just after Sunny's first coma, the brief coma that had come after Claus reportedly lay inactive beside his unconscious wife throughout an entire day. According to Alexandra, Claus told her that he and Sunny had been arguing about divorce "late into the night." He had watched her drink "a great deal of eggnog" and then take Seconal. The next day, "when she was unconscious," he had watched her, "knowing that she was in a bad way . . . and finally when she was on the point of dying he said that he couldn't go through with it, and he called and saved her life."

No doubt, this testimony cuts both ways. Claus is not seen telling his girlfriend that he tried to kill his wife, but that he almost let her die. The difference is considerable. Alexandra's statement could not convict a man of attempted murder, but it could show him in a most unflattering light, as a husband who devoutly wished his wife dead and came within minutes of watching his wish be fulfilled. Is Alexandra's story the spiteful tale of a spurned lover? Perhaps. But it does concur with Maria's account of the same day. And taken together with the other health crises Sunny would suffer over the coming year, it does little to lift suspicion from Claus.

When the verdict was announced at the second trial, official efforts to discover what happened to Sunny von Bülow came to an end. Much of the evidence used against her husband was discredited by a well-prepared defense, but one troubling premise in the case remains: despite the doubts raised by the lawyers, the most likely cause of Sunny's comas was insulin, given by injection. As Claus's lawyers did well to point out, this is not a certainty. But consider the reports about Sunny's first coma: her blood sugar was low when she entered the hospital and fell even lower after the first push of glucose. An injection of glucose should cause an immediate rise in blood sugar. Doctors consulted for this book have mentioned only two possible explanations. Either there was an unnaturally high level of insulin in Sunny's body, or there was a bad test result at the lab.

The test for insulin when Sunny reached the hospital in the second coma came back at a shockingly high 216 mg. %. A defense expert at the second trial argued that this was an invalid test result, because it was one of four wildly different readings from the sample. One of the readings was much higher, the other two much lower. Technically, the defense expert may have been correct. But throwing out the test results begs a question: what was the actual level of insulin in Sunny's blood? If it was anywhere near the reported level, there are two medical explanations: a pancreatic tumor or insulin administered from outside the body. Sunny had been tested for a pancreatic tumor. She didn't have one.

None of this makes anyone guilty beyond a reasonable doubt. There are too many other unanswered questions. The theories can be spun endlessly:

Claus did it and got away with it.

Sunny did herself in and Claus was an innocent bystander

who may or may not have been framed. Someone else did it and framed Claus.

Claus did it but Sunny's family felt compelled to manufacture evidence to assure a conviction. If this is the case, the irony is that the manufactured evidence helped free a guilty man.

Claus was innocent but Sunny's family was so convinced he was guilty and so protective of Sunny's reputation that they manufactured evidence to assure a conviction.

The story of Claus and Sunny is one of those mysteries that is almost certain to remain mysterious forever. As a whodunit, it has a certain elegance and charm. But as a reflection of life, there is something in it that makes it hard to get beyond the sadness and the disappointment. Here are people who had more than almost anyone on this planet. People who quite literally had everything money could buy, but could not buy happiness, or love, or rest, or peace of mind.

Postscript

Claus von Bülow, now 76, resides comfortably in London near his daughter Cosima, dotes on his grandchildren, and writes occasional reviews for *The Sunday Times*.

Sunny von Bülow, now 70, remains in a coma in a nursing home on the upper east side of New York. Her children remain estranged from Cosima and Claus.

7

The Price of Being Born Again

The Case of T. Cullen Davis

The jade shattered like so much dime store junk, and the ivory splintered and flew in creamy chips. The gold and the jewels skittered and bounced on the dark gray pavement. Cullen Davis and an evangelist preacher named James Robison were smiting false idols on the driveway of Cullen's $6 million mansion in Fort Worth, Texas. They were using hammers.

The graven images being smashed to smithereens were worth about $1 million. There were Hindu gods and dragons. There was a four-foot-tall jade pagoda topped with gold and decorated with temple dogs. Cullen had collected all these Oriental knick-knacks in an earlier lifetime, before he was born again. He had given them to the preacher to support his television ministry. But at the last minute, the preacher had read Deuteronomy 7:25. It said "the carved images of their gods" were an abomination not to be coveted, but to be burned – or in this case, smitten. So Cullen and the preacher stood in Cullen's driveway and smited righteously, until they were surrounded by a pile of shards. These they dumped into a lake, to shield the rest of us from temptation.

It was late in 1982. Cullen had been born again about two years before. He could afford to take a hammer to his Oriental art collection. In fact, he could afford damn near anything he wanted, because he was personally worth about $250 million at the time. The maze of companies he and his older brother controlled were selling oilfield equipment, oil drilling services, armored cars, and other assorted goods at the rate of over $2 billion a year.

Cullen was doing pretty well, considering that so many people thought he was a killer. He still had the distinction of being the Richest Man Ever Tried for Murder. It had only been five years since three eyewitnesses testified he had shot dead his twelve-year-old stepdaughter and his ex-wife's six-foot, nine-inch boyfriend, severely wounding his ex-wife and partially paralyzing another man in the course of the same rampage. Then there had been the accusation that Cullen had tried to hire a hit man to knock off fifteen people he didn't care for, including two judges and his own younger brother. But Cullen had endured. And now he was Saved.

Despite his infamous adventures in recent years, Cullen was in some ways typical of second-generation Texas oil money. The founders of these oil patch fortunes had been a hardbitten bunch, as proud, as rugged, and as downright mean as the cattle barons who had preceded them at the top of the Texas social heap. Cullen's old man had certainly sprung from this mold. He was Kenneth W. Davis, known to friend and foe as Stinky. The elder Davis did not earn his nickname by the way he smelled, but by the way he conducted business.

Stinky Davis was a solid little man, about five feet five, who had played semi-pro baseball, flown in World War I, and kicked around various small-time jobs before finding his niche in the Texas oil boom of the 1920s. In 1929 he bought an interest in a tiny oil field equipment company called Mid Continent Supply, which then had four employees. Stinky took over Mid Continent and, over the course of the ensuing thirty-nine years, proceeded to nail together an empire that included almost eighty companies, all privately held. The corporation at the top of the chart was named, appropriately enough, for Stinky himself: KenDavis Industries International, Inc.

Stinky had an ego and a drive a lot bigger than he was. According to another millionaire who was his pal, "He was the only man I ever knew who could strut sitting down." He was said to have an amorous nature, and a quick hand for a shapely secretary's bottom. He did not part easily with money, whether solicited for a social cause or by one of his three sons. When the boys were college age, he did not send them to a fancy Eastern school but to Texas A&M, because – according to one report – "it was the cheapest, hardest place he could think of." Stinky's offspring were Ken Jr., a cool and distant customer who would run the bulk of the empire, Thomas Cullen, and William Selden, who would be forced out of the family business in a power struggle with his older brothers.

For boys with so much money, none of the brothers was particularly conspicuous, and Cullen was the least conspicuous of all. His high school yearbook lists no accomplishments or club memberships under his name. Even as a young man, he dressed and acted conservatively, frequently appearing in a suit and tie. Cullen would grow into an enigmatic figure, a dark, small-framed man, handsome enough, but with a hooded and reptilian gaze that could be unsettling. He did not make conversation easily, but could exercise a dry, tough-guy wit when he felt like it. Until the time of his second marriage, his only noticeable passion was his business, though he did take an interest in the Dallas Cowboys, and shooting pool, and skiing. He was said to have a fiery temper, but even this trait went largely unnoticed until people began comparing notes when he was charged with murder.

Cullen's first wife Sandra bore him two sons before filing for divorce because of his violent outbursts, according to one report based on the gossip of the time. He already had a new love interest anyway, a curvaceous platinum blonde named Priscilla Wilborn, whose husband was a well-to-do used-car dealer. It was 1967, and Cullen was thirty-three years old. He and Priscilla met on the tennis courts of a country club, sparks flew, and a full-blown affair was soon in progress. On New Year's night of 1968, Priscilla and Cullen were cuddling in a Fort Worth hotel when the door was kicked down and a bunch of private eyes with cameras around their necks barged in and started snapping pictures, followed by Sandra Davis and Jack Wilborn. Cullen's divorce was already in progress. Priscilla's came soon after.

Cullen married Priscilla the same day old Stinky Davis died, on August 29, 1968. The new woman in his life seemed to bring a change over Cullen. He became a lot more visible around the town he had grown up in. Relative to his old retiring ways, he became almost flamboyant. No doubt it was tough to be invisible and unflamboyant in the company of a woman shaped like Barbie, who favored cowboy boots, skin-tight hot pants, bikini tops, and diamond necklaces that spelled out "Rich Bitch." Much has been made of Priscilla's silicone-implanted breasts and racy costumes. The fact is she had been a poor little girl and she was having a helluva good time being a rich big girl. Scandalizing Fort Worth society was part of the fun.

Priscilla was a high school dropout from a blue collar background. Her father was a rodeo rider who had left the family when she was small. She had married at sixteen, become a mother and divorced the same year. At eighteen she married Jack Wilborn, who was forty at the time. She had her second child a year later and her third at age twenty-two. Marrying Jack Wilborn gave Priscilla a life of luxury. Marrying Cullen Davis put her into the stratosphere. Whatever may be said about Priscilla, she had moxie. People who wondered what Cullen saw in her must have overlooked the fact that, maybe more than anybody else Cullen had encountered, she was very much alive.

The newly vitalized Cullen seemed to be enjoying himself. He and his new wife were just as likely to be seen in a redneck honky-tonk as in the exclusive Petroleum Club. At one golf tournament, while Priscilla was wowing 'em with her halter top, Cullen was showing *Deep Throat* in a Winnebago with some of his pals. Up to this point, Cullen had lived modestly for a man of his means. Now he set about building a monument to his new life: a $6 million house on a 181-acre estate Stinky had acquired thirty years before. The trapezoidal structure has been compared to everything from a Mayan temple to a national park visitors' center. Depending on one's point of view, it gives the impression of a museum or a monstrosity. It is 19,000 square feet of walnut, marble, and mirrors. It held art collections gathered on impulse buying trips around the world. The game room accommodated three pool tables. The master bedroom featured a gigantic bed covered in silver fox fur, a camera and projection system, and a mirrored, hot-pink bath.

But even this pleasure palace would not serve as a guarantee of happiness. Cullen's violence was still a problem. Priscilla would claim he broke her nose on one occasion and her collarbone on another. He beat her teenage daughter Dee, and in one fury hurled a kitten that belonged to Dee against the kitchen floor and killed it. In a rare public fit of temper that has been widely reported, Cullen grew tired of waiting for a valet to bring up Priscilla's white Lincoln Continental during a rainstorm at a debutante ball. He looked for the car keys on the country club's wooden rack, but couldn't find them. Before astonished onlookers dressed in tuxedos and evening gowns, he then ripped the rack off the wall and threw it in the mud. He screamed at Priscilla to get into another couple's car and the Davises drove off, leaving the cream of Fort Worth society to search the mud puddles for their car keys.

The separation came in July of 1974. Priscilla stayed in the mansion. Cullen moved briefly into a hotel and then took refuge in the home of his new girlfriend, Karen Master. Karen was younger than Priscilla, but also blonde, and also shapely, and also a high school dropout. She had been named Miss Flame by the Fort Worth Firefighters Association in 1965. A previous marriage had given her two sons, who had been injured as babies in a head-on collision with a drunken driver. The accident had left both boys disabled, and one of them deaf.

While Cullen seemed to be settling back into his accustomed inconspicuous ways, Priscilla seemed prepared to take her notoriety to a new level. She kept a menagerie of animals – a pack of mongrel dogs, several cats, and a horse named Freedom – and to this she added a human menagerie. The new guests at the mansion were not your basic High Society types. They were bikers, construction workers, and alleged dope peddlers. Rumors of drug and sex orgies at the mansion began to be heard around Fort Worth. Priscilla denied all this and later explained that she had these folks around because she wanted to rehabilitate them. One rehabilitation project was a scruffy electrician named W. T. Rufner, who had received a suspended sentence for possession of LSD and pethidine with intent to deliver. According to trial testimony, Rufner abandoned his houseboat on Possum Kingdom Lake to live with Priscilla in the mansion for a period of several weeks (Priscilla's version) to several months (Rufner's version). An assortment of other houseguests, some with criminal records, came and went.

In the spring of 1976, Priscilla formed a serious attachment to a thirty-year-old man named Stan Farr. Stan was a giant, though by all accounts a gentle one. He had played center for the TCU basketball team in the late 1960s, and he stood every inch of six feet nine. Stan had suffered through a number of failed business ventures, mostly bars and restaurants, and had become a partner in a country disco called the Rhinestone Cowboy when he moved into the mansion with Priscilla and her eighteen-year-old daughter Dee in the early summer. According to Priscilla, she and Stan were serious enough to have started talking about marriage, and about getting a place of their own.

Meanwhile the Davises' divorce was grinding along at a snail's pace. The case was already two years old. Too much money and too many lawyers were involved for anything about it to be a simple matter. There were two major questions to be settled: who would get the house and how much money would be awarded to Priscilla. July 30, 1976, was Priscilla's thirty-fifth birthday. It was also the day domestic relations judge Joe Eidson held a hearing on the divorce. Cullen and his lawyers had hoped to make the divorce final on this date but, by their lights, Priscilla was holding up the process with her unreasonable demands. The July 30 hearing was a victory for Priscilla. Judge Eidson granted her request for an increase in temporary support payments, from $3,500 to $5,000 a month. The judge further ordered Cullen to fork over $42,000 for Priscilla's attorneys' fees and expenses. Cullen had already been enjoined from entering the house his money had built. According to press reports, Cullen first learned about the judge's latest ruling on the afternoon of August 2.

Priscilla's twelve-year-old daughter Andrea Wilborn, who normally lived with her father, happened to be visiting the mansion at this time. Her half-sister Dee had just driven her back from Houston, where she had been attending vacation Bible school. On the night of August 2, Dee went out to a party. A friend of hers, Beverly Bass, had arranged to come to the mansion later to spend the night. Stan and Priscilla left at around 9:00 p.m. to meet friends for dinner and drinks. They watched Andrea lock the door behind them, and Priscilla activated the electronic security system. Andrea was alone in the big house. She was last heard from at around 10:30 p.m., when she spoke to friends on the phone.

According to the eyewitnesses who were there, this is what happened just after midnight that night:

When Priscilla and Stan returned home and approached the front door, Priscilla noticed a light on the security panel. This meant someone had opened a door into the house. She assumed it was one of her daughters. The breakfast room door was unlocked.

Stan went up to the master bedroom and Priscilla went into the kitchen. She noticed a light on in the basement. Then she saw the bloody handprint. It was halfway up the basement door. She screamed for Stan and started for the bedroom, but she was stopped by a man who stepped out from a laundry room. He was dressed all in black and wore a woman's shoulder-length black wig. Both his hands were in a plastic garbage bag, and in his hands was a .38 revolver. Priscilla has never expressed any doubt about who the man in black was. She says he was Cullen Davis.

The man in black was there to kill people. In a perfectly

normal voice, he said "hi" to Priscilla and then shot her in the chest. By this point, Stan Farr was running down the stairs toward the kitchen. Priscilla says she screamed, "I've been shot! Cullen shot me! Stan, go back!" She knew Stan was on the other side of the closed kitchen door because she watched the gunman struggle trying to open it. Then he fired through the door. Priscilla heard Stan cry out, and saw the man in black push the door open. He wrestled briefly with the big man before shooting him again. Stan fell and the man in black stood over him and shot him two more times. Priscilla watched Stan die.

The killer picked up Stan's feet and began dragging his huge body toward the basement. Priscilla took this opportunity to try to escape through a sliding glass door. When she fell outside the house, she found the killer standing over her. She remembers pleading with him, saying, "Cullen, I love you, I have never loved anybody else, please let's talk." He responded by pulling her back into the house. He was speaking softly, as a man might speak to a child, and all he said was, "Come on, come on." For some reason he left her near the front door and went back to Stan's body. Priscilla ran out the front door and hid in the shrubbery. She saw the killer walking toward her, but he was distracted by voices from the driveway. Beverly Bass and her date, Gus "Bubba" Gavrel, Jr., had just driven up. In her panic, Priscilla thought the girl she heard was her daughter Dee.

The young couple had heard Priscilla saying, "I love you," and the killer's response. They had seen Priscilla being dragged back to the house. As they walked to the front door, the man approached them and told them to follow him inside. Beverly claims to have recognized Cullen and called his name. He then turned and shot Bubba, from a distance of about three feet. Beverly ran and escaped into the darkness, perhaps because the killer's gun was empty. With a bullet lodged against his spinal cord, Bubba was unable to move his legs. He watched the man he later identified as Cullen Davis run to the locked front door, then fire through the window and climb into the house. Unlike

Beverly and Priscilla, Bubba Gavrel was at first unsure who had shot him, but he would soon testify that it was Cullen.

In the meantime Priscilla ran more than a thousand yards to the home of a neighbor. She banged frantically on the front door, screaming, "Cullen is up there killing my children! He is killing everyone!"

By the time police arrived, the killer was gone. Past the bloody handprint and down the basement stairs, they found the body of twelve-year-old Andrea Wilborn on the concrete floor of a storage room. The little girl had been killed with a single shot. The investigation revealed that the bullets that had killed Andrea and Stan Farr came from the same gun. The other bullets were too mangled for positive identification. The bloody handprint was too smeared to reveal prints. The wig and torn parts of the garbage bag were found upstairs in the house.

While Priscilla was in surgery to remove the slug from her chest – another fraction of an inch, the doctors said, and she would have been among the dead that night – and while young Gus Gavrel was learning that he would have to live without the use of all of his body because the bullet against his spine could not be removed, police were looking for Cullen Davis. Cullen's older brother Ken Jr. called him at Karen Master's house around 4.00 a.m. to tell Cullen the police were looking for him in connection with murders that had happened at the mansion that night. According to Ken, Cullen was remarkably calm. "Well," he said, "I guess I'll go back to bed." He wouldn't sleep long, because by 4.30 a.m. the police had surrounded Karen's house and ordered him to come outside. The arrest took place without incident.

In Cullen's white-over-blue Cadillac, parked in Karen's garage, police found a total of four handguns – three in the trunk and one under the driver's seat. None of these guns matched the murder weapon.

At the jail a detective named Claude R. Davis interviewed Cullen and Karen Master. The officer reported that Karen told him she had taken a sleeping pill around 10.00 p.m., had gone to sleep before Cullen arrived and had not seen Cullen until the phone rang around 4.00 a.m. In the course of a forty-five-minute interview with Cullen, the detective asked why two people had died that night. According to officer Davis, Cullen responded, "Sometimes you don't need a reason for it." The detective's statement was inadmissible at Cullen's murder trial. Officer Davis would not publicly repeat what Cullen had told him until he testified in a civil trial eleven years later.

Cullen was charged with murder and released the next day on $80,000 bond. One newspaper reported that he then spent three nights in a psychiatric clinic. Three weeks later, as he was about to board his Learjet for a business trip, he was rearrested. The charge had been changed to capital murder – which can bring the death penalty in Texas. The DA's reasoning was that Cullen had committed murder during the course of a felony, i.e., break-ing into the house then controlled by Priscilla. Perhaps the prosecution feared a man with Cullen's resources and his own jet might flee the country. One ramification of the capital murder charge was that Cullen could be held without bond.

A total of five indictments were returned against Cullen. Two capital murder charges, for the deaths of Andrea Wilborn and Stan Farr; two attempted murder charges, for shooting Pricilla and Bubba Gavrel; and felony trespassing for entering the mansion against Judge Eidson's order. He would be tried for the death of Andrea Wilborn, the only crime for which there were no direct witnesses. Why? Maybe because the prosecutors were sensitive to the element of the Old West that remains alive in Texas. In those parts, a man who kills his wife's lover may still expect some sympathy. A man who kills a twelve-year-old girl cannot.

As it turned out, Cullen would stay in jail for more than a year. The first capital murder trial opened in Fort Worth in February 1977, but a mistrial was declared because of phone calls made by a juror. District Judge Tom Cave filed his own motion for a change of venue, and the case was moved to Amarillo, a town of 150,000 souls in the Panhandle of far northwest Texas. The Amarillo trial opened on August 22, 1977. It would last three months.

As more than one legal eagle has observed, Cullen would have been a goner without his bank balance to protect him. Three eyewitnesses were ready to testify he had been shooting people. Take away the money and the case became a common homicide: a typical, open-and-shut story of an estranged husband gone berserk. We all may be equal in the eyes of the law, but a man with a quarter of a billion dollars to spend is more equal than the rest. The difference is that that man can afford the best lawyer money can buy, and in Texas that means Richard "Racehorse" Haynes.

Remove Perry Mason's conscience and you have Racehorse Haynes. Racehorse is a Houston-based criminal lawyer who got his nickname from his high school football days and inherited his unofficial Best Lawyer Money Can Buy mantle from his hero Percy Foreman. He also inherited Foreman's favorite courtroom tactic: put the victim on trial and discredit the witnesses. The technique is frequently successful because the rules of evidence in U.S. courts prevent the prosecution from doing the same thing to the defendant. The stories about Racehorse approach legend. One favorite is about the time he couldn't subpoena a crucial witness. No problem. Racehorse cross-examined an empty chair and won his case. Another oft-repeated tale concerns the trial where Racehorse won the acquittal of a motorcycle gang accused of nailing a woman to a tree. As the story is usually told, Racehorse nailed his own anesthetized hand to the jury box, to prove crucifixion really doesn't hurt that much. Racehorse modestly denies this aspect of the story. True, he *thought* about the tactic, but realized that if he cried or winced he'd lose the case. He won without resorting to the nail and hammer.

The Amarillo trial cost Cullen a reported $3 million, and as it turned out the money was well spent. A major investment was made in pretrial investigations. The three eyewitnesses were a primary target. There was plenty of dirt to be had about Priscilla

– suspected drug addiction, association with dope dealers, and enough sexual gossip to fill a rack in an adult book store. Beverly Bass had paid for an abortion with Priscilla's money. Gus Gavrel, Jr. allegedly had marijuana on his person the night of the killings. Potential defense witnesses were ready to testify that Stan Farr had been a player in drug deals. Then there was the investigation of potential jurors. Cullen's money paid for a study to profile the characteristics of the ideal jurors for his purposes. The result: straight-laced, conservative, forty or over, passive and used to taking orders, and believers in the accumulation of wealth through hard work. A team of five full-time and up to twenty part-time investigators fanned out across Amarillo, photographing potential jurors' homes, interviewing anyone who might know them, and evaluating their lives from every angle. The suggestion of a single step outside the norm was enough to disqualify a prospect. As one attorney on the team told a writer, "We were looking for good, solid, basically conservative citizens who would have no affinity for Priscilla and might even find her revolting." To defuse the perception that Cullen's defense team was made up of high-priced out-of-towners, a popular Amarillo attorney was paid merely to show his face each day at the defense table.

From the opening day, the strategies of both sides were evident. District Attorney Tim Curry and his prosecutors were there to try Cullen, with fairly straightforward I-saw-him-with-the-smoking-gun testimony. Racehorse and his team were there to try Priscilla. The trial was a hit in Amarillo, and widely covered by the media. A faithful covey of Cullen groupies, mostly middle-aged ladies, soon developed. Oddly, since Cullen was after all on trial for killing a child, the mood of the spectators – and of most of the courthouse and jail officials – was decidedly pro-Cullen and anti-Priscilla. Cullen enjoyed privileges in the jail that included catered meals, trips to the chiropractor, and more space than the other prisoners. At times he wandered around the premises virtually unguarded, and once even answered the jail phone when nobody else was around to do so. Reporters at the trial soon renamed the jail the Cullen Hilton.

Priscilla was grilled on the stand daily for two weeks. She told her terrifying story of the bewigged Cullen killing and maiming in cold blood. In the course of questioning by the prosecution, Priscilla spoke of Cullen's violence toward her and her children, revealed that Andrea had been terrified of Cullen, that Cullen had a master key to the mansion, and that he was a good shot who kept an arsenal of pistols hidden in his house and car. If this had been all the jury heard, Cullen might well have gone from Amarillo to death row. But each time Racehorse got hold of Priscilla, the whole proceeding was transformed from a murder trial to a morals trial.

On the second day of Priscilla's testimony, Racehorse approached the witness stand holding up a poster-sized blowup of a photograph. The picture showed Priscilla standing beside her former boyfriend W. T. Rufner. Both were smiling broadly at the camera. She was fully dressed but W.T. was wearing only his birthday suit and a red and white Christmas stocking, which adorned his most private part. (Soon thereafter, W.T. himself could be seen around the courthouse hawking T-shirts with the legend "W. T. Rufner Socks It To 'Em.") Upon objection from the prosecution, Judge George E. Dowlen ruled that the Christmas stocking picture could be placed into evidence, but could not be shown to the jury. This ruling was purely academic, since Racehorse had had the big print made on transparent paper, and held it up against the light so the jury could hardly miss the image it revealed.

Racehorse had more photographs, said to be overt depictions of sexual acts, but these were not admitted into evidence. There were suggestions that Priscilla had corrupted her daughter Dee's teenage friends. One teenager told about a sexual group grope with Priscilla, W. T. Rufner, and a convicted felon named Larry Myers, who was a frequent guest at the mansion. The comings and goings of Priscilla's colorful acquaintances at the mansion were discussed with a maximum of innuendo, and the criminal records of some were revealed. The lawyer got Priscilla to admit it was "highly possible" that she suffered from a long-term addiction to the painkiller Percodan, and had taken as many as two hundred pills a week during her recovery from her gunshot wound. The jury heard this admission, but was out of the room when Priscilla denied using other narcotics.

Gus Gavrel, Jr. testified that Cullen was the man who had shot him and left him partially paralyzed. An ambulance attendant testified that Gavrel was in possession of two small baggies of marijuana when he was taken to the hospital. Gavrel denied this.

Beverly Bass, nineteen at the time, unhesitatingly identified Cullen as the man in the black. Then Racehorse made her admit, in tears, that she had undergone an abortion and that Priscilla had paid $600 for it.

Through all this, Cullen Davis watched as calmly as any other spectator, looking the part of the powerful and respectable corporate executive. There was no way the jury would hear him say a word, because Racehorse wouldn't put him on the stand on a bet.

It was now the defense's turn to present witnesses. Testimony was heard that Gus Gavrel was unsure who had shot him at the time he entered the hospital. W. T. Rufner talked about his relationship with Priscilla, and Racehorse suggested that he was acquainted with the mansion security system and might have had a motive for killing Stan Farr. More was heard about the drug scene at the mansion and about Priscilla's sex life. It was said that Stan Farr may have lived in fear of an alleged drug dealer who had been shot to death shortly before the trial.

Racehorse produced a surprise in the form of a nurseryman with the ornate name of Arthur Ulewayne Polk. Polk told the court Priscilla had failed to pay him for hundreds of plants he had delivered to the mansion, and he had gone to the mansion under cover of darkness to take the plants back. The night of the plant raid, he said, happened to be the night of the murders. As he stood at the edge of the mansion grounds, Polk happened to check his watch. He remembered that it showed precisely 11.11 p.m. At just that time, Polk ran into a man dressed in dark clothes. He followed the man up to the mansion and watched him put something on his head. The man, according to Polk, was definitely not Cullen Davis. Polk then thought better of his plant recovery plan and went home.

Despite the fact that the mansion murders had been a leading news item in Fort Worth for over a year, Polk admitted under cross-examination that he had waited until the Amarillo trial to come forward with his story. Polk's story was somewhat defused when the prosecution produced his estranged wife Paige Polk, who testified that Arthur's watch was not working at the time he claimed to have referred to it. Because the judge ruled it inadmissible, the jury did not hear Mrs. Polk say that Arthur had told her about an aborted trip to take back his plants days before the murders. Nor did the jury learn that Mr. Polk had been convicted of armed robbery and once indicted for arson.

Racehorse had a pharmacologist testify that addiction to Percodan may produce a "Jekyll and Hyde" personality and a tendency to tell tall tales. But the testimony that was by far the most beneficial to Cullen came when his girlfriend Karen Master had a surprising change in her memory of the fatal night. Suddenly Cullen had what amounted to an alibi.

When Karen had been interviewed by police on the night of the murders, she said she had taken a sleeping pill at 10.00 p.m. and had not seen Cullen until the phone rang at 4.00 a.m. She repeated basically this same story before a grand jury ten days later. Now, under questioning by Racehorse Haynes, Karen said she had awakened "very briefly at 12.40 a.m.," noted the time on a bedside clock, and seen Cullen lying beside her on the king-sized bed. The mention of 12.40 a.m. was critical, because this was approximately the time Priscilla and Beverly Bass had alerted people on either side of the mansion of the killings. If Cullen was the killer, it would have been virtually impossible for him to have made it from the mansion to the king-sized bed in Karen's house in the allotted time. When prosecutor Joe Shannon asked Karen why she had not mentioned this crucial detail to either the police detective or the grand jury, she answered that "It didn't seem significant." The prosecutor underlined the irony: the man she lived with, loved, and intended to marry had been arrested for murder, and it didn't seem significant that she had seen him in bed with her at the time of the crime.

During closing arguments, prosecutors pled with the jury to remember who was on trial. It was not Priscilla Davis, and the question before them had nothing to do with drugs or sex. It had to do with whether Cullen Davis had murdered his twelve-year-old stepdaughter in cold blood. Racehorse took his turn, ranting about the "scuzzies, scalawags, rogues, and brigands" who populated Priscilla's world, and pouring out his sympathy for the unfortunates Gus Gavrel and Beverly Bass, drawn as they were into a conspiracy against Cullen by the evil "Queen Bee" Priscilla.

The jury deliberated just over four hours before returning a verdict of not guilty. In interviews with journalists after the trial, jurors made it clear they had not necessarily believed Cullen innocent, but could not pronounce him guilty beyond a reasonable doubt. For most, the deciding factor had been Priscilla's character and perceived lack of credibility.

Cullen was a free man. After the longest and most expensive murder trial in Texas history, the District Attorney seemed reluctant to pursue the other indictments against him. Still, his days in court were far from over. Gus Gavrel, Jr. and the family of Stan Farr had filed lawsuits, and Priscilla would soon be joined by her ex-husband Jack Wilborn in a wrongful death suit for the murder of their daughter Andrea. Then there was the divorce from Priscilla, which had yet to be settled.

The divorce proceedings dragged on through the winter, the spring, and the following summer. By August of 1978, the divorce had become a four-year-long ordeal. This must have been particularly frustrating for Cullen, because he was forced to beg Judge Eidson's permission to sell stock, arrange loans, and make other major financial transactions. At one point Cullen's lawyers asked that Judge Eidson be disqualified because he had testified about the divorce at the murder trial. Priscilla's attorneys opposed this, arguing that Cullen only wanted Judge Eidson out because he "could not control" him. Judge Eidson stayed. Cullen and his attorneys were forced to answer a list of nearly 2,000 questions about his financial dealings. The answer – filed on August 2, the anniversary of the mansion killings – ran to 251 pages. Cullen was then forced to answer in court questions about the state of his finances, and to testify for the first time about such touchy subjects as his physical abuse of Priscilla and her daughter Dee. On August 10, over the strong protests of Cullen's lawyers, Judge Eidson sided with Priscilla by granting a postponement of the divorce trial until September 18. On August 11, Cullen and Priscilla were reported to be more than $20 million apart in their negotiations. Then, on August 20, 1978, an amazing development put Cullen back on the front page of the newspaper. Cullen was arrested for soliciting the murder of Judge Eidson and fourteen other people.

It seemed that an acquaintance of Cullen's named Charles David McCrory had voluntarily gone to the FBI on August 17. McCrory's story was that Cullen had asked him to hire a hit man to kill the judge and the others. The FBI wired McCrory for sound and sent him out to discuss this with Cullen that very afternoon, on the parking lot of Coco's Famous Hamburgers. Enough interesting things were said in this conversation that, two days later, the FBI men set up an elaborate ruse to convince Cullen that Judge Eidson had been rubbed out on his orders. They taped and photographed McCrory bringing Cullen the news. On tape and in pictures, T. Cullen Davis was caught in the act of talking about having people killed, apparently paying for at least one killing, and apparently accepting delivery of a .22 pistol equipped with an illegal silencer, which McCrory claimed he had ordered earlier. Once again, it appeared that Cullen was without a prayer. The official charges were solicitation of capital murder – for Judge Eidson – and possession of an illegal weapon, the silenced pistol. Conviction could mean imprisonment for life.

Until this point, Charles McCrory had been only a bit player in the Cullen Davis drama. He and his wife Judy had been friends with Cullen and Priscilla during the happier days of their marriage, and he had been a karate instructor at a martial arts school owned by a mutual friend named Pat Burleson. Charles and Judy McCrory were the couple who had dinner and drinks with Priscilla and Stan Farr the night Stan Farr was killed. Judy, by this time divorced from Charles, was still a close friend of Priscilla's. Charles had created a stink by giving conflicting affidavits, one for each side, during preparation for the murder trial. By the time of the trial itself, he appeared to have taken Priscilla's side. The summer of 1978 found him down on his luck and out of a job.

According to McCrory, Cullen got him a job as assistant to the president of one of his companies, Jet-Air, Inc. In June, Cullen began asking him to do some investigatory work on the side. He says Cullen wanted to know two things: where Beverly Bass and Gus Gavrel, Jr. bought drugs, and whether it could be proved that Priscilla's lawyers were "in bed with" Judge Eidson. From the story, it appeared that Cullen was working two fronts: gathering ammunition for a possible new murder trial – or the civil suits regarding the murders – and looking for an advantage in his divorce from Priscilla. McCrory says he was paid $5,000 for these chores but turned up nothing of interest. Apparently this didn't bother Cullen, because McCrory says he then began placing orders to have people killed.

McCrory and Cullen began a series of secret meetings and McCrory placed calls to Cullen's office using a prearranged alias. McCrory testified that Cullen first discussed killing Beverly Bass, because "he said Bev Bass was the only witness that the jury believed in Amarillo." Cullen could have formed this opinion from reading the newspapers, since jurors interviewed after the trial had been quoted to this effect. Cullen had reason to believe Beverly's testimony would be heard again in at least three civil trials, if not in a criminal trial for the murder of Stan Farr or the attempted murder of Priscilla or Gus Gavrel. There is a venomous sort of logic to the idea of eliminating the only credible witness. But according to McCrory, Cullen wanted more than the blood of Bev Bass. In the course of a subsequent conversation, he expanded his hit list to include Gus Gavrel, Jr. and his father, Judge Eidson, Judge Tom Cave (who had held Cullen in jail without bond for over a year), W. T. Rufner, a businessman named A. J. Pascal (who was involved with Cullen in a hassle over money), an unnamed friend of Pascal's, Priscilla, Priscilla's daughter Dee, Cullen's own brother William (still bitterly estranged after Cullen and Ken Jr. had forced him out of the family business), and four other people, presumably to be named later.

McCrory says he told Cullen he had made contact with a hit man affiliated with Murder, Inc. According to McCrory's testimony, Cullen offered a number of his own brainstorms to make the killer's job easier. Maybe dope could be planted near the bodies of Bev Bass or Gus Gavrel, so their deaths would look like a drug killing. Maybe Bev's body could be cut up into tiny pieces and strewn about to make identification impossible. Maybe Judge Eidson, who enjoyed watering his lawn, could be kidnapped with hose in hand and killed off the premises. Leaving a brown beret and a Mexican-American's driver's license near the judge's body could give the appearance of a political killing by a prominent activist group of the time, the Brown Berets. For Cullen's brother William Davis, a scuba diving accident might be just the thing. And so on. A price tag was reportedly placed on each person's head. Priscilla was worth $200,000 to $500,000. A judge would bring $80,000. Beverly, Gus, and W.T. could command only $25,000 each.

It may seem an ambitious, not to mention suspicious, undertaking to contract for the killing of fifteen people, especially when those people are so easily identifiable as enemies of – or threats to – the contractor. Nevertheless this is for all the world what the FBI tapes appear to show Cullen Davis doing. The first recorded meeting reveals McCrory showing Cullen the .22 Ruger pistol he has bought, and the two of them discussing the manufacture and delivery of the silencer. They talk about the hit man's price for killing Judge Eidson. He wants $100,000. Cullen says, "Bullshit." They appear to discuss arranging alibis for themselves, and a price for Priscilla's killing, and the best way to kill Judge Eidson. At one point, Cullen tells McCrory to "go back to the original plan." When McCrory asks what he means, he replies, "Get the other one . . . who we started this out with." McCrory asks if he means Priscilla. Cullen says no. He means Bev. They discuss the possibility of killing Bev, Gus, and Gus's father all at once, and Cullen says, "Let's plan on getting all three of 'em . . . it's the best way." McCrory later explains that his hit man is an unpredictable character who "may just waste the shit out of a bunch of 'em and get a bunch of it over with at once." Cullen's response: "That suits the shit out of me." The chilling conversation lasts a total of twenty-three minutes.

The repartee at the next meeting, recorded just after 8.00 a.m. on Sunday morning, August 20, was even more grisly. Cullen is apparently under the impression that McCrory's hit man has done the job on Judge Eidson, and McCrory is bringing him the proof. This had been arranged by the FBI. Agents had staged and photographed a death scene by having the judge crawl into a car trunk wearing a T-shirt doctored with cigarette burns – to look like bullet holes – and liberally doused with ketchup. The resulting picture is authentic enough. Before getting into McCrory's car on the Coco's parking lot, Cullen stopped and tried to peer into the van where the agents sat with their recording devices and their cameras. He was unable to see anything. After this, the first words he spoke on the tape, to a very nervous Charles McCrory, were, "Just paranoid."

McCrory asks, "Who do you want next?" and Cullen replies, "The ones we talked about . . . the three." McCrory asks if he means Bev and Bubba Gavrel, and Cullen says "Yeah." Presumably the third party was Gus Gavrel, Sr. McCrory confirms again that Cullen wants Bev killed next, and says the hit man plans to "operate again tonight." Cullen warns that it may take him a little time to line up the money for that hit. McCrory says, "I got Judge Eidson dead for you," and Cullen – clearly and calmly – says, "Good." As though he wants to be sure he has enough incriminating evidence on tape, McCrory adds, "You want a lot of people dead, right?" Cullen answers, "All right." He instructs McCrory to ask the hit man, "Does he want to leave and come back, or do it [presumably this refers to the killing of Bev Bass and/or Bubba Gavrel and his father] and then wait three days for the money." McCrory apparently shows Cullen the picture of the "dead" judge, takes delivery of $25,000 in $100 bills as a partial payment for the murder of Judge Eidson and leaves Cullen the .22 Ruger, now silencer-equipped.

With police surveillance teams watching on the ground and from an airplane overhead, Cullen then departed, making several U-turns and switching his Cadillac back upon its tracks as though to evade anyone who might be following. He finally stopped at a Kentucky Fried Chicken and stepped into an outside phone booth. He was arrested just as he finished his call. The arresting officers found it strange that Cullen did not seem at all outraged that he was being arrested, and did not even inquire why he was being arrested.

Within hours, Racehorse Haynes was back in the saddle and the defense team that had won Cullen's acquittal in Amarillo was reassembled. But this one had the look of a horse race even Haynes couldn't win. Cullen Davis could be clearly seen and heard in the act of soliciting murder. There was widespread speculation that Race would be forced to have Cullen plead insanity.

The defense appeared to gain a slight advantage when the trial was moved from Fort Worth to Racehorse's stomping grounds in Houston, and to the courtroom of his good friend Judge Wallace Moore. As it turned out, Judge Moore held Racehorse under tighter rein than had Judge Dowlen in

Amarillo. Pretrial hearings began on October 9, 1978, and the trial opened on November 6. It would drag on for eleven weeks.

During the presentation of the state's case, the jury heard the tapes and saw the pictures over and over again. There were also tapes of telephone conversations between Cullen and McCrory, where money arrangements for the murders were apparently discussed. One of Cullen's secretaries testified that he had stowed a thick envelope in his office safe a few days before his arrest on August 20, and another secretary related that he had called her at 8.00 a.m. the morning of August 20 to ask for the combination to the safe. The inference was that Cullen had made the trip to his office that Sunday morning to collect the murder money he delivered to McCrory a few minutes later. The jurors heard how McCrory and his wife had laundered $50,000 of Cullen's money at the gaming tables in Las Vegas. They heard McCrory claim Cullen had repeatedly threatened to have him and his family killed if he didn't do as he was told. Racehorse managed to poke holes in McCrory's credibility and to show he had a faulty memory, but attacking McCrory would do nothing to erase the troublesome tapes.

Little by little Racehorse's central strategy became clear. He would not deny that the voice on the tapes was Cullen's. He would not stoop to claiming that Cullen was crazy. He would show that Cullen was the victim of a "creeper peeper" conspiracy, and that the real mastermind behind it all was not Cullen but, lo and behold, Priscilla! Despite the fact that Judge Moore would not allow the talk of drugs and sex that had been such a sensation in Amarillo, Racehorse had found a way to dust off his Amarillo tactic and reintroduce it with a new twist. Here was the theory in a nutshell: Priscilla had conspired with karate school owner Pat Burleson and their mutual friend Charles David McCrory to entrap and frame Cullen. Her motive was to take away more of Cullen's millions in the civil suits and the divorce case. Perhaps she was helped and/or financed in her evil enterprise by Cullen's brother William. The conspiracy, Racehorse hinted darkly, might even extend to the District

Attorney's office, the FBI, and the Texas Rangers – who had been in on the bust.

There was at least a bit of a skeleton to hang the creeper peeper story on. It was Pat Burleson who had advised McCrory to talk to the FBI, and the agent McCrory had first approached had in fact been one of Burleson's karate students. Burleson had met with Priscilla several times during August, and one of these meetings had occurred on the same day he suggested McCrory should talk to the FBI agent. In fact Burleson had been meeting with Priscilla at the mansion on the morning of Cullen's arrest. Both Priscilla and Pat Burleson claimed their meetings had only to do with planning Priscilla's new security arrangements. The divorce court had recently removed its order that Cullen had to pay for Priscilla's bodyguards, and she was shopping for new protection. Priscilla and McCrory said they hadn't been in each other's presence in at least a year.

As for William Davis, there was nothing to suggest that he was even vaguely involved except the fact that he had helped Priscilla with unrelated expenses and had hidden out during the trial, successfully avoiding subpoenas. Racehorse made the most of his absence, interjecting suggestions that Cullen's brother was aligned with Priscilla and ending with a version of his famous question-the-empty-chair routine during final arguments.

Racehorse produced a series of surprise witnesses in an attempt to put the glue to his loosely knit conspiracy theory. A thirty-seven-year-old secretary testified that she had seen Priscilla, Pat Burleson, and Charles David McCrory together in a car in mid-July. If true, this would give the lie to the claim that Priscilla and McCrory hadn't seen each other, and cast doubt on their testimony. The fact that the secretary had waited five months to tell her story took some of the shine off the revelation. So did the fact that she was employed by one of Cullen Davis's companies. Another witness said she had seen Priscilla in Las Vegas that summer, when Priscilla had testified she hadn't been there. The husband of this witness, as it turned out, worked for another of Cullen's companies.

It would get better. An ex-con named Larry Gene Lucas claimed McCrory had offered him $10,000 to kill Cullen Davis during the early summer. When he turned down the offer, he said, McCrory upped the ante to $20,000. This bombshell was defused when the prosecution produced Lucas's girlfriend, who testified that he had written her from prison about his plan to make a bunch of money by telling the story he had told in court. Lucas was charged with aggravated perjury. Racehorse had the audacity, perhaps with tongue in cheek, to put Lucas's mother on the stand as a character witness on his behalf.

The "contract on Cullen" theme had been established when Cullen's girlfriend Karen Master testified that McCrory had warned her in early June that Priscilla and Gus Gavrel, Sr. had put a price on Cullen's head. Karen's testimony also suggested that the money Cullen handed to McCrory on August 20 was really McCrory's money. Karen claimed Cullen had, for some reason, been holding a large amount of cash in an envelope for McCrory and had taken it to his office in July.

All this was interesting stuff, but Racehorse knew the cold-blooded tones of Cullen's voice on the tapes were still ringing in the jury's ears. Somehow, he would have to explain why his client had said all those nasty things about killing people. He was forced to do what he had never even contemplated in Amarillo. He put Cullen Davis on the stand.

Cullen gave some fascinating testimony. He revealed that McCrory was in league with hired killers working for Priscilla. Cullen wanted these killers to testify against her in the divorce trial. To give them assurance that he wouldn't double-cross them, he played along in making tapes of the murder conversations with McCrory, thus incriminating himself on purpose. He said McCrory was taping the conversations on his own as evidence of Cullen's good intentions toward "Priscilla's killers." The envelope he was shown by McCrory did not contain a photograph of a "dead" judge, but the cassettes of previous conversations. He knew all along Judge Eidson had not been killed, even when he answered "Good" to McCrory's

"I got Judge Eidson dead for you" remark. He had no reason to want Judge Eidson dead. It had all been make-believe.

Besides, Cullen explained, he thought he was working for the FBI at the time. On August 10, he said, he had been called by a man who identified himself as FBI agent James Acree. Cullen was acquainted with Acree because he had spoken to him earlier during the investigation of an extortion plot against himself. According to the story, the FBI agent told Cullen that McCrory was part of a plot to frame him for a crime. Cullen should play along, and presumably the FBI would step in at some point, rescue him, and arrest the bad guys.

This part of the testimony becomes a bit incredible when one considers that Cullen never once asked to speak to Agent Acree, or mentioned after his arrest that he was "playing along" under FBI instructions. Instead he sat in jail for months and waited to tell his I Was Undercover for the FBI story at his trial.

The defense did what it could to tie this thread into a fabric of conspiracy with the testimony of a golf pro named Harold Sexton. Sexton claimed he had met McCrory during the summer, and the two had talked over a meal at a Sambo's restaurant. McCrory said he understood that Sexton had been down on his luck and offered a way to make some easy money. The job was to call Cullen Davis and impersonate a police officer. Sexton said he turned the job down. He thought no more about it until he had read about Cullen's trial in the newspapers. Despite the fact that he had waited so long to come forward, Sexton seemed credible enough until the prosecution pointed out that the Sambo's location he described had burned down well before the date he claimed to have been there with McCrory.

All in all, the defense had presented an underwhelming case, populated in the main by incredible witnesses who told incredible stories. But it had presented a *long* case. The jurors had to absorb eleven weeks of conflicting and confusing testimony. Racehorse had spent hours going over minutiae in the course of seemingly insignificant examinations. Where there is the money to support it, this is a favorite tactic of defense lawyers, because the longer a trial drags on the more chance there is for judicial errors to be made and for the case to become reversible on appeal. Judge Moore was not amused. He was quoted as saying, "The entire system has been abused . . . this trial should have been over weeks ago . . . the jurors can barely remember the testimony."

As it turned out, four of the jurors could not be convinced beyond a reasonable doubt that Cullen Davis was guilty. The jury became hopelessly deadlocked and a mistrial was finally declared after forty-four hours of deliberations. Technically, the mistrial was a tie. Realistically, it was a victory for Cullen. A defendant's chances are generally better at a second trial, and this rule held true. The trial process was repeated in Fort Worth, beginning in July of 1979. After three months of testimony, the jury deliberated for two and a half days before voting to acquit Cullen. The District Attorney then announced that all remaining charges against him would be dropped.

Cullen and Priscilla were finally divorced in April of 1979. He got the mansion and kept roughly ninety-eight percent of the assets. She got a $3.3 million settlement, certainly not chicken-feed but a far cry from the $20 million – and the mansion – she had held out for for so long. He married Karen Master one month later.

The next spring, with the evangelist James Robison at his side, Cullen got down on his knees on the carpet at his mansion and got born again. He would become a very public Christian, testifying before a crowd of seven hundred of his employees on the mansion grounds, supporting Robison's conservative political causes, and railing against heathen practices like the teaching of humanism in the public schools. Humanism, Cullen said, was "the underlying reason our society has been crumbling," the driving force behind everything from "child disobedience" to crime to sexual perversion. He said a "humanist conspiracy" had been going on for centuries, and that its tentacles now reached into our government, our schools, and our churches. It was in the midst of this fervor that Cullen and James Robison struck down the false idols on the driveway. "Anything that represents a god to anybody," Cullen explained to a reporter, "is an abomination to the Lord and must be destroyed."

In 1983 it was reported that God had told Cullen to sell the mansion and build a new home "more suitable for prayer meetings." The price for the house and its 181-acre grounds was said to be $60 million. The buyer was a real estate developer. The plans for a complex of residential and commercial properties fell victim to the Texas real estate bust a few years later.

The downturn in the state economy hit Cullen as well, and hit him hard. In May of 1987, Cullen and his brother Ken were chucked out of the management of thirteen of their companies by a bunch of bankers who were owed a combined $500 million by KenDavis Industries. The holding company Stinky Davis had founded was bankrupt. Cullen himself filed for bankruptcy later that year, reportedly listing debts of $865 million and assets of $1.8 million. The plunging price of oil and a series of disastrous real estate investments were cited as the cause of Cullen's downfall.

There was another reason 1987 was a troublesome year for Cullen. He and Priscilla were back in court over the wrongful death suit brought by Priscilla and Jack Wilborn for the murder of their daughter Andrea. Jack and Priscilla were asking for more than $16 million. The trial was in many ways a replay of the murder trial in Amarillo, but this time the rules were different. The judge wouldn't let Cullen's lawyers talk about drugs and sex, and – because it was a civil procedure – only ten of the twelve jurors had to vote against Cullen to bring in a verdict in Priscilla's favor. Cullen testified, and for the first time the public learned where he was the night of the murders, before he crawled in bed beside Karen shortly after midnight. He was at the movies by himself. He saw *The Bad News Bears*.

The civil trial lasted a month. The jury deadlocked at eight to four against Cullen and a mistrial was declared. The jury foreman, angry and in tears, accused the four jurors who had supported Cullen of gross misconduct, saying they applied a standard of reasonable doubt rather than one of a preponderence of the evidence, as required in a civil trial. Cullen and Priscilla eventually reached a $5 million settlement out of court, but by this time Cullen had filed for protection from creditors in his bankruptcy and his lawyer predicted that Priscilla will never "be paid a penny."

Cullen is rarely in the news these days. He seems to have reverted to his old inconspicuous self. Not much is heard about Priscilla either. When asked, she still maintains with the same certainty that the man who shot her and killed her daughter and Stan Farr was T. Cullen Davis. "I will go to my grave," she says, "knowing Cullen killed my child." She says Cullen once told her he could get away with anything because of his money. Maybe he was right.

Postscript

Priscilla Davis died of breast cancer at her home in Dallas in February of 2001. She was 59 years old. As she had predicted, she died convinced that Cullen Davis was "the man in black."

Cullen, meanwhile, has added to his already staggering string of victories in court. In 1999, the 5th U.S. Circuit Court of Appeals in New Orleans ruled that Cullen's bankruptcy protects him from having to pay $300,000 to his first wife as a result of earlier court decisions.

8

Death Plays Doctor

The Murders of Joan Robinson Hill and John Hill

John Hill loved music. It was his passion. It was the current that carried and sustained him. When he stood in surgery with an unconscious patient stretched before him and his scalpel slicing flesh to mold a woman a new pair of breasts or free a man of a deformity, the air around him danced with Mozart or Vivaldi, booming forth from speakers he had installed himself.

He was clearly a remarkable man, but not because he had escaped the obscurity of Edcouch, Texas – a crossroads town across the border from Mexico where his parents ran the only store – to a life as a flourishing plastic surgeon and an accomplished classical musician. John Hill was remarkable because in his short lifetime he appears to have presented two radically different faces to those who knew him intimately. To some, John Hill was a monster, a psychopathic Jekyll and Hyde who murdered his wife and once admitted the killings of at least three other people, including his own father, brother, and close friend. To others who knew him just as well, John was the essence of gentility, a kind and cultured man who became the undeserving victim in a tragedy of classic proportions.

One thing about John Hill would seem indisputable. He was shot dead by a bumbling hit man at his own front door. Yet even with a corpse in evidence, one thoroughly strange story would suggest that the evil genius Dr. Hill somehow staged his own death and is still walking the world today.

The career that ended in such violence and infamy had begun

with great promise. John Hill graduated *summa cum laude* from college and breezed through medical school and internship at the Baylor College of Medicine in Houston. In 1957, while still a young resident in surgery, he did what many another impecunious medical student has dreamed of doing. He married a beautiful woman with a lot of money.

Joan Robinson was the darling of the local society gossip columns. She was rich, blonde, vibrant, and highly visible in the haunts of moneyed Houstonians of the day. She had a passion as intense as John Hill's for music, but hers was for horses. She won her first ribbon at a horse show at age five, and by the time of her death at age thirty-eight had racked up seven world championships in the five-gaited class.

Joan had the leisure and the funds to pursue her passion because of her doting Daddy, a crusty and swaggering old oil man named Ash Robinson. Ash had adopted Joan as an infant. According to one hotly disputed story, he had also fathered her in the course of an illicit romance. Real daughter or not, Joan was Ash's passion. He and his wife Rhea lived and breathed the life of their only child. Their home in Houston's exclusive River Oaks neighborhood was a shrine to Joan, with hundreds of ribbons, trophies, photographs of her and her horses, and closets full of scrapbooks detailing every aspect of her life and every victory in horse rings around the world. Ash Robinson was a fierce old bird, one of that breed of jackbooting wildcatters who made Houston the freewheeling town it is, and nothing about him was fiercer than his love for Joan.

By most accounts, it could be the kind of love that smothers. When Joan went off to school, at Stephens College in Missouri, Ash and Rhea went with her. Rhea was installed full-time in a hotel suite next to campus, and Ash visited on weekends. Joan never made a move without their knowledge. When Joan was seen around Houston with a new boyfriend, Ash had his private detectives check the guy out, and if he didn't like what he learned he did everything in his considerable power to break up the romance. When Joan had two disastrous early marriages, the central disaster – according to the stories of the time – was the meddling of Ash Robinson.

Even with the prospect of Ash as a father-in-law, Joan must have seemed an ideal catch to the young John Hill. She not only had good looks and good breeding and the money to sustain him through his early practice, she had the social connections and the name to bring in the kind of clientele who can afford a plastic surgeon. If John Hill did have problems with Ash, he was not loath to take advantage of the old man's largesse. At Ash's insistence, the young couple moved into the Robinsons' house while John finished his residency. They stayed for six years. Ash bought John a car and gave him the use of a chauffeured limo to get back and forth to the hospital.

In 1960, Joan gave birth to the couple's first and only child, a boy named Robert Ashton Hill who was immediately christened Boot by his proud grandfather. With his father busy with the demanding life of a surgeon and his mother occupied with her horse shows, little Boot spent the first years of his life under the protective wings of Ash and Rhea. Ash paid the bills that came with the new baby.

In 1965, John found the house he thought was just the thing for the rich and prominent doctor he hoped to become. It was an imposing colonial-style structure just down the street from the Robinsons', at 1561 Kirby Drive. Ash made an interest-free loan for the down payment. The doctor's fledgling practice was going nicely. True, there had been a rough start when a partnership with an older plastic surgeon had ended bitterly. The older man would later call John Hill "an avaricious doctor," a "psychopath," and accuse him of making love to a woman patient in the office. There had also been a tragedy. John's younger brother Julian, also a doctor – an aspiring psychiatrist – and a classical musician, had committed suicide in 1963. Julian was said to be a homosexual, in despair over a broken love affair.

None of this kept John Hill from success in his chosen profession. He had too many assets going for him: a willingness to cram as many operations in a day as humanly possible, an undisputed surgical skill, Joan's money and connections, and his own good looks and charm. One reporter referred to his "Rock Hudson-like" features. He had a piano installed in his consulting room, and often delivered an impromptu sonata for the benefit of the lady who had come to see about making her eye bags disappear. It was a winning combination.

Still, the prosperity and the independence that came with the new house would not be enough to hold the Hills' marriage together. The passions were not shared. Joan was outgoing and social. John was introverted and taken by his moods. John's spare time was given to practicing his instruments, performing, and moving in the rarefied atmosphere generated by classical musicians and music lovers. Joan, while she supported her husband in his endeavors and joined the proper musical and medical societies, would take a rough-talking horse crowd anytime. With Ash's money, she had opened a breeding stables and riding school called Chatsworth Farm, and much of her time went to making it succeed. Both husband and wife were quoted as complaining publicly about their mates. And then there was the conflict over John's grand dream: his music room.

What he wanted was no less than the most exquisite environment for listening to music in any private home in the world. Whether he achieved this is a matter of conjecture. Certainly, after spending more than the purchase price of the entire house, he achieved some excellent acoustics, and he could listen to his massive record library on one of the most sophisticated sound systems then in existence. Once completed, the music room had more the air of Versailles than Houston. The color scheme was white and royal gold. There was a carved marble mantel on the fireplace. An intimate listening and performance area opened onto a forty-by-eighty-foot ballroom. There were four miles of wiring and 108 speakers. The room would eventually be crowned with a ten-foot-long, handmade Bösendorfer piano to accompany the other grand piano already in residence there.

Sometime during the construction of his music room, if not

before, John Hill developed a wandering eye. In 1968, at age thirty-seven, he commenced an affair with a thirty-nine-year-old divorcee named Ann Kurth. Ann had been married three times and had three sons. She was the daughter of a prominent architect and no stranger to Houston high society. She had attended Stephens College just ahead of Joan Robinson Hill. Because she provides by far the most damaging statements about him, Ann Kurth's credibility is almost as important to this story as John Hill's. This is complicated by the fact that opinions about her seem to be as evenly divided as opinions about him. Whatever the truth, there can be no doubt that the tale she tells is a strange one. But more of that later.

To carry on his liaison, John Hill took an apartment. He was not discreet, and it was not long before Ash Robinson had his private detectives on the street. In November of 1968, John filed for divorce from Joan. In December, Ash summoned John for a private conference. Somehow, Ash convinced him to sign a curious paper that was part confession and part IOU, which Ash would claim was dictated by John. If the dictation was John's, the sentiments – and the handwriting – had clearly come from Ash. The paper begged for Joan's forgiveness. It said that John would deed the home on Kirby Drive to Joan in the event of another separation. It further promised that John would pay off the house, increase Joan's household allowance, and put $7,000 into Joan's bank account. It seems exceedingly strange that a man in the midst of a divorce proceeding would sign such a paper. According to Ann Kurth, Ash obtained John's signature through "broad hints" about his "Mafia connections." Whatever his reasons for signing, John Hill does not appear to have taken the paper very seriously. He did move back into the house with Joan and he did stop the divorce process, but he kept the apartment and he kept seeing Ann Kurth.

An odd bit of business has been reported about John picking up his things from Ann's house, to give the appearance of reconciliation with Joan. John claimed he was afraid of Ann's temper, and ended up taking one of Ash's private detectives along with him for protection. Ann was understandably surprised by this development, and there was an uncomfortable scene while the possessions were removed.

Thus began a period in which John Hill presented himself as the faithful husband at home while doing all he could to keep a girlfriend happy on the side, and wedging in his medical practice in between. He celebrated Christmas in two households, with Joan and their son and with Ann and her sons. He frequently stayed away from home overnight, supposedly because of the demands of his surgical schedule. In March, the Hills had houseguests: two women friends of Joan's, one of whom was negotiating with Ash about a job as manager at Chatsworth Farm.

On Sunday night, March 9, John appeared with a treat for the three women. He had bought some pastries for dessert. He insisted on assigning a specific pastry for each person. This strange ritual was repeated the following Tuesday night, and again on Thursday. Three times during the week John infuriated Joan by staying away from home until the early hours of the morning. On Friday night the couple attended a party, where John performed with a doctors' musical group called the Heartbeats. The evening ended in a bitter argument when John claimed he had to leave and check his patients. Uncharacteristically, Joan slept into the next afternoon, explaining that John had given her a sedative that had knocked her out the night before. On Saturday, she learned for the first time – from her eight-year-old son – that John was still keeping his apartment. She was furious. That night there was a nasty scene in which Joan announced to her friends that she would visit a divorce lawyer on Monday.

On Sunday, Joan complained of the flu. She was nauseous. She threw up several times. John gave her one or more injections. He would later claim the shots were Compazine, a drug that relieves vomiting. On Monday the houseguests left, expressing concerns for Joan's health. John told them she had a virus, and Joan herself assured them she would be all right.

Before leaving for his office, John instructed the housekeeper, Effie Green, to let Joan rest. During the day, Effie checked on her mistress and found her weak and distraught. John prescribed an antibiotic called Mysteclin-F. He also provided Kaopectate and an antidiarrhea drug called Lomotil. According to Effie, the next day – Tuesday, March 1 – John Hill called her upstairs during the early morning. He was dressed and leaving. He would play a tuba solo at an elementary school before reporting for his rounds. He instructed the housekeeper to "clean up Joan's mess" and to be sure she took her medicine. Effie has said she then realized for the first time that Joan was desperately ill. Underneath Mrs. Hill on the bed were two white towels, and underneath these was a loose bowel movement and what Effie took to be blood. The feces looked dried, as though they had been there for hours. Joan complained that she was "burning up" from the neck down. Effie helped her to the bathroom, and there was another loose and green-tinged bowel movement on the way. Joan's face appeared to Effie to be turning blue. Effie said a prayer for Joan. She and her husband Archie tried to call the Robinsons but got no answer. They called John's office and left a message that Joan was critically ill.

Sometime between 10.30 and 11.00 a.m. John Hill stopped at his house after his musical performance. The message from his office had reached him at the school. By coincidence, his mother-in-law had been dropped off by the house at about the same time, to see if her daughter's "flu" had improved. John announced that he was putting Joan in the hospital. He had not called an ambulance; he would drive her himself. She was obviously in bad shape. She told her mother that she could not see. John made a decision that would be reviewed and re-reviewed by students of the case for years. He chose to drive his wife not to one of the hospitals in the relatively nearby Texas Medical Center, where the most sophisticated medical technology in the world was available, but to an obscure suburban hospital in Sharpstown where he was a minor investor, almost twice as far away. Sharpstown Hospital had little to offer in the way of emergency facilities. John would later claim he chose Sharpstown because he had an operation scheduled there that morning, and he wanted Joan in the same hospital where he would be.

Joan was placed under the care of a doctor named Walter Bertinot merely because, as John explained, Joan had spoken well of him after meeting him socially. The unsuspecting Bertinot had never treated Joan before. He found himself responsible for a difficult case. Joan's blood pressure was only sixty over forty. She was clearly in shock, and yet she was conscious and talking. Bertinot at first suspected food poisoning. While he battled to raise Joan's blood pressure, John Hill performed his previously scheduled plastic surgery, the operating room alive with classical music. By early evening, Joan's kidneys failed. A kidney specialist was called in. When he phoned to ask John Hill's permission to begin peritoneal dialysis – a process by which the body's peritoneal cavity is used to purify fluid – John was in his music room at home, lost in a melody. He would not appear at the hospital until almost two hours later. Sometime after midnight, John bedded down on a couch at the hospital. At about 2.30 a.m., Joan suffered cardiac arrest and died. She was thirty-eight years old. Only a few days before, she had appeared to be in perfect health.

Then a still unexplained sequence of events occurred that would seal Joan Robinson Hill's death in mystery forever. When a person dies within twenty-four hours of admittance to a hospital in Texas, the law requires that the county coroner perform an autopsy and rule on the cause of death before the body is released to a funeral home and embalmed. In the confused wee-morning hours after Joan's death, while Dr. Bertinot was trying to reach the hospital's staff pathologist to request an autopsy, John Hill reportedly asked another doctor friend to call a mortuary. The mortuary got there first. By the time Dr. Arthur Morse, the hospital pathologist, found Joan's body in a funeral home at around 10.00 a.m. the following morning, it had already been embalmed. The blood and other fluids had been drained from the body, and in their place the embalming fluid had coursed through, destroying any bacteria or viruses that may have been present along the way, just as it is designed to do. All the doctors involved knew the law required that the county Medical Examiner be called. No one had called him.

The press would report that Dr. Morse thought Joan had died of "acute fulminating pancreatitis." This would be the first in a prolonged series of medical opinions about the cause of Joan Robinson Hill's death. The same newspaper report assured the public that "Dr. Hill said he ordered the autopsy to find the cause of his wife's unexpected death." Pancreatitis is a severe inflammation of the pancreas that normally occurs in people much older than Joan Hill. As other pathologists have pointed out, a diagnosis of pancreatitis would have been an easy trap to fall into under the circumstances, because the job of the pancreas is to produce digestive juices, and the first thing the pancreas does after death is digest itself.

Had Joan Robinson Hill been a common citizen, chances are the story of her death would end right here. True, she had died suddenly, but a pathologist had given an opinion on the cause of death, and there was nothing on the surface to indicate the cause was anything other than natural. But Joan, even in death, had an uncommon advantage: a father named Ash Robinson. From the moment he learned of his beloved daughter's death, Ash set out like an avenging angel. He had one goal and one obsession. He wanted John Hill's head.

Joan's funeral was scheduled for noon on March 21, 1969. Bright and early that morning Ash appeared in the District Attomey's office clutching a sheaf of notes. He made his case, based on his own interviews with Joan's houseguests, the housekeeper, various doctors, and others he had buttonholed over the previous two days. Ash was not a man to mince words. He was accusing Dr. John Hill of murder.

The immediate upshot was that the DA's office called the Harris County Medical Examiner, Dr. Joe Jachimczyk, who learned to his displeasure that Joan Hill's death had never been reported to him, and that her body had been autopsied only after it was embalmed. Jachimczyk dropped his other work and made a crash study of the case. He learned that blood and urine samples taken at the hospital had been thrown away. He called Dr. Morse and found out what tissue samples were still available. Morse had by this point changed his mind about his diagnosis of pancreatitis, but hadn't come up with an alternative. Then Jachimczyk went to the funeral home and stared at Joan's corpse along with the mourners. He had been put in a highly uncomfortable position. He had the authority to stop the funeral and examine the body himself but apparently decided the little he could learn by this exercise was not worth the sensation it would surely cause. Joan's body was, at least temporarily, given over to the earth.

Dr. Morse handed over tissue slides of Joan's stomach, kidney, liver, heart, brain covering, and blood to Dr. Jachimczyk. No traces of poisons were found in the tissue. Based on the limited evidence he had to work from, the Medical Examiner concluded that Joan had died as a result of a severe case of hepatitis, or infection of the liver. He was not prepared to say for certain what had caused the infection, but thought the most likely cause was a virus. Thus the public was exposed to the second in the series of opinions on what killed Joan: "virus hepatitis."

Ash Robinson wasn't buying this diagnosis. The investigation of Joan's death had become a full-time cottage industry at the Robinson household, and every tidbit Ash gathered left him more convinced his son-in-law had killed his only child. Ash was prepared to spend anything it took to make sure the world shared his opinion. He hired the former District Attorney to facilitate bringing the case before a grand jury. Ash's bitter quest took on a fresh dose of inspiration when, less than three months after Joan's death, John Hill married Ann Kurth.

In June of 1969, Ash got the grand jury investigation he had been pushing for. Knowing that he had to do something to stop the campaign against him, John proposed an unusual question and answer session with the DA's men. He would not agree to a standard polygraph examination, but he would agree to being under the influence of Sodium Pentothal, if administered by an anesthesiologist in a hospital. The result was less than conclusive. John certainly and without hesitation denied having killed his wife, but he also gave incorrect answers to some factual questions. Ann Kurth would later claim that John prepared for the session by studying the effects of Sodium Pentothal and giving himself an "antidote." The anesthesiologist present took offense at this, saying there could be no antidote and that his professional judgment was that there was no doubt John Hill "went under." He would admit, however, that a pathological liar or a psychopath might have no trouble maintaining his story under the effects of the drug.

With so little hard evidence to go on, the first grand jury did not return any indictments in the death of Joan Robinson Hill. This did not stop Ash Robinson. He remained convinced that John had killed Joan by giving her some evil substance, and all he had to do was prove it. He came up with a new tactic. He would hire the world's greatest pathologist, have Joan's body exhumed, and establish the truth once and for all. At the time, it was generally accepted that the world's greatest pathologist was Dr. Milton Helpern, the Chief Medical Examiner of New York City. Ash contacted the eminent doctor, who was no stranger to headlines, and interested him in the case. A second grand jury was now in session. Ash was allowed to plead his case for an exhumation. He would pay all expenses. Permission granted.

Dr. Helpern left behind a description of the second Joan Robinson Hill autopsy in a collection of memoirs that was published after his death. It seems to have been quite a show. No fewer than eleven doctors were present, including the pathologists Dr. Jachimczyk – who had been a student of Dr. Helpern's – and Dr. Morse, and two medical teams representing John Hill and his antagonist Ash Robinson. At this point, the subject's body had not only been embalmed, it had lain in the earth for almost six months. Nothing could be expected from microbiological or toxicological testing at this late date. Nevertheless, the autopsy went on for seven grueling hours. Dr. Helpern would rely on "visual appearances" and on the microscopic sections from this

autopsy and the previous one. There was one macabre development that would give rise to a minor controversy. Dr. Helpern
announced that Joan's heart and brain were missing. Dr. Morse
explained that he had removed these organs during the first
autopsy. In fact, he happened to have slices of the brain in the
trunk of his car, parked just outside. He was in the process of
transfering some specimens from one lab to another. The brain
tissue was produced and Dr. Morse helpfully offered that it would
show decided evidence of meningitis. The upper end of the spinal
cord proved to be free of this disease, and the two teams of doctors
became bitterly divided over the issue of whether the upper spinal
cord always shows evidence of meningitis at the same time as the
brain. Meanwhile a newspaper headline trumpeted "Wrong Brain
Hinted."

But the most startling development in the second autopsy, from
a layman's point of view, came when Dr. Helpern first ordered
the casket opened. There was mud inside. Clearly, someone had
dug up the grave and opened the casket. Upon investigation, it
developed that John Hill had had the body dug up himself just a
few days after the burial. He had obtained the proper permits. He
said he wanted to retrieve a ring that was of sentimental value.
The odd thing about this explanation was that the funeral home
remembered a specific request that Joan be buried without
jewelry, and a friend of Joan's remembered John making this
request himself. John would be quoted as saying he searched for
the ring on Joan's body at the grave but couldn't find it. Ann Kurth
claims she was told John made his visit to the grave in the
company of "some woman," and spent an undetermined amount
of time with Joan's body, having sent cemetery workers away. In
any case, Dr. Helpern could see no evidence that the body had
been tampered with after burial. The revelation was still
alarming. What possible reason could a husband have for digging
up his wife's dead body? In February of 1970 a third grand jury
would begin considering an indictment of Dr. John Hill for the
death of his wife. One member of this grand jury had a particular
interest in the case. He was Cecil Haden, a wealthy, longtime pal

of Ash's who had had an avuncular relationship with Joan throughout her life and had been a pallbearer at her funeral. Haden had been closely informed on developments in Ash's efforts to nail John Hill, and he was hardly objective. Still, those involved with the process would make the less than credible claim that his service on this particular grand jury was pure coincidence.

In April, the grand jury considered the long-awaited autopsy report from Dr. Milton Helpern, which had been eight months in the making. Dr. Helpern flew into town at Ash Robinson's expense and presented the report himself. The bottom line of Helpern's report was that Joan had died of "an acute inflammatory and probably infectious disease," the origin of which could not be determined under the circumstances. The "portal of entry" was probably "by way of the alimentary tract." In other words, Joan most likely swallowed whatever it was that killed her. The meningitis, the kidney failure, the hepatitis, the pancreatitis, etc. had all been end results of this massive infection. This was the technical side of Helpern's report. But there was a nontechnical section that would prove more damaging to John Hill. Dr. Helpern quoted reports from the housekeeper and houseguests to support his contention that "failure to provide adequate medical attention at home and the resultant delay in hospitalization . . . aggravated a situation which proved fatal."

This would open the door to the tactic the prosecution would eventually use to pursue John Hill for murder. Citing well-scattered precedents, the DA's men would argue that John Hill was guilty of "murder by omission." As Joan's husband, he was responsible for her welfare. As her doctor, he was doubly responsible. If he let her die when he could have saved her, he was her killer. The third grand jury returned an indictment alleging "malice aforethought by failing to provide and by withholding proper medical treatment and timely hospitalization."

While these developments went forward, John Hill and Ann Kurth had been enduring a wild and woolly marriage. Their time together must have been, to say the least, intense. John would claim she broke his nose with a fair right cross (he drove to a hospital and set it himself, using a mirror, before an admiring audience of medical students), went on jealous tirades in which she ripped apart and burned mementoes of Joan's, denied him sleep through all-night harangues, and terrorized his office staff during attempts to learn about the details of his appointment schedule and his income. Ann would have far worse to say about her time with John.

By this point John Hill was being defended by Richard "Racehorse" Haynes, the same wily lawyer who would later defend Cullen Davis. The Hill case was in fact an important springboard for Racehorse in his ascent to the legal limelight. The doctor reportedly began pleading with his lawyer to free him of Ann Kurth. The lawyer pleaded with his client to keep the wife no matter how troublesome she might be. As a wife, she could not testify against her husband. As an ex-wife, particularly as a bitter one, she might go over to the Robinson camp. John would not be swayed. He wanted a divorce, no matter what the consequences. Lawyer and client conspired to an odd maneuver whereby John drove Ann to Louisiana under pretense of a reconciliation, while Racehorse had Ann's things removed from the house on Kirby Drive. Shortly thereafter, Ann reportedly appeared on Ash Robinson's doorstep. The day after her divorce from John, in March of 1970, Ann testified before the grand jury that would indict her ex-husband. She said he had tried to kill her and had confessed the killing of Joan Robinson Hill. She would repeat this story at his trial and expand on it in the book she wrote later.

John and Ann's divorce was an early volley in a fusillade of legal activity that would keep lawyers on all sides busy for years. John was suing Ash for $10 million for conspiring to have him indicted. Joan's will was being contested, because John and Ash had produced two conflicting versions of the document. Ash's version, which appeared to be the most recent, cut John out entirely. John said Ash's version was a blatant forgery. But all this was a sideshow. The centerpiece of the legal drama was the preparation for John Hill's murder trial.

The judge at the trial had a memorable name. He was Fred Hooey. Jury selection did not begin in Judge Hooey's courtroom until March 16, 1971. These jurors would hear about the sad state of the Hills' marriage, and of Joan's plan to see a divorce lawyer the day before she died. They would hear Effie Green's story about how desperately sick Joan had seemed and how inattentive John had seemed, and they would see Racehorse demonstrate that Effie could be confused about details. But this was just a warm-up. Both sides knew the most dramatic testimony would come from Ann Kruth. She was the only witness prepared to say without hesitation that John Hill was a killer.

A long struggle ensued over whether Ann should be allowed to testify. Racehorse maintained that she had been married to the defendant at the time the events she would describe took place, and that John was thus protected by the "ancient legal maxim" that prohibits a wife from testifying against her husband. The prosecution offered legal precedent to show that the husband–wife privilege can be lifted in regard to specific acts of violence committed by one spouse or another. In other words, Ann Kurth should be allowed to testify about the times she claimed John Hill tried to kill her. Implied in this was the argument that anything John Hill said to her in the course of the act of violence should also be admissible. This was crucial, because both sides knew Ann's story was that John had confessed to killing Joan while he was attempting to kill Ann. Judge Hooey bought the prosecution's argument with the caveat that he might stop Ann's testimony at any time.

So Ann Kurth took the stand. Her testimony began with the period before she became Mrs. Hill. She told about her affair with the handsome doctor. She said that he "hated" his then wife Joan. Then she described a scene she said took place the week before Joan's death, at John's secret apartment. In the bathroom, she spotted three petri dishes under a gooseneck lamp "with red something in them and little dots of something." When John found her in the room, he quickly led her out and explained he was "doing an experiment." The same day, she spotted pastries in boxes in the refrigerator, and John told her not to eat them.

Over Racehorse's continued objections, Ann was allowed to continue her testimony the next day. She described an evening in June of 1969, a month after her marriage to John. After an argument over the dinner table at a restaurant, John suggested a drive. He cruised in an aimless fashion for more than an hour, to the sound of music on the radio in his Cadillac. When Ann realized they had arrived at Joan's horse stables, Chatsworth Farm, she asked where they were, and John replied, "That's where somebody lived who doesn't live anymore . . . and now, neither do you!" With this, he jammed down the accelerator and crashed the passenger side of the car into a bridge. Ann was not wearing a seat belt, and she had the presence of mind to jump over to John's side of the car before the crash. Disappointed to see her still alive, he produced a syringe and tried to inject something into her chest. She struggled and he dropped the syringe on the floorboard. Like a movie monster who refuses to die, he produced a second syringe. Just as he was about to plunge this into Ann, she was saved by motorists who had stopped to inquire if anyone was hurt in the wreck. He threw the syringe into some weeds and accepted a ride to the hospital with the motorists.

Maybe the shot was just a sedative to calm her down after the wreck, the prosecutor suggested. How did she know, her husband being a doctor and all, that he intended to harm her with the needle? "Because" Ann replied, "he told me how he had killed Joan with a needle." This brought Racehorse up and screaming for a mistrial. After some consideration, Judge Hooey gave it to him. The only trial John Hill would face for the murder of his wife had come to a sudden and unexpected end. Judge Hooey had apparently never been comfortable with the idea of Ann Kurth testifying about incriminating things John said and did while they were married, especially when confessing to the crime for which he was on trial. Both sides would prepare for a second trial, but John Hill would not live to see it.

Thus a jury would never hear the bulk of the evidence that suggested John Hill was guilty of "murder by omission." The state was not after all trying to prove he killed Joan with a pastry or a needle, but that he let her die through negligence. The jury had likewise heard only a condensed, edited-for-television version of Ann Kurth's Gothic tale. She would give it its full scope in her own book, and it would be retold as a TV movie.

The John Hill Ann knew was a truly sweet, considerate, and romantic guy. Most of the time. "He was a wonderful person," she said when interviewed for this book, "still the neatest person I've ever met. He just had this terrible, deadly habit." Of killing people. The problem was, John Hill had an evil side. According to Ann, he was no less than a classic, true-life Dr. Jekyll and Mr. Hyde. He even registered himself and Ann at motels as Mr. and Mrs. Hyde. Ann first witnessed the werewolf-like transformation the night John tried to do her in with a Cadillac and a bridge. The jury was spared the most lurid details of that evening in early summer, but they are re-created in the torrid prose of Ann's book:

"His face was a mask of evil; his eyes piercingly cruel and his features contorted. His voice had taken on a diabolical tone . . . 'I got some Petri dishes from the lab and then I grew some cultures . . . I saved every form of human excretion. Urine, feces, pus from a boil on a patient's back . . . First, I gave it to her in some pastries. Nothing happened. Then I gave her some ipecac [an emetic] in a Coke. She threw up everything but her toenails . . . So I gave her [an injection of] a broad-spectrum antibiotic . . . mixed in with the results of the cultures, and from then on, it was just a matter of time. By the time I took her to the hospital, she was in irreversible shock.'" Why did he do it? Because Joan and Ash would never give him a divorce. When Ash wrote out the agreement he forced John to sign, "'Her own father had . . . authored her death certificate.'"

Is this means of murder plausible? Various medical authorities have said it is. Feeding somebody a concoction of dung and pus – despite Dr. Helpern's assertion that Joan "most likely" swallowed something deadly – might do little more than make them queasy. Giving it to them in a shot could kill them.

Ann goes on to claim that one of the syringes her husband tried to plunge into her after the car wreck was recovered and found "after exhaustive tests" to contain "procaine hydrochloride which would have made my heart fibrillate, causing death in seconds . . . I would have appeared to have died in shock following the wreck." When John Hill was asked about the same night, he reportedly remembered nothing about syringes. His version of the wreck was that he and Ann were having one of their frequent violent arguments, and this one turned into a rolling free-for-all. She grabbed the wheel and the car veered into the bridge.

Perhaps the most questionable thing about Ann Kurth's story is that it recounts an incident that happened one month into a nine-month-long marriage. How could anyone in their right mind continue living with a madman who had done and said what Ann claims John Hill did and said that night? On that night alone, Ann had the opportunity to talk to the motorists, the hospital staff, and the police who investigated the accident (the official report quotes John as saying he fell asleep at the wheel). According to Ann, John would go on to do other strange and dangerous things, and yet she continued living with him and lying down beside him every night. She apparently never breathed a word to anybody about the other side of Dr. Jekyll until she and John were in the process of divorce. In her book, Ann Kurth goes to some lengths to explain away this discrepancy. The bottom line is she was "immobilized by fear." She knew if she tried to get away and "botched it, I wouldn't live to try again. I would try to remain safe and alive until I could get us all [herself and her children] away." This process of remaining safe and alive while looking for an escape route went on for months. And during those months, Mr. Hyde would emerge in all his nastiness on several occasions.

During the drive to Louisiana, while Racehorse was busily arranging to have Ann's things moved out of the house on Kirby Drive, John somehow felt compelled to talk about "'several strange and sudden deaths I have been associated with.'" His voice "taking on that peculiarly dreadful tone" and his face "indescribably changed," he hinted that he had killed his brother Julian – after "'a delightful evening'" in which the two Hill boys played piano duets – with an overdose of morphine, and made the death appear a suicide. He went on to confess he had "'prescribed some medicine that was certain to be fatal'" to his father, who had a heart condition and subsequently died of a heart attack. Dad had been asking too many questions about Julian. Then there was John's "'good friend Andrew Gordon,'" a doctor who died of an overdose. His mistake was becoming "'very jealous'" of John. The recitation trailed off with the suggestion that the list of "strange and sudden deaths" went on.

One troubling thing about Ann Kurth's descriptions of the appearances of Mr. Hyde is that there is no one to corroborate them. All the scenes have only two players, Ann and a man who has been declared dead. Could John Hill have been so anxious to divorce a woman who had so much on him, and who would become an instant threat the moment she could legally testify? And what about the next Mrs. Hill, who lived with John twice as long as Ann and never met Mr. Hyde?

This was Connie Loesby, who became John Hill's new ally before the trial, stuck with him – doing legwork and research to support his case – throughout the ordeal, and married him four months after the mistrial was declared. By all appearances, Connie was the woman John Hill should have been with all along. Her passion was music. She had taken a Master's degree in the subject, had sung in choirs under the direction of Leonard Bernstein and toured Europe with the Robert Shaw Chorale. Connie met John through musical connections and remembers their time together fondly. She not only never saw the evil transformation, she never heard a word in anger. The only irregular behavior she recalls in her eighteen months of marriage to John Hill is one night when he failed to show up at home. She called the hospital and was told he was sound asleep in the doctors' lounge.

Together with Connie, John Hill worked at rebuilding the medical practice that had been virtually destroyed by the scandal attendant to the trial. Connie opened a music school. The couple lived as low-key and inconspicuous a life as possible under the circumstances. The second trial was postponed by legal maneuvering three times, and had eventually been set for November 1972. All this delay rankled Ash Robinson. His pressure campaign to have John Hill tried in Joan's death never let up.

In September of 1972, the Hills were due to attend a plastic surgeons' convention in Las Vegas. Neither of them being Las Vegas types, they spent most of the time in San Francisco. John Hill's mother Myra was staying with young Robert, now twelve, in the big house on Kirby Drive. The weekend the couple was due back, Myra Hill received two phone calls from a man who called himself James Gleason, who needed to talk to the doctor and wanted to know exactly when he would return. She told him. When John and Connie arrived from the airport by taxi on Sunday evening, September 24, "James Gleason" was waiting for them inside the house.

At about 7.15 p.m. a man with a green pillowcase over his head and only his eyes showing through cut slits forced his way into the house and bound and gagged Myra Hill, then in her seventies, and the twelve-year-old boy. He was carrying a pistol. Sometime during the binding his pillowcase either came off or was removed, and both child and grandmother had a good look at him. When Connie Hill rang the doorbell a few minutes later, the old woman tried to scream a warning and was kicked in the throat for her trouble. The boy was kicked in the head.

When the man greeted Connie at the front door, the pillowcase hood had been replaced. Before she realized what was happening, she was pulled inside the house. John Hill was just behind her. He pushed her out of the line of fire and confronted the intruder. He was shot three times, and after each shot he tried again to stop the man who was killing him. John Hill died just inside his own front door. He had been hit in the wrist, the right shoulder, and just below the right rib cage with hand-loaded .38 caliber slugs. It was the abdominal shot that killed him, severing the aorta and piercing the diaphragm and the stomach. When the cops found him, his mouth, nose, and eyes had been sealed with adhesive tape, assuring that he would die of suffocation if not of blood loss. The killer had said, "This is a robbery" to both Myra and Connie

Hill, and John's briefcase and wallet were missing, but the tape on his face strongly suggested a professional hit.

Houston Homicide detectives Jerry Carpenter and Joe Gamino worked the case for six months. The .38 was found just down the street from the Hills' house, buried in the mud behind a manicured suburban hedge. The gun pointed the way along a trail that led from River Oaks into another world entirely, a world where oil fortunes and charity horse shows and passions for classical music are unknown. A trace on the pistol took the Houston cops to the east Texas town of Longview, where a high-rolling black doctor told them it had been stolen from him by a white whore whose trick name was Dusty. Dusty turned out to be a twenty-three-year-old dope addict named Marcia McKittrick, who worked for a sometime burglar and sometime pimp in Dallas. His name was Bobby Vandiver. Bobby was a thirty-three year old three-time loser. He was definitely a hardcase, but killing people was not a part of his accustomed repertoire. Nevertheless, when Carpenter and Gamino finally laid hands on him and grilled him and he realized his best move was to deal for the twelve-year sentence he was offered, he confessed to the murder of John Hill.

Killing Dr. Hill had not been Bobby Vandiver's idea. He had never met the man. The hit was a paying job and, after a long run of bad luck, he took the job because he needed the money. According to the story Bobby told, he had taken the assignment from a fifty-four-year-old woman named Lilla Paulus, who worked a string of underworld connections behind a respectable middle-class facade in a neighborhood near Rice University in Houston. Bobby said Lilla had told him the contract was on a doctor who had killed his wife, and the man buying the contract was the dead wife's father. As it turned out, Lilla Paulus had known Ash Robinson for a long time. The murder of John Hill was beginning to look less like a botched robbery and more like an assassination.

John Hill's life had been worth $5,000 to Bobby Vandiver, and Bobby said $1,500 of this had been kicked back to Lilla Paulus. Bobby had been led to believe the doctor was carrying as much as $30,000 in his briefcase, but only about $700 was to be found there. Bobby's real intention, or so he claimed, had been just to take the briefcase and run, but the doctor had fought back hard and gotten himself killed after all.

Murder indictments were returned against Bobby Vandiver, Marcia McKittrick – who Bobby said had told him about the contract and driven the getaway car – and Lilla Paulus. The DA apparently did not feel enough evidence existed to try Ash Robinson at the time. Bobby Vandiver would never go on trial or testify in court about what he knew. He got himself killed by a policeman in a Longview bar. When detectives Carpenter and Gamino finally ran down Marcia McKittrick, she admitted her role in the Hill killing and told them she had seen Ash Robinson meet with Lilla Paulus on several occasions, give her money, and hand her a diagram of John Hill's house. Marcia believed Lilla had taken in $25,000 on the contract, but had only offered $5,000 to Bobby Vandiver.

In the fall of 1974, Marcia McKittrick accepted a verdict of guilty for the murder of John Hill, and the ten-year sentence that came with it, in the hope that the judgment would be reversed on appeal. Lilla Paulus's trial as an accomplice to murder was delayed until February of 1975. It was a drawn-out and interesting event. Lilla presented herself as a frail, respectable matron who was falsely accused in the twilight of her life. The prosecutors knew she had been busted herself for prostitution a number of times in the 1940s, had operated a whorehouse in Galveston, was a tough-talking, habitually armed confidante of Houston underworld characters, and had been married for twenty years to a big-time bookie named Claude Paulus, who died shortly before the hit on John Hill. How much of this side of Lilla could be communicated in a trial was an open question. As it turned out, quite a bit could be. Marcia McKittrick testified about the contract arrangements and told the court Lilla had told her the source of the contract was Ash Robinson. The prosecution offered telephone records to support Marcia's story, as well as a scrap of paper found in Lilla's house that had an unlisted phone number for Ash.

Lilla denied all this in her own testimony and still had some hope of carrying off her wronged little-old-lady routine until the prosecution put her own daughter on the stand. The daughter, Mary Jo Paulus, testified that she had heard her mother and father talking about Ash Robinson's desire to pay somebody to kill John Hill. Mary Jo confirmed earlier testimony that put Lilla and Ash together as horse show enthusiasts. Then she put the final pin in Lilla's balloon by revealing that her mother had forced her into a life of prostitution, beginning at the age of four. Lilla Paulus was found guilty and given a thirty-five-year sentence.

Ash Robinson was never charged in the death of his son-in-law. In 1977, the Hill family, including Connie and Robert, filed a $7.5 million wrongful death suit against him for the murder of John Hill. Ash appeared on the stand and made a direct, emotional appeal to his seventeen-year-old grandson to believe that he had nothing to do with his father's death. The old man made an impressive and impassioned speech. Lionel Barrymore could not have been more eloquent in the part, and the jury could hardly fail to have been moved. The Hills' case was weakened by, among other things, Mary Jo Paulus's unwillingness to repeat her earlier testimony, and Lilla Paulus's reliance on the Fifth Amendment. Marcia McKittrick did testify, and in a strange development that perhaps has more to say about the accuracy of lie detector tests than anything else, Marcia passed a polygraph exam saying Ash had caused the death of John Hill, while Ash passed another saying that he hadn't. The jury found that there had been a conspiracy to cause John Hill's death, but vindicated Ash Robinson.

Ash Robinson died in February of 1985 at the age of eighty-seven. His wife Rhea died two years later. Robert Hill is about to graduate from law school. Connie has remarried and is still living in Houston. Ann Kurth is running a dress shop in central Texas.

Shakespeare told us that "the evil that men do lives after them." So what about the evil Mr. Hyde? In a twist somehow appropriate to this horror story, Ann Kurth claims he's still alive. In the clincher to her book, Ann relates that a friend of hers reported a possible sighting of the good doctor – alive and well but incognito, and still plying the medical trade – "outside Guadalajara" in Mexico. Ann suggests that, being a plastic surgeon, John Hill could have duped someone else into looking just like him, gotten his impostor killed in an elaborate plan to fake his own death, and rearranged his own features before his Phoenix-like appearance in Mexico. She claims someone called her not long after the Mexico story and played Rachmaninoff over the phone, as John Hill had once done. When interviewed for this book, Ann revealed there have been new developments since she wrote her story down. She's read the autopsy report on John Hill, and found a corpse described who's the wrong height, with the wrong color eyes. Reports of John in Mexico, she says, continue: "Supposedy he's happily-ever-after in Mexico somewhere, traveling to Europe quite a bit."

No matter that the doctor's death was witnessed by his wife, his mother, and his son, and none of these people had any doubt that the man who died that Sunday evening in 1972 was John Hill and no one else. No matter that the faked-death theory would require either the full cooperation or a mind-boggling deception of Connie Hill. Or that there's so much evidence of an assassination plot against John Hill, and none of a faked-death plot of his own making. In this tale, the ground can shift as quickly as the voice that tells it. Since the night Joan Robinson Hill died so abruptly and so mysteriously, what you believe about this murky case depends on who you believe. It is likely always to be so.

Postscript

Ann Kurth died in 1990 at the age of 59. Some in her family suggest the berry aneurysm that killed her could have been brought on by a certain deadly doctor.

Robert Hill now works as a prosecutor in California and is an avid horseman.

9

Killing for Candy

The Disappearance of Helen Brach

In 1950, Frank Brach made some changes in his life. He divorced the woman he had been married to for seventeen years and started over with the redheaded hat-check girl he had picked up at a country club in Miami Beach. He did this knowing it would cost him a bundle, but that didn't seem to matter. Money was one thing he had plenty of.

There was a minor scandal during the divorce, but Frank Brach was ready to pay that price too. When he had divorced his first wife twenty years before, she had stood up in court and claimed he liked to beat her up. He knew the second wife would do the same thing, and she did. He must have guessed rightly that nobody would stop buying the candy his company made just because he knocked his wives around a little.

The next year, Frank married the redhead. He was sixty-one and she was thirty-nine. It was not hard to see why he had paid the price. Helen Vorhees looked like she had stepped out of the pages of a fashion magazine. She was a leggy five feet ten, with a peachy complexion, a smile like a beacon, and knock-you-dead brown eyes. For Frank Brach, it was a change of women. For Helen Vorhees, it was a whole new world. There must have been times in those early days when she identified with Cinderella. Despite her good looks, there had not been much excitement in her life: at thirty-nine, she was living from one skimpy paycheck to the next. Suddenly and with a single stroke of fate, she was transformed into one of the richest women in the city of Chicago. This transformation is the second-most remarkable thing about the story of Helen Vorhees Brach. The first is her unexplained disappearance from the face of the earth twenty-six years later.

While he was changing women, Frank Brach made another change that could not have seemed so significant at the time. He hired a new chauffeur, a man in his late twenties named Jack Matlick. Matlick showed the proper qualities of loyalty and dedication at his job. Over time, he would become in effect the majordomo of the Brach household, responsible for the progress of all things domestic. He would also become the most enigmatic figure in the drama that was still two and a half decades in the future.

There is nothing on the record to show that the marriage of Frank and Helen Brach was anything but happy. He seems to have indulged her every whim, buying her candy-colored cars, changing the Brach's Candy logo to her favorite color – pink – and giving her all the money she needed to make life comfortable for her family back in her Ohio hometown. The couple traveled extensively, built vacation homes, and remodeled and enlarged Frank's big house at 935 Wagner Road in Glenview, Illinois, a suburb of Chicago.

Chicago was Frank's town. He had been born and raised and earned his millions there. Frank had the good fortune to be the son of the Henry Ford of the candy game, a German emigrant named Emil Brach. Through his tinkering with machinery and his innovative recipes, old Emil revolutionized the mass production of various forms of candies. The Chicago candy store he opened in 1905, the Palace of Sweets, grew into a candy kingdom called E. J. Brach & Sons. Frank Brach was the son in charge of marketing and sales, and as much an innovator in his own way as his old man. Candy was good to Frank Brach. When he died in January 1970 at the age of eighty, he left his wife the bulk of his estate. Being Frank Brach's widow made Helen worth roughly $21 million at the time.

The money was held in a trust, and the trust was watched over by Frank Brach's longtime accountant, a man named Everett Moore. Helen had access to the principal anytime she wanted it, but showed no particular interest in spending large amounts of money. Maybe it was her upbringing. The Vorhees clan did not spawn many spendthrifts. They were a hardworking, solid lot who descended from one of the earliest settlers of the Appalachian hills of southeast Ohio.

Helen Marie Vorhees was born in 1911, in a small town known as Hopedale. Following the local custom, she married early, to a man with the infelicitous name of Hanlin Littlecock. Mr. Littlecock was said to be a womanizer, and this was said to be the reason Helen found herself divorced at the age of twenty-one and working as a ticket seller on a trolley line. She would later hold a job as a bookkeeper, and then sell tickets for a dancing club outside Columbus. The latter position had a suggestion of glamour about it, with the occasional glimpse of a big-name musician or a big-money patron, and led to her escape from her Ohio roots to the more glitzy club in Miami Beach, where she would strike it rich on the arm of Frank Brach.

Even after becoming Mrs. Brach, Helen seemed to remain a small-town girl at heart, preferring the company of her childhood acquaintances in Ohio to that of her peers among Chicago's monied elite. After Frank's death, she apppeared to withdraw further into reclusiveness and eccentricity. Her Glenview neighbors rarely caught a glimpse of her. Chores outside the home were performed by the ever-present Jack Matlick, who served as an effective shield between Helen and the world at large.

Most of her communications were carried out by telephone. In fact, she became a compulsive telephone user, spending up to several hours a day in conversation with friends or relatives in Ohio or Florida, or with others who shared the central interests of her life.

Interest number one was the welfare of animals. When Helen Brach gave money to a cause, she was much more likely to give it to help animals than people. Her two favorite dogs, Sugar and

Candy, were buried beside her husband in the $500,000 memorial complex she had built in a Unionport, Ohio graveyard. Her own crypt awaited her there, molded in the form of a gigantic box of chocolates topped with roses carved in marble. At the time of her disappearance, three ragged mutts named Luvey, Tinkerbelle, and Beauty were sharing her home and dining on choice cuts. Her favorite charity was the Animal Protective Institute, a California-based outfit whose founder, Belton Mouras, had helped Helen expose a crooked dog pound in Ohio. The API reportedly received up to $100,000 a year from widow Brach.

Interest number two was spiritualism. Helen made daily calls for consultation with a psychic and card reader in Florida. The final call was received on February 16, 1977, the day before the last confirmed and credible sighting of Helen Brach on earth. Helen had developed the habit of arising each day at dawn to practice spirit writing. She would meditate herself into a trance and allow the spirits from the other side to guide her pen across the page.

As one source close to the case put it when interviewed for this book, "She was, all in all, a very strange lady . . . a lady who was most concerned about herself." Perhaps this self-absorption had something to do with the ironic atmosphere following her disappearance, when all involved seemed much more interested in what would happen to Helen's money than in what had happened to Helen.

Roughly three years after her husband's death, Helen Brach – then sixty-one years old – developed a new and unexpected interest. She became an avid follower of the horseracing game. She had begun dating a man named Richard Bailey, who bought and sold race horses and operated an upscale riding stables in the Chicago suburb of Morton Grove. Bailey was seventeen years younger than Helen Brach. He was a small-framed but handsome man with a reputation as something of a playboy. He was involved in a rough business. A number of the horse traders round about Chicago at the time had a habit of engaging in bloody feuds with one another, in the course of which a barn might be burned down, or a horse poisoned, or, on occasion, a man killed. While Bailey was not known to be directly implicated in these affairs, he did business with people who were. The worst that was alleged about Richard Bailey was that he had a penchant for bilking rich old ladies out of their money by selling them questionable horses at inflated prices.

Helen Brach did buy horses through Richard Bailey, from his brother P.J. – a former jockey – and from others of his associates. She reportedly bought a total of nine horses over a period of time, paying between $200,000 and $300,000 for them. One of the more expensive horses was ironically named Potenciado, or "Powerful One." Helen Brach paid P. J. Bailey a reported $50,000 for Potenciado, only to learn he had a debilitating bone disease and would be forever lame. There is another story that Helen gave Richard Bailey a large amount of money – $100,000, according to one version – for a horse-buying trip to South America, and that Bailey returned horseless. Whatever their relationship, Richard Bailey and Helen Brach did take several trips together, to Ohio, to Florida, and once to New York City for New Year's Eve. Bailey is said to have proposed marriage on more than one occasion, but to have been turned down.

In early 1977, Helen Brach became concerned about her health. She had noticed a swelling in her ankles. For status-conscious Chicagoans, the premier health care facility within easy striking distance is the Mayo Clinic in Rochester, Minnesota. Helen Brach could certainly afford the Mayo. The problem was that even wealthy patients normally could not be taken on short notice there. Richard Bailey had a connection at the Mayo and he solved the problem, just as he reportedly had for another wealthy woman client not long before. Helen Brach checked into the Kahler Hotel just across from the clinic. Her medical examinations were completed on February 16, and she was to learn the results the next day, Thursday, February 17. She arose that morning to good news. The clinic had given her a clean bill of health. She was advised to exercise more and to lose a little weight, but otherwise she was pronounced a remarkably healthy sixty-five-year-old.

On the way back from the clinic Helen Brach stopped in a shop called the Buckskin. There she purchased some cosmetics and a set of bath towels for a total of $41, paying with her American Express card. The saleslady in the Buckskin may have been the last person to see Helen Brach alive. She described a tall, still-attractive woman with tinted red hair, wearing a full-length fur coat. Helen Brach remarked to the saleslady that she was in a bit of a hurry because her "houseman" was waiting for her. The saleslady was unsure, when questioned later, whether this meant he was waiting just outside or in Chicago.

Helen had a reservation on Northwest Airlines Flight 352, due into Chicago's O'Hare Airport at 3.00 that afternoon. Her ticket for the flight was used, but none of the flight crew remembered a woman of her description on the plane. Because of her height, her carriage, and her clothes, Helen Brach was too striking to be easily overlooked. On the other hand, the flight crew was not interviewed until weeks after the fact. A lot of passengers had occupied their seats in the meantime.

From there the story of Helen Brach is picked up by the "houseman," Jack Matlick, then fifty-two years old. He is the only source of her actions over the next couple of days. Suffice it to say that if Matlick's account were presented as fiction, it would be rejected as beyond belief.

Matlick claims he met Helen's Northwest Airlines flight at O'Hare and drove her to the house in Glenview. She was crabby because the ride was not in her lavender Rolls, or one of her three candy-toned Cadillacs, or her pink Continental, but in a lowly Jeep. Jack explained that he had not had time to change cars. Normally, Matlick stayed overnight at the Glenview house only when Mrs. Brach was out of town. When she was at home, he spent evenings with his wife and family at a house on a farm in Schaumburg, Illinois, owned by Helen Brach and provided as a perk of his job. This weekend, Jack Matlick says he spent every night in Glenview, explaining that he had some extra work to do.

Wherever Helen Brach was, the telephone was constantly in use. But between Thursday night and Monday morning – when Jack Matlick claims she left for Florida – none of the people she called regularly reported hearing from her. She appears to have placed not a single call. There were the usual number of incoming calls, but callers talked only to Jack Matlick. They were told Helen was in the tub, or indisposed, or unavailable. The only caller who reported talking to Mrs. Brach was an elderly part-time maid who, as it turned out upon investigation, was often confused.

On Sunday night, according to Matlick, Helen Brach went out with a man and returned to the house around midnight. Matlick reportedly told some people the man was Richard Bailey – who was in Florida at the time – and told others he had never seen the man before. If this unknown man exists, he has never come forward, despite all the publicity the case has generated, to admit he had a date with Helen.

Early Monday morning, Jack Matlick says, he drove his employer across the frostbitten city and let her off at O'Hare Airport. He says she was off to Florida, to close a deal on a condo she was buying. He last saw her at the airport terminal at 6.50 a.m. No planes were scheduled to take off for Florida for more than two hours. Helen Brach despised waiting, and – according to her friends – never flew in the morning because of the early hours involved. Matlick says she carried only a small overnight bag. She normally traveled with all the baggage the airline would allow. There was no ticket purchased in Helen Brach's name, and no flight crew member or ticket agent remembered seeing anyone of her description. No one in Florida had been alerted to expect her arrival, despite the fact that she habitually called her friends there to tell them she was coming, and ask that they meet her at the airport. In fact, she had called her Florida friends from the hotel in Minnesota and told them she had decided to postpone her trip to Florida indefinitely. No one in Florida, or anywhere else, would ever see her again.

Sometime over the weekend, someone had signed Helen Brach's name to a number of checks, totaling around $15,000, made out to Jack Matlick or benefiting him in one way or another. One of these checks was a belated "Christmas bonus" for $3,000, from a woman who reportedly had limited her previous Christmas gifts to employees to $50 or less. Everything except the signature on the checks was typed in. Jack Matlick would claim he saw Mrs. Brach sign the checks on Sunday. Even to the untrained eye, the signatures did not resemble Helen's. Matlick said this was because her hand had been injured by a falling trunk lid while she was packing some things to be shipped to Florida. Two graphologists would later call the signatures an outright forgery. The same two experts examined Jack Matlick's handwriting and reported that the forgeries were not his. No one else's handwriting – that of Matlick's wife, for example – was considered.

Ten years later the aforementioned wife, now divorced from Matlick and remarried, would surface to shoot more holes into Jack's already gaping story. Joyce Nowak testified in court that Jack had given her a different account of Helen Brach's last weekend at home than he gave the rest of the world. Joyce said Jack called her Thursday night, February 17 – the night Helen Brach was due back from the Mayo Clinic – and told her Mrs. Brach had not shown up. Telephone company records confirm a call that night from the Glenview house to the farm in Schaumburg. During the call, Joyce testified, Jack said he would have to spend the weekend in Glenview, waiting for Mrs. Brach. Joyce reaffirmed earlier reports that Jack Matlick never stayed overnight in Glenview when Mrs. Brach was there. When she was away, he was expected to stay on the premises to watch over the house and take care of the dogs. According to his ex-wife, Jack unexpectedly appeared at their home on Sunday night, saying Mrs. Brach had returned and that he would have to take her to the airport in the morning. He got up at 4 a.m. to do so.

After Helen Brach's disappearance, Joyce Nowak said, the Matlick family benefited from an unusual influx of cash. Jack would give her $100 bills to do the grocery shopping, which had previously been paid for with a check. Joyce said she never inquired about this because she and Jack were less than close at the time: "I was more or less like the maid, and he never told me nothing. . . . I was just glad he wasn't home." Just before Frank Brach died, Joyce said, Jack Matlick had installed a large safe on rollers in their house, in which he kept gold coins, money, and some guns. She noticed that the coins began appearing in large numbers after Frank Brach's death. Jack was secretive about his hoard of coins and the other contents of his safe, and she rarely caught a glimpse of it. During the same court hearing, there was discussion about a reported $75,000 of unexplained income and spending by Jack Matlick in the nine months after Helen Brach disappeared.

At the time of the disappearance, Jack took some other actions that would have seemed ordinary under other circumstances. Timed as they were, they took on a suspicious tinge. On Monday – according to his story, on the way back from the airport – the Brach houseman had the pink Cadillac he was driving cleaned and waxed, including a complete shampoo of the interior. The next day, he had a decorating service at the house in Glenview, repainting two rooms and replacing a carpet. He had called the decorators over the weekend. The car shampooers and the decorators later told police the work Matlick had commissioned did not appear to be out of the ordinary. They had seen no gross evidence of a crime.

The first red flag about the whereabouts of Helen Brach was raised by a man who wanted her money. Belton Mouras, of the Animal Protective Institute in California, was expecting a large donation he hoped to use to erect a new headquarters building. He had been one of the callers who reached not Helen but Jack Matlick during the mysterious weekend, and he kept calling. Finally, almost two weeks after the last time he claimed to have seen Helen Brach, Jack Matlick appeared at the Glenview

Police station to report her missing. He was told a relative would have to file the report, and he then called Helen's brother Charles Vorhees, who still lived in Hopedale, Ohio. By the time Charles Vorhees reached Glenview, it had been twenty days since Helen Brach left the Mayo Clinic. It took that long for anyone to care enough about her absence to ask the cops to look for her.

But before Charles Vorhees visited the Glenview Police, he joined Jack Matlick in a very curious action. Jack and Charles burned Helen's spirit writings and her diaries in the oil-burning furnace at her house. Charles has said he found a note he knew to be in his sister's handwriting on top of the spirit writings that said, "Burn these in case something happens to me." Jack Matlick said his employer had given him similar instructions. The odd thing was that at this juncture the two men supposedly had no way of knowing anything had "happened" to Helen Brach. Both Helen's brother and her houseman denied looking at the writings or the diaries before they destroyed them. If this is true, no one will ever know what the writings contained. The ashes were found in the furnace during a later search of the house.

Charles Vorhees was Helen's little brother. Not long before she disappeared, he had retired from a career of inspecting railway cars for Conrail. Like his and Helen's parents, he had been a direct beneficiary of the good fortune of her marriage to Frank Brach. In the mid-1950s, Helen and Frank had installed Charles and his family in a luxurious ranch-style home in Hopedale, complete with the town's only outdoor swimming pool. Besides this, as Charles would later tell a court in an attempt to get some of his sister's money released to him, Helen had bought him ten cars, paid for medical expenses and vacations, and helped send his children to college.

Charles's contention was that, were his sister around, she would have still been giving him money. He wanted her trust to do this in her stead. There were other people – Belton Mouras, for one – who felt the same way. These requests were an example of the numerous problems that arose to prove how messy it is to disappear when one has a lot of money. Under Illinois law, Helen Brach could not be declared legally dead for seven years. Once she was officially dead, her will could be probated and that would be that. But in the meantime, her affairs were in limbo, and the courts were put in the position of making her financial decisions for her. Continental Illinois Bank, which administered and was co-trustee of Helen's trust, sued to clarify matters and to gain the authority to make decisions regarding the Brach money. The accountant Everett Moore, who was used to managing Mrs. Brach's funds, had other ideas. In the course of this legal wrangle, the court appointed a lawyer named John Cadwalader Menk, a former president of the Chicago Bar Association, to represent the interests of the missing Helen Brach, and another lawyer named Arthur Gorov to represent other interested parties. The two lawyers became ersatz investigators working to solve the mystery.

More would be learned about the Helen Brach case in the course of these unofficial investigations than in any official inquiry. One grand jury did consider the case, but no criminal charges were ever filed and no criminal court proceedings were ever held. Both Menk and Gorov expressed frustration over this puzzling lack of interest by the responsible authorities. The cops working the case were frustrated, too, and at least a part of their frustration sprang from the very nature of the investigation. As one source within the Glenview Police Department put it when interviewed for this book, "I don't have a body, I don't have a murder; I have a missing person. Who am I gonna bring up on charges for that, and what am I gonna charge 'em with?" One good charge might have been forgery. Helen Brach's name was apparently signed on the checks made out to Jack Matlick by somebody who wasn't Helen Brach, but the State's Attorney – for reasons that have never been explained – chose not to pursue this angle.

While the civil procedures ground on in Helen Brach's absence, she was earning an income that exceeded $1 million a year, and this money was being spent. Households were being maintained in three states, race horses were being boarded and exercised even though they never raced, and Luvey, Tinkerbelle, and Beauty were being cared for. Jack Matlick stayed on in his job for a year after his boss disappeared. He was eventually fired by Everett Moore. Belton Mouras got his contributions, though these were interrupted when the IRS reportedly charged that the Animal Protective Institute was a fraud set up to separate rich widows and other animal lovers from their cash. Most of the money Helen Brach had given API, so the IRS investigators claimed, had gone to administrative expenses and big salaries for executives like Belton Mouras. When IRS tax-exempt status was restored to API after a lengthy court battle, Belton Mouras went back on the list of recipients of money from the absent Helen Brach. Charles Vorhees was granted an annual stipend.

Over the years, the court authorized three rewards for information leading to the discovery of Helen Brach. The first was for $100,000. The ante was then upped to $200,000, and later to $250,000. People began seeing Helen Brach all over. Psychics saw her in their minds' eye, and less clairvoyant types spotted her pushing shopping carts, riding airplanes, driving cars, and dining in nightclubs in Illinois, Ohio, Florida, Colorado, and elsewhere. None of these sightings produced Helen, dead or alive.

About a year after the disappearance, the court became interested in whether Helen Brach had authored a will. Jack Matlick claimed he had given a copy of her will to the Glenview police, but the police said he hadn't. The attorney for Everett Moore claimed to have a copy of the will but refused to produce it because of attorney–client privilege. A judge then ordered a search of Helen Brach's house. The search commenced on April Fool's Day of 1978. The will was found in a kitchen cabinet. In a storage room upstairs, the search party located what appeared to be a suitcase Helen Brach had used on her trip from Rochester to Chicago just before she disappeared. Both these finds were a little on the fishy side because police investigators had been through the house before and found no will and no significant suitcase. John Cadwalader Menk described the exercise as an "Easter egg hunt," with planted goodies waiting to be discovered.

Easter egg or no, there was nothing to indicate the will was not a genuine article. It was dated October 15, 1974. It said that almost all of Helen Brach's money was going to the dogs. The Helen Brach Foundation, which favored giving to animal causes, got almost everything. Charles Vorhees and Everett Moore were directors of the foundation. Charles Vorhees got a $500,000 trust. Jack Matlick got a ten-year, $50,000 annuity policy that would pay him $5,000 a year.

The contents of the will were not surprising. In fact the most perplexing thing about the will was what it did not reveal. It did not reveal anyone with a particularly strong motive for killing Helen Brach. All the people who benefited from the will stood to make just as much – or more – money by keeping Helen Brach alive as by making her dead.

If this was true, what happened to Helen Brach, and why did it happen to her? Any number of theories have been proposed. The most grisly is the meat grinder theory. This has been attributed to a colorful private eye named Ernie Rizzo, who worked the case for a time on behalf of Belton Mouras and the Animal Protective Institute, and who would later be busted on a wiretapping charge. It seems that Jack Matlick bought a nine-pound meat grinder from Marshall Fields sometime during the mysterious weekend. There were three dogs on the premises who were used to Matlick feeding them a supper of fresh meat. The ground outside the house was frozen to a considerable depth, making a burial an arduous task. Could Helen Brach have disappeared into the ravenous stomachs of her own beloved dogs? Probably not. The meat grinder was an attachment for a kitchen blender. Helen Brach weighed 160 pounds, a sizable meal for any pack of dogs. And these dogs, as Sergeant Joe Baumann of the Glenview police delicately phrased it, "were little mutts . . . the kind of dogs that if you yelled at them, they'd wet the floor." One was part Chihuahua.

A more comprehensive theory has been proposed by John Cadwalader Menk, the lawyer who was appointed to protect Helen's interests, and who took up the investigation with the zeal that could be expected from the crime buff that he is. Menk told a newspaper interviewer he thinks Helen Brach was killed within a few hours of leaving the Mayo Clinic. He thinks she was picked up in Minnesota by someone she trusted, and never made it to the Northwest Airlines flight. Why was she killed? Menk liked the racehorse theory. Helen Brach had reportedly bought at least nine, and perhaps as many as twelve, horses. As Menk has said, she was "really rooked" on these ponies. "She didn't know anything about horses. She had never done anything with the millions Brach had left her . . . and then suddenly she gets into this big racing thing. It was out of character for her." Maybe, Menk suggests, Mrs. Brach was ready to talk about being ripped off in her equine investments. Being a multi-millionaire, she had the resources to create a lot of heat for crooked horse traders. Menk still stands by his theory today.

Aside from Helen Brach's expensive flirtation with the racing game, there is no direct evidence to support the racehorse theory, but there are some intriguing suggestions. Helen Brach's sometime escort Richard Bailey did occasional business with some of the toughest players on the racing scene. One of these was a millionaire horse trader named Silas Jayne. Silas was not a nice man. He was given a six-to-twenty-year sentence for the hired killing of his own younger brother in 1970. The year before, Silas had killed another man, purportedly one of his brother's bodyguards, purportedly in self-defense. Silas and his clan were associated in the minds of those who followed their activities with horse-doping, horse-poisoning, barn-burning, and other nefarious pastimes.

Three of the horses Helen Brach had paid for reportedly disappeared around the same time she did. Just when the news was breaking about the discovery of the will in Helen's kitchen, some odd, spray-painted graffiti appeared near her house. One message said, "Richard Bailey knows where Mrs. Brach's body is. Stop him! Please!" Another was less verbose. It said, "Bailey killed Brach." Similar slogans were reported near Bailey's stables in Morton Grove. The graffiti artist was never apprehended.

Richard Bailey was finally questioned about his involvement with Helen Brach in a court deposition taken in 1979. In response to sixty-three questions from John Cadwalader Menk, he took the Fifth Amendment sixty-three times. He even declined to incriminate himself in regard to such pressing issues as his current address and whether or not he was married. This response, or lack of it, did little to remove the cloud of suspicion surrounding Mr. Bailey.

According to a cop familiar with the investigation, this uncooperative stance was characteristic of Richard Bailey. When interviewed by police, Bailey always seemed "put out, offended . . . he did his talking, almost exclusively, through his attorney." Jack Matlick, on the other hand, would talk to the Glenview police "at length, but would tell us nothing."

As recently as 1988, leads that suggest the horse connection were still being pursued. By this time, the police had reportedly heard a story that at least one of Helen Brach's horses had come from a stable in which Silas Jayne had an interest, and that she had been threatening to go to the authorities about the questionable horseflesh her money had bought. An inmate in the Mississippi state prison at Parchman, the same prison that inspired the blues songs about "Parchman Farm," appeared to be ready to supply the next chapter to this story. Maurice Ferguson, then thirty-six, had been a cellmate of Silas Jayne's at the Vienna Correctional Center in Illinois. In 1979, according to Ferguson's story, Jayne offered him $10,000 to move Helen Brach's body from a horse stable in Morton Grove, Illinois, to another spot. Ferguson was then due to be paroled. He was free for only a month before being jailed again in Mississippi. The problem with Ferguson's story is that each time he tells it the location of Helen Brach's unmarked grave keeps changing, and that despite repeated diggings by concerned authorities he has failed to produce a single bone belonging to the woman he says Jayne described as "the candy lady."

Ferguson, who made his living on the outside by armed robbery, had led the police on three previous wild goose chases in a forest near Glenview, a riding stable near Northbrook, Illinois, and another place in Wisconsin. In 1988, he claimed he was ready to reveal the real location of Helen Brach's remains because Silas Jayne had died and he no longer feared revenge. Helen was resting, he said, in a cemetery in either Minneapolis or St. Paul, Minnesota. He had reburied her at night, nine years before, so he wasn't entirely sure of the location. When the convict could not locate the cemetery or the grave after several days of looking, a police officer who had been along for the ride concluded, "I think we are one of his forms of recreation . . . This is like a trip to Club Med for him." Smiling to reporters as he boarded the police plane that would take him back to his cell at Parchman, Ferguson said, "I enjoyed Minnesota." Thus ended the latest attempt to find Helen Brach.

Helen Brach was declared dead in 1984. By that time her estate was estimated to be worth about $45 million. Today the Brach case is no nearer a solution than it was the year Helen disappeared. There have always been two main suspects—the houseman and the horseman. Jack Matlick's outlandish story certainly makes it difficult to think of him as innocent. And if Richard Bailey had nothing to hide, why was it necessary for him to take the Fifth Amendment in a court deposition? Yet if one assumes both these men had something to do with Helen's disappeance, one must assume they were working together. It could be inferred from John Menk's racehorse theory that Matlick may have been the "someone she trusted" who delivered Helen into the hands of the horsemen. But there is not a single piece of evidence that this happened, and no apparent motive to make it happen.

Because it is so hard to escape the notion of partners in the crime, Menk and others have promoted the idea of granting immunity to either Matlick or Bailey, in the hope that the truth would finally be learned and at least some of the guilty parties would be punished. Police familiar with the case have expressed doubts that this tactic would be productive with either Matlick or Bailey, assuming that either man knows anything worth telling. A grant of immunity is always a gamble, because the real instigator of the crime might walk away scot-free. In this case it is hard to see what damage that might do. If someone did kill Helen Brach, they are free as it is. For whatever reason, the immunity strategy was never used. And the perfectly good forgery case, which might have yielded some new leads in the disappearance – if Jack Matlick did not sign the checks, who did, and what did this person know? – was never pursued. Given the public clamor over Helen Brach, there is no adequate explanation for the passive approach prosecutors seem to have taken in the case.

Without the twist of fate that made her rich, few outside Helen's family would even know her name. Her good fortune had appeared out of nowhere. And with another twist of fate, as suddenly, she herself would walk away to nowhere. The people who know what became of her are determined to be as silent as she is. Assuming, that is, she is not speaking from the other side to someone whose pen is guided by her spirit. That may be the only way the world will ever hear the end of her story.

Postscript

In 1995, a federal judge sentenced Richard Bailey to life for soliciting the murder of Helen Brach. The largely circumstantial case included the testimony of two men who said the horseman had offered them $5,000 to kill Brach shortly before her disappearance. John Cadwalader Menk, who died in 2000, was pleased by Bailey's sentence but still believed "others were involved." Many wonder if those "others" might include houseman Jack Matlick. Matlick gave up his share of Helen Brach's estate in 1993 in response to a lawsuit by the other heirs.

10

Murder in the House of the Lord

The Lord Lucan Murder Case

> "The only thing a gambler needs
> is a suitcase and a trunk . . ."
>
> *House of the Risin' Sun*

George Bingham, the sixth Earl of Lucan, dropped dead quite
unexpectedly one day in January 1964. He had been a good and
kindly man and he was mourned. But the sad event was a stroke
of luck for at least one other man, who worshipped luck as some
men worship gods. His father's passing did two things for
Richard John Bingham. It made him the seventh Earl of Lucan,
a peer of the realm. And it gave him the money to realize his
destiny: to live out his days as a high-rolling gambler.

On the face of it, no man could seem better suited for this
fate. Fortune had smiled lovingly on the new Lord Lucan,
known to his closest pals as Lucky. For anyone who chooses to
romanticize the British aristocracy, there could be no figure
more ideal than Lucky Lucan. He was dashingly handsome,
four inches more than six feet tall, a dedicated sportsman with a
fastidious sense of proper manners and of Doing the Right
Thing. In short, the seventh Earl of Lucan was a beautiful
example of what used to be called good breeding. He was in fact
a beautiful example of a lot of things that used to be: a man from
yesterday, a genuine endangered species.

As things would turn out, he was more endangered than
anyone could have known. Because one day Fortune would end
her loving gaze on Lucky and look another way, and on that day

he would disappear into thin air, accused of the hideously brutal murder of a young woman and the attempted murder of his wife.

Lucan's upbringing had been typical of an Englishman whose flawless pedigree reached back into Anglo-Saxon times. He had attended Eton and served in the Coldstream Guards. He had raced speedboats and ridden on the Army bobsled team in international competitions. Upon his father's death, he took his place in the House of Lords. His political views were just to the right of Genghis Khan's. He had worked, but not with too much diligence, as a merchant banker until he came into his inheritance. But he was much better at gaming than at working, and as soon as he could afford it he devoted himself to gaming full-time.

Despite his impressive family tree, Lucan's forebears were something of an embarrassment to him. An Elizabethan Richard Bingham, military governor of Connaught in western Ireland, had ordered the slaughter of shipwrecked Spanish sailors in the aftermath of the Spanish Armada. Lucky's great-great grandfather, the third Earl of Lucan, had ordered the disastrous Charge of the Light Brigade at Balaclava in 1854. Generations of schoolchildren on both sides of the Atlantic have had stuffed down their memories the famous poem about the noble six hundred who rode into the valley of death against the volleying and thundering cannons that day, and the "someone" who "had blundered" in the poem was none other than a nineteenth-century George Bingham. Military historians are divided about whether the earlier Lord Lucan deserved full blame for the disaster, but the affront to his genetic code was still chafing on the seventh Earl 120 years after the fact.

As if this was not enough, Lucan's own parents had somehow acquired liberal views. The sixth Earl had been commander of the Coldstream Guards and served with distinction in World War II. His failing was that he had not developed into a proper Tory. He had in fact been Chief Opposition Whip for the Labour Party in the House of Lords during the last ten years of his life. Lucan's mother was also a prominent activist in Labour Party politics. To Lucan and his ultraconservative circle of friends, she might as well have been in league with the Kremlin.

In 1960, Lady Luck intervened to decide the course of the balance of the future Lord Lucan's life. During a two-day session of *chemin de fer,* a card game similar to baccarat, the twenty-five-year-old Richard John Bingham won £20,000. From that memorable card game forward, Lord Lucan was convinced he had the touch of Midas in games of chance.

On November 28, 1963, Lucky took a wife. The former Veronica Duncan was elevated through the marriage from a solidly middle-class life. Her father had been an Army major, and her stepfather a hotel manager. His sister had married a millionaire friend of Lucan's named Bill Shand Kydd. Veronica and Lucky had met at a golf tournament and married after an engagement of only one month. Veronica had a pretty face, a keen intelligence, a sharp wit, and – according to Lucan's friends – an equally sharp tongue. She stood a full head and shoulders beneath her husband and weighed less than a hundred pounds. She looked sensitive and frail. She reportedly had suffered from emotional disorders as early as age eight.

In the beginning there was said to be a genuine attachment between Lord and Lady Lucan. They took up residence in a three-story home at 46 Lower Belgrave Street, in a blue-blooded section of London known as Belgravia, within a quarter-mile of Buckingham Palace. Together they produced three children, two girls and a boy. But as time wore on it became painfully clear that little besides the children was holding the marriage together. Veronica had dreamed of the grand life of an aristocrat, with dazzling dinner parties and weekends in great country houses. Instead she found herself increasingly isolated, with a husband who spent his days and nights in gambling clubs. What little social life the couple had came when Lady Lucan joined him, as an unwelcome and sometimes carping visitor. She was not a popular figure with Lucan's thoroughly patrician pals.

Lucky's favorite haunt was the Clermont Club, a private gambling establishment run by an old school chum of his named

John Aspinall. When he wasn't feeding the gentry at his club, Aspinall fed his collection of tigers at the private zoo he maintained on the grounds of his country home. The Clermont was as exclusive as exclusive gets, catering to that subset of the rich and the titled who had been to the right schools and held the right opinions. It was situated in Berkeley Square, about a mile and a half from Lucan's home, and housed in the last masterpiece designed by the architect William Kent, dating from 1742. One of the regulars in the small world of the Clermont was a Dane named Claus von Bülow, who – like his friend Lord Lucan – would later be accused of the attempted murder of his wife.

Like many another gambler, Lucky Lucan appears to have suffered from an inflated sense of his own skills and his standing with the goddess Fortune. On the whole, the time he spent at the Clermont was a downward slide. By the early 1970s he had squandered most of his liquid assets and had been reduced to the role of a house player, used by Aspinall to attract other gamblers with his title, his good looks, and his charm. Not too surprisingly, his already shaky marriage shook apart at about the same time. In early 1973 Lucan moved out of his house on Lower Belgrave and installed himself in a basement bachelor's flat on Elizabeth Street, about a half-mile away. The whole problem, he told his friends, was Lady Lucan. He claimed, perhaps with some justice, that she was batty. So batty she was unfit to look after the children. Lucan wanted custody of the kids, and a long legal struggle ensued. Several people who knew him well, including his own mother, have described him as "obsessed" with getting the children away from his wife.

Lucan had begun complaining in public about his wife's mental problems as early as 1967, after the birth of their son George. He tried to put her in a psychiatric hospital that year, but she refused to be admitted. She did, however, submit to injections of mood-controlling drugs, and to consultations with psychiatrists. After reported episodes of hallucinations and paranoid fantasies, Lucan tried again to commit his wife for treatment in 1971. She got as far as the hospital door before making a run for it.

During the custody battle Lucan took to carrying a concealed tape recorder to demonstrate to the world how unbalanced his wife was. The recorded conversations, now in the possession of the police, were said to reveal him speaking in the coolest and most reserved tones, tossing out bait to which Veronica rose angrily. He also recorded interviews with the children, the nannies, and anybody else who could say anything that reflected badly on Lady Lucan's state of mind. He spent more than he could afford on private detectives to maintain surveillance on his house and follow his wife when she went out. At one point only weeks before the custody hearing, he and two private detectives scooped up the children, nanny and all, from a park and took them to live in his flat. Despite his tape recordings and his medical testimony and the affidavits of his friends, Lord Lucan lost the custody case in June of 1973. It did not help when Veronica claimed he had once tried to strangle her, and her statement was supported by a nanny. He had spent a reported £40,000 in his unsuccessful struggle.

It was a fight Lord Lucan had expected to win. He was, after all, the heir to centuries of privilege. His ancestors had literally *been* the law in their domains. It must have seemed his world was ending around him. He began to fret aloud about the miscegenation of the British people, and he and his far-right Clermont cronies discussed bloody solutions that bordered on the neofascist. To add insult to injury, the Clermont had been sold to Playboy and was no longer the exclusive retreat it had been.

With the loss of the custody case, Lucan seemed to settle into a siege mentality, and to take on the appearance of a desperate man. Combined with his gambling losses, the custody fight had left him in serious arrears. His income would not cover his overdrafts at at least two banks, or his debts to his landlord, his gunsmith, and assorted others – even the cleaners who looked after his coronation robes and the jewelers who had sold him his crocodile watch strap were after him for money. By selling some of the family silver, he raised enough to support his gambling habit for the time being. He had begun drinking heavily and gambling more recklessly. At the age of thirty-nine, his life had settled into a relentless routine, contained within the few square miles of London's West End with which he was most familiar.

He rose late each day and began with martinis at the Clermont Club. His lunch order could have been imprinted on the ticket: it was invariably the same meal of smoked salmon and lamb cutlets. The afternoon was given to backgammon or bridge and the evening to *chemin de fer* or blackjack. He had become an insomniac and he played until he felt he could sleep. He then retired to his flat and the next day repeated the same actions in the same order.

The routine ended abruptly and violently on Thursday night, November 7, 1974. The Lucan children – Lord Bingham, 7, Lady Frances, 10, and Lady Camilla, 4 – were being bedded down as usual in the house on Lower Belgrave Street. The children's nanny, a twenty-nine-year-old woman named Sandra Rivett, normally had Thursdays off. This Thursday she had a cold and had remained in the house. The cold would be fatal.

The house had four levels. The first was a basement containing a kitchen and a breakfast room. Lady Lucan's bedroom was on the third level, and the children's bedroom on the fourth. Lady Lucan habitually descended to the basement just before 9.00 p.m., when the television news came on, to brew a pot of tea. On this night the eldest child, ten-year-old Lady Frances, was still awake and watching television in her mother's room. Sandra Rivett knocked on the door and offered to go down and make the tea. When she reached the ground-floor level and tried to switch on the light at the basement stairs, nothing happened. She had no way of knowing it, but someone had unscrewed the bulb and left it lying on a chair. She started down the stairs in the dark. She was near the same size and shape as Lady Lucan. As she reached the breakfast room, someone struck out in the darkness and hit her squarely on the front of the head with a length of lead pipe. It was a crushing blow, and there were nine or ten more to go with it. At least four blows caught her in the head, cracking her skull. The others landed on her shoulders, her neck, and her arms. She died within a couple of minutes, probably while unconscious, of suffocation caused by internal bleeding into her throat. Her blood covered the breakfast room floor in a thick pool, and splattered the wall. Her attacker then bent her body double and stuffed it into a heavy canvas U.S. Mail bag.

Roughly fifteen minutes later, Lady Lucan began to wonder what had become of Sandra and her tea. According to the account she gave the police and later a coroner's inquest, she then descended the stairs herself. On the ground floor, she noticed there was no light coming from the basement. She heard a sound from the ground-floor cloakroom at the entrance hall, and as she moved toward this sound someone stepped out and hit her on the head with a heavy club. He then hit her several more times.

Lady Lucan was luckier than Sandra Rivett. She survived the attack. She swears that the man swinging the club was her husband. She says she first knew it was he when she screamed and she recognized his voice as he said "shut up." She says he then "thrust three gloved fingers down my throat," and a deadly hand-to-hand struggle commenced. He tried to strangle her and to gouge out her eyes. She remembers being on the ground and then somehow getting a firm grip on his testicles. This caused him to turn her loose.

The two combatants were exhausted. According to Lady Lucan, upon catching their breath they agreed, as only two proper English aristos could under the circumstances, to sit down and have a chat about recent developments. While they talked, she was rapidly losing blood from several serious head wounds. She says she asked about the nanny and he admitted killing her. He said he had mistaken Sandra for her. After this revelation, Veronica said she was thirsty and Lucky got her a drink of water. Then they went upstairs to her bedroom. The ten-year-old Lady Frances was still watching television. She viewed her blood-drenched parents and was sent upstairs to bed. Together, Lady Lucan says, she and her husband examined her injuries in the bathroom and she then lay down on the bed, on a towel he provided. While he was in the bathroom wetting another towel to clean her wounds, she jumped from the bed and escaped.

The story is then picked up by the witnesses who were innocently hoisting flagons in a pub called the Plumber's Arms, just thirty yards from the Lucans' front door. An extraordinary thing happened in the Plumber's Arms at around 9.45 that Thursday night. The door was thrown open and a small woman in a nightdress burst in drenched in blood from head to foot. She was screaming "Murder, murder, I think my neck has been broken . . . he tried to kill me." She went on to say, according to reports from these witnesses, "I think I am dying, please look after my children," and she made it clear that the nanny had been murdered and the children were still in the house with a murderer.

Unfortunately no one in the pub thought this was a good enough reason to spring out to protect the children, or otherwise to right the wrong that had so obviously been done. Maybe this is a sign of our times. Sign or no, if the pub drinkers had poured out en masse and rushed the thirty yards to Lady Lucan's house there might have been no mystery to solve. They might have apprehended whoever was in the house, that person could have been given a proper trial, and the matter would have been effectively brought to an end. As it was, the people in the pub stayed put and called the police like responsible citizens.

The cops who first arrived at Lady Lucan's house found the front door locked. Once inside, they discovered Sandra Rivett's body, still warm and still doubled up in the mailbag. There was an awful lot of blood, concentrated mainly in two areas – in the basement breakfast room, and on the stairs at the ground floor hall. The pool of blood in the breakfast room had within it fragments of smashed teacups and saucers. On the ground floor the police located an object that had the look of a murder weapon: a nine-inch length of lead pipe, wrapped in adhesive tape, covered in blood and curved and twisted by the heavy work it had done that night. Upstairs in Lady Lucan's bedroom was more blood, particularly on a well-soaked towel that lay across the pillows on the bed. On the next level were the children, unharmed, the two younger ones asleep but the ten-year-old still wide-awake and wide-eyed, staring back at the cops in front of a TV set that was blasting out at near full volume.

Lady Lucan spent the next six days in the hospital. She had passed out in the pub and arrived at the emergency room in deep shock, suffering from seven blows to the head and from cuts inside her mouth.

On Sunday, November 10, the police located a car Lord Lucan had been driving near the English Channel at the south coast port of Newhaven, sixty miles from London. The car was a Ford Corsair Lucan had borrowed from a friend about two weeks before. The front seats, dashboard, glove box, and steering wheel were liberally smeared with blood stains. The trunk contained a sixteen-inch long piece of lead pipe wrapped in adhesive tape, which proved to have been cut from the same original length of pipe as the murder weapon. This pipe was not bloodstained or bent. Lord Lucan was nowhere to be found, and has never been found since. The car was said to have been parked and abandoned in the early-morning hours following the murder, and two fishermen claimed to have seen a man of Lord Lucan's description near the Channel at about the same time.

All this provided a fairly tidy package in which to wrap the official theory of the case. Lord Lucan, the theory goes, let himself into his own house with his own key and waited in the basement, knowing his wife's habits and fully expecting her to descend at any time with tea set in hand. The nanny's descent was unexpected, since Lucan would have assumed she had the night off. He either mistook the nanny for his wife in the dark or decided he had to kill her anyway, stuffed her in the mailbag, and resumed waiting for his wife to come down. When she did, he tried to kill her too, but failed. The mailbag was there because Lucan's plan had been to cart off Lady Lucan's body in the back of the borrowed car, which had a larger trunk than his own Mercedes, and drive it to Newhaven. There he would transfer the body to a speedboat he owned, weight it down, and sink it in the Channel. He was well familiar with the Channel and its varying depths from his speedboat racing days. If the murder had gone as planned, Lady Lucan would have simply turned up missing. There would have been no body and therefore no murder case. It had been well established that she was a bit on the unstable side, there were suggestions that she may have attempted suicide at least once, and people might well think she had simply wandered off. This theory was given more substance by reports gathered from the more cooperative of Lucan's acquaintances. One said Lucan had spoken of solving his financial problems by killing Veronica, and another gave a second-hand account that suggested he had actually rehearsed the dumping of the body in the Channel.

Alas, all these well-laid plans were ruined by the appearance of Sandra Rivett on the basement stairs. Two vanishing acts would have been a bit much. The police theorized that after failing to kill his wife Lucan panicked and set out for the coast without any body in his trunk, then either killed himself or went into hiding.

Neat and reasonable as it may seem at first glance, there are some serious problems with the official theory. The most glaring is the choice of murder weapon. Murder with a piece of lead pipe is a very messy business. And a bloodspattered basement is hardly consistent with an unexplained disappearance. With his children upstairs, Lucan certainly could not have allowed in his plan for the time to mop up as thoroughly as would have been required after so violent an attack. Still, what was the big mailbag for if not to carry off a body?

Lucky Lucan has never had the opportunity to defend himself at a trial. His version of events is known only through accounts of one face-to-face conversation he had with a friend, two phone conversations with his mother, and three letters he wrote in haste before his disappearance.

Shortly after his wife ran into the Plumber's Arms, Lucan apparently arrived on the doorstep of a friend named Madeleine Floorman, who lived near his house in Chester Square. Mrs. Floorman's children attended school with the Lucan children. She reported hearing her doorbell ring at length just before 10.00 p.m. that Thursday night. She was alone in her house and afraid to go to the door, so she didn't answer. A short while later, Mrs. Floorman received a phone call from a man who didn't identify himself. She was sure the voice on the other end was Lord Lucan's, but claims to remember nothing of his remarks except that they were incoherent. Bloodstains were later found on the Floorman doorstep.

At about the same time, Lord Lucan called his mother, told her there had been a horrible catastrophe at the house on Lower Belgrave, and asked her to go and take care of the children. He said that both Veronica and the nanny had been badly injured. He explained that he had been passing the house, as was his frequent habit, and had happened to look in through the blinds into the basement. There he saw his wife trying to fight off the attack of a large man. He entered the house and the man escaped. If he offered a reason why he himself had left the premises, his mother did not report it. The call to his mother was placed sometime between 10.00 and 10.25 p.m. She arrived at the house to collect the children at 10.45.

Apparently Lord Lucan then got into the Ford Corsair and started driving. He arrived at the home of friends in Uckfield, Sussex, forty-four miles from London, at about 11.30 p.m. Mrs. Susan Maxwell-Scott would testify that she had opened the door to a disheveled Lucan, had given him a drink and listened to a shocking story. Again he told of passing the house, seeing the fight with the intruder and going inside. This time he added the detail that he had slipped down in a pool of blood, explaining the wet patch Mrs. Maxwell-Scott noticed on his trousers. He had left the scene because his wife had been hysterical and had accused him of hiring the man to kill her. He said Veronica had gotten the idea of a husband using a hired killer to dispose of a troublesome wife from an American TV movie, and had harped on it in the past. He tried to clean her wounds, but she had run from the house while he was in the bathroom. He knew she would tell the police he had tried to kill her, and he had decided the best course was to remove himself from the situation. Mrs. Maxwell-Scott said Lucan's story "came out in bits," did not sound rehearsed or made up, and that she believed it.

While at the Maxwell-Scott house, Lucan again phoned his mother. He asked about the children and learned they were safely installed in bed at his mother's home. The Dowager Lady Lucan told him the police were there and asked if he wanted to talk to them. He said he would contact them in the morning. He asked Mrs. Maxwell-Scott for notepaper and wrote two letters, marked with bloodstains on the envelopes. Both letters were addressed to his friend and brother in-law, Bill Shand-Kydd. Mrs. Maxwell-Scott posted them the next day. The first letter said this:

> Dear Bill,
> The most ghastly circumstances arose tonight, which I have described briefly to my mother, when I interrupted the fight at Lower Belgrave Street and the man left.
> V. accused me of having hired him. I took her upstairs and sent Frances to bed and tried to clean her up. She lay doggo for a bit. I went into the bathroom and she left the house.
> The circumstantial evidence against me is strong in that V. will say it was all my doing and I will lie doggo for a while, but I am only concerned about the children. If you can manage it I would like them to live with you.
> V. has demonstrated her hatred for me in the past and would do anything to see me accused.

For George and Frances to go through life knowing their father had been in the dock accused of attempted murder would be too much for them.

When they are old enough to understand explain to them the dream of paranoia and look after them.

Lucky

One curious thing about this letter is that it refers only to "attempted murder." The dead nanny is not mentioned. The "dream of paranoia" alludes to Lady Lucan's mental problems.

The second letter to Bill Shand-Kydd dealt with financial matters, giving instructions about family silver to be sold at Christie's and creditors to be paid with the proceeds. After finishing the letters and refusing the offer of a bed for the night, Lord Lucan left the Maxwell-Scott house at around 1.15 a.m., presumably headed for Newhaven to begin "lying doggo."

At some point Lucan wrote a third letter, apparently using notepaper he found in the car he was driving, addressed to the car's owner Michael Stoop. Stoop was a wealthy businessman and a dedicated backgammon player. He had been a longtime friend of Lucan's and a member of the inner circle at the Clermont Club. Postage on the letter had to be paid because it arrived with no stamp, and the police never knew where it was posted because Stoop had destroyed the envelope. Here is what the letter said:

My dear Michael,

I have had a traumatic night of unbelievable coincidence. However I won't bore you with anything or involve you except to say that when you come across my children, as I hope you will, please tell them that you knew me and that all I cared about was them. The fact that a crooked solicitor and a rotten psychiatrist destroyed me between them will be of no importance to the children. I gave Bill Shand-Kydd an account of what really happened, but judging by my last efforts in court no one, let alone a 67-year-old judge, would believe – and I no longer care, except that my children should be protected.

Yours ever,

John

This letter, presumably written later in the night, has more of a dashed-off and rambling quality than the letters to Shand-Kydd. Lucan's reluctance to "bore" Stoop with the events of the night, as though murder was after all a rather humdrum affair, is typical of the icy affectation of his social set. The mention of the solicitor, the psychiatrist, and the judge are all references to the custody case. Is the man who wrote this letter a raving maniac hoping to put the best face on things before he disappears, or a victim of "unbelievable coincidence" – the worst bad luck – who really believes he cannot get a fair trial?

The coroner's inquest into the death of Sandra Rivett, held seven months after the murder, shed some light on this question, and the light did not shine favorably on Lord Lucan. The police contended that the fight in the basement could not have been seen from outside the house, and that Lucky could not have happened onto the disturbing vision of his wife being attacked as he claimed. But there is a further difficulty. It was Sandra Rivett, not Veronica Lucan, who was attacked in the basement, and Sandra was attacked at least fifteen minutes before Lady Lucan. Forensic testimony from the police authority on blood groups confirmed that there had been two main arenas of violence in the Lucan house that night: the basement and the ground-floor hall.

Blood in the basement was Type B, Sandra's type. Blood in the hall on the ground floor was Type A, Lady Lucan's type. Oddly, a bit of Type A blood was found on the U.S. Mail bag that held Sandra's body. The bloody and bent lead pipe held both blood types on its surface, and both blood types were found in the abandoned Ford Corsair. The clear implication was that the same lead pipe had been used on both women, and whoever rode in the car had either attacked or handled both women.

At the same time, the testimony of the medical expert created a new puzzle in the case. Using relatively new fiber-identification techniques, the expert had established to her satisfaction that traces of the same grey-blue wool fibers were found in the basement, on the presumed murder weapon, on Lady Lucan's washbasin, on a bath towel Lord Lucan had reportedly handled to begin to clean her wounds, and in the abandoned car. This suggested a direct connection between Lord Lucan and the murder weapon, an important connection because there were no fingerprints (in Lady Lucan's well-turned phrase, her attacker had "thrust three *gloved* fingers down my throat"). It appeared that Lord Lucan's no doubt stylish garment made him look like a murderer. But the curious thing about all this was where the grey-blue wool fibers were *not* found. They were not found on the U.S. Mail bag or on Sandra Rivett's body. Lucan appeared to be leaving a trail of wool fibers everywhere he went. Could he have killed Sandra and stuffed her in a mailbag without brushing up against the bag in the process?

Then there was the problem of time. Using the telephone, Lord Lucan had reserved a table for four at the Clermont Club that night. He had invited several of his friends to join him for dinner after they attended a theater performance. The dinner reservation had been placed at about 8.30 p.m. At around 8.45, Lucan drove by the Clermont and spoke to the doorman through the rolled-down window of his Mercedes, asking if any of his friends had arrived. The Mercedes was later found, devoid of bloodstains, at the flat on Elizabeth Street. If the official theory is right, Lucan would have wanted to be waiting in the basement when his wife descended the stairs to make her tea, just before 9.00 p.m. Lady Lucan said Sandra Rivett went down for the tea about 8.55. Her daughter Lady Frances, using TV programs as her guide, put the time about fifteen minutes earlier. In either case, Lucan would have had to perform a challenging act of moving through space. He would have had to drive through two miles of city traffic from the Clermont to his flat, park the Mercedes and pick up his lead pipe and mail-bag, walk or drive in the Ford the half-mile to the house on Lower Belgrave Street, let himself in, unscrew the light bulb and stand waiting to attack, all in ten minutes if you accept Lady Lucan's timing, and in less than no time if you accept Lady Frances's. Of course it can be argued that Lucan drove by the Clermont when he did precisely for the purpose of establishing an alibi, but by doing so he would have been cutting things perilously thin. If the Clermont doorman had his time right, it would have been diffi- cult for Lord Lucan to have killed Sandra Rivett.

On the other hand, the sighting at the Clermont does not work entirely in Lord Lucan's favor. He told Mrs. Maxwell- Smith he was passing the house on Lower Belgrave on his way to "change for dinner." But the house is between the Clermont and the flat on Elizabeth Street. Since the unstained Mercedes was found parked at the flat, Lucan could not have been casually passing on his way to change clothes. He had to be making a special trip, out of his way, past the house on Lower Belgrave.

The coroner's inquest was essentially a one-sided affair. Lucan's side of things was presented only through the readings of his last three letters and the testimony of those he had talked to. No one developed and presented his case, and without a defense the evidence against him was convincing. For the last time in England, a jury in an inquest not only established a cause of death, but named a party responsible. Lord Lucan was identified as the murderer of Sandra Rivett, and bound over for trial. One month later, a bill was introduced in Parliament to limit the power of coroners' courts and prevent them from naming a responsible party. The bill, later passed, was inspired by the Lucan inquest.

The inquest verdict did not sway the opinions of Lucan's highly opinionated friends. With very few exceptions, they had closed ranks to protect Lucky's interests in the face of the scandal. Sometimes referred to in the press as members of the "Eton mafia," these people swore for public consumption they were convinced of Lucan's innocence, but there was within their attitudes the strong suggestion that they would protect him even if he was guilty as hell. The implication was that Lord Lucan had a right to kill people if he felt it necessary, and the law be damned. Among the Clermont set, Lady Lucan was seen as a millstone around the neck of an otherwise promising and delightful fellow. "She had no money," John Aspinall – who owned the Clermont and the tigers – sniffed to a reporter, "she wasn't particularly pretty, and she had a shrewish temperament." Aspinall reportedly added, when interviewed by the police, "If she'd been my wife I'd have bashed her to death five years before, and so would you." Attitudes toward the dead nanny were no less callous. At the inquest, Sandra's family had wondered with some justice why so little attention was being paid to the victim of the crime, and so much to the high-born accused. An attempt at black humor attributed to a Lucan friend may hold the answer: "Such a pity. Nannies are so hard to find nowadays."

Seven of Lucan's friends held a meeting at the Clermont Club the day news of the murder broke to discuss how to handle the situation and how to get money or other help to Lucan if he should request it. At least this was the business of the meeting as reported to the press. Could Lucan have already been receiving help in making his escape, and could this have been the real purpose of the Clermont meeting?

This question must have crossed the minds of the Scotland Yard detectives who set off scouring the world in search of the elusive aristocrat. It appeared that Lord Lucan had dematerialized in Newhaven, somewhere between the parked Ford and the English Channel. Those who thought he had committed suicide speculated that he might have roared out into the deepest part of the Channel in his speedboat, opened the drain plug, tied himself aboard, and gone down to a watery grave. An even more imaginative theory held that Lucan killed himself like one of the noble Romans he admired, and then was fed by his devoted friends to John Aspinall's tigers. The tigers had reportedly tried a meal of human flesh before – as the result of an accident – and found it tasty. The suicide theory was given added weight by the fact that Lucan had called on a pharmacist the afternoon of the murder, and inquired about a pill he said his wife was taking. He was told it was a sleeping pill. Mrs. Maxwell-Scott reported that Lucan had asked her for sleeping pills while at her house, saying he thought he would have trouble going to sleep after such an eventful night. She had no sleeping pills, but gave him four Valiums which he pocketed and took with him.

In any case, no body has ever been found. This was not for lack of effort. Shortly after the abandoned car was spotted, fourteen divers searched Newhaven harbor and nearby coves and rock pools, while fourteen dogs sniffed the passages of a Napoleonic fort that overlooks the harbor from a cliff top. Aerial photography with infrared and ultraviolet film revealed the bodies of rodents and other small game amongst the underbrush, but no Lord Lucan.

It is more fun to suppose that Lucky Lucan is still alive, playing nightly high-stakes games in some exotic outpost under cover of a new identity and savoring the romantic grief of exile. There is in fact more to support this assumption than the suicide idea. None of Lucan's farewell letters reads like a suicide note. In fact, the closest he comes to revealing his plans is when he says "I will lie doggo for a while." Lucan's tight circle of patrician friends were close, loyal, and rich. They tended to look at the world as a few of us against a lot of them. They had connections around the globe, ready resources to support a man on the run, and they had made it clear that they would help Lucky in any way they could.

There has been no shortage of Lord Lucan sightings to encourage those who believe Lucky is alive. Some of these have appeared to have some substance. In June of 1975, two Scotland Yard detectives traveled to the French port of Cherbourg, where Lucan had reportedly been staying at the Grand Hotel near the harbor bridge. The hotel owner and several members of the hotel staff positively identified a photograph of Lucan as the man who had checked in and out of the hotel three times between March and May. Lucan was said to have friends in this area of France. This report was dismissed as nonsense by Lucan's friends in England, because the hotel owner said her guest, an insomniac who appeared to be "laboring under great stress," spoke fluent French. Lord Lucan's stockbroker told *The Times* of London he had traveled to France with his famous client, and doubted whether "he could manage half a dozen words in French."

The Cherbourg Lucan, with or without a command of French, had dropped from sight. But there would be other Lucans – hundreds of them – in Belgium, Brittany, the Netherlands, Ireland, Australia, South Africa, South America, and elsewhere. A sighting in Johannesburg in 1976 was reported by a man who claimed to have known and done business with Lucan in England. He said the South African incarnation had shaved off his trademark mustache and dyed his dark hair blond. In January of 1978 Scotland Yard checked out a story that a British citizen living in Barbados was sending money to Lucky Lucan, who was then living in South America. In 1982, Lucan was supposed to be in the Caribbean.

The fact that none of these sightings resulted in an arrest does not rule out the possibility that Lord Lucan may be alive today. Thanks to the glory days of the British Empire, there are any number of quite livable places throughout the world where an Englishman with the proper upbringing could live and prosper without drawing undue attention. Especially if that Englishman had taken the precaution of changing his appearance.

While the fruitless search went on, the tragedy of Lower Belgrave Street seemed to be spawning other tragedies. In September of 1975, a high-society painter named Dominic Elwes stretched out across his bed in his London flat and died of an overdose of barbiturates. Elwes had been one of those at the Clermont meeting, and described himself as one of Lord Lucan's best friends. A talented and sensitive man who had been the court jester of the Clermont set, Elwes was the only close friend of Lucan's who had publicly expressed doubts about the Earl's innocence. The stuffy Clermont types thought he had cooperated with a reporter who published a story sympathetic to Lady Lucan, and blackballed him from the Clermont and a restaurant favored by the clique. His suicide note said he hoped that the people who had shunned him "are happy now."

In February 1985, Christabel Boyce, the nanny who had replaced Sandra Rivett in the Lucan household, was brutally murdered and dismembered. Her body parts were found scattered in London's East End. Christabel had apparently been killed by her husband, as the result of a domestic dispute that had nothing to do with Lord Lucan. The husband confessed to the crime and was given a six-year sentence for manslaughter and two years for concealing the body. But Christabel's death did have a minor impact on the Lucan case. It turned out that she had also worked as the Lucan children's nanny before Sandra Rivett. Searching through her effects, police came upon a locked diary she had kept at the time of Sandra's murder. Eight days after the killing on Lower Belgrave Street, Christabel had made a diary entry that detailed a ninety-minute telephone conversation she had just had with Lady Lucan. She wrote that Lady Lucan said her husband had proposed a suicide pact after he admitted killing the nanny. He did this, according to the diary, while the couple were together in Lady Lucan's bedroom. He had in mind an overdose of Veronica's sleeping pills. This revelation did little except give some encouragement to those who thought Lucan had taken his own life.

There was another detail in the diary that had been left out of Lady Lucan's public accounts. Christabel quoted Lady Lucan as saying her husband told her he had planned to put her body in the safe. There was a safe in the basement big enough to accommodate a body. If Lucan said this, it could mean he had intended to stow his wife's body in the safe while he went out and established a tighter alibi for himself, perhaps by joining his friends at the table he had reserved in the Clermont. Then, at his leisure, he could return and drive the body to the English Channel for disposal.

For her part, Lady Lucan continued to have problems long

after her husband disappeared from her life. In February of 1982, she was hospitalized after a reported suicide attempt. A year later she was again taken to the hospital for treatment after "being found wandering in Belgravia."

The Scotland Yard file on Lord Lucan remains open. He has never been declared officially dead. Under British law, this would require a request from his family, and the request has not been forthcoming. One consequence of this is that his son George has not yet taken his seat in the House of Lords. Occasional Lucan sightings are still reported and duly noted in the ever-thickening file.

The evidence against Lucan is all but overwhelming, and the version of events he offered cannot be supported by the facts. The discrepancies in forensics and timing suggest he may have had an accomplice who killed Sandra Rivett. It is much easier to believe a paid hit man could have mistaken the nanny for Lady Lucan than that her husband could have done so. Following this line of thought, Lucan could have arrived at the house a few minutes after the killing and found his wife still alive and himself the victim of incredible bad luck. This would explain why he referred only to "attempted murder" as a crime he might be charged with in his letter to Bill Shand-Kydd. Still, the existence of a hit man is pure speculation, without so much as an underground rumor to support it. Whether he suffered from a poor choice of helpers or an "unbelievable coincidence," it appears that Lucky Lucan gambled all he had that fateful Thursday night in London, and he lost.

Postscript

In 1999, the British High Court issued a certificate declaring Lord Lucan dead for purposes of probate. Speculation on his whereabouts continues. His children, educated on the proceeds of the family silver, seem remarkably well adjusted and successful given their experiences in early life.